Is Globalization on the Wane?

About the Author

Dr. V. Krishna Rao (b. 1942) is presently the Director of Sania Institute of Social Action, a non-government organization. Earlier, he was a Reader in Political Science at S. V. College, Suryapet, Andhra Pradesh, from where he retired in 2000. Also, he was awarded Senior Fellowship by the ICSSR, New Delhi for the Years 2004-2006.

Besides 47 research papers published in national and international journals of repute, Dr. Krishna Rao has to his credit many books, including Communism in Andhra Pradesh, Expansion of Cultural Imperialism through Globalization and ABC of Globalization.

Is Globalization on the Wane?

Dr. V. Krishna Rao

Readworthy
New Delhi

First published 2009

Readworthy Publications (P) Ltd.

Regd. Off
A-18, Mohan Garden
Near Nawada Metro Station
New Delhi – 110 059-06
Phone: 011-2537 1324
Fax: +91-11-2537 1323

Branch
4735/22, Prakash Deep Building,
Ground Floor, Ansari Road, Daryaganj
New Delhi – 110 002
Phone: 011-43549197
Fax: +91-11-23243060

Email: info@readworthypub.com
Web: www.readworthypub.com

Cataloging in Publication Data--DK
Courtesy: D.K. Agencies (P) Ltd. <docinfo@dkagencies.com>
Krishna Rao, V. (Vaidyulu), 1942-
Is globalization on the wane? / V. Krishna Rao.
p. cm.
Includes bibliographical references (p.).
Includes index.

ISBN 13: 978-93-80009-16-2 ISBN 10: 93-80009-16-X

1. Globalization--Economic aspects--India. 2. Globalization--Economic aspects. 3. Globalization--Social aspects--India. 4. Free enterprise--India. 5. Liberalism--India. 6. India--Economic policy. I. Title.

DDC 338.954 22

Printed at Salasar Imaging Systems, Delhi - 35

Preface

For some critics, in globalization there is nothing new—the world has been 'globalised' from the time that there were international trade routes in ancient eras, and colonization and internationalization and other forms of inter-country relationships have existed for a very long time.

However, the word 'globalization' has come to represent certain new structures of economic practices, social, organisational principles and ideological positions. A few key areas have combined to create new formations which determine certain modes of interaction in a variety of spheres, and which taken as a whole, should be seen as a change from earlier times.

The first is, of course, global finance. The flow of financial capital completely ignores traditional barriers or boundaries like national borders or specific economic sectors.

Second is the growth of global corporations. Rupert Murdoch's News Corporation, is seen as the best example of the new huge, cross-nation, cross-media formation. It owns about 150 newspapers around the world, book publishing firms, including Harper Collins', the Twentieth Century Fox Production Centre and Library, the Fox Broadcasting System in the US, satellite broadcasting systems in Europe; it controls the STAR network in Asia and operates children's and news channels in Latin America.

Sony, another huge media conglomerate, brings together both hardware and software, distribution and production. Sony and General Electric are conglomerates, which are more diversified. Sony manufactures television sets and other equipment, but their software holdings are also extremely large and diversified. Music contributes more than half of their profits;

Columbia Pictures is owned by Sony and they own about three-quarters of the lucrative market of the world's video games. Sony has television operations in Asia, Europe, North America, Latin America and in India. General Electric are the largest manufacturers of electronic goods; they also control many of the television channels in the US and globally own media publication networks; even Discovery Channel is owned by the General Electric.

Another feature of globalization is global production. Production process is global and the mobility of finance makes it possible to seek out the best deal in the global market place.

Another aspect that affects a country like India, is globalization of the service sector. This is only a beginning now in India, and will rapidly increase in accordance with the World Trade Organisation (WTO), but services are no longer located in one nation. Offering training in medical transcription is nothing but providing very cheap labour to American hospitals and American companies, is something to note. The data processors for airline companies form out the actual labour to countries like India. All of these new modes of financial interaction have created a situation where it is no longer possible to talk about and discuss the contemporary world in the traditional terms like the first world, second world and third world which have become obsolete, just as of many other configurations that were very much part of the common currency until recently.

In the present globalised world, there are increased levels of deprivation just as there are increased levels of affluence in a variety of locations around the world. These zones of poverty and affluence are no longer determined in terms of geographical location. Capital and certain kinds of labour have become physically mobile, while other kinds of labour have become mobile through the use of information technology. We can see this in the way IT professionals and managers of large corporations are globally mobile. However, this mobility is not affecting the other side of this coin, the workers or the labour force are not mobile. Today, we no longer have mobility of workers—physically they are not migrant—but the services are globalised.

These aspects of globalization also imply that the first world-third world relationship can no longer be defined in traditional terms of the nation-state political boundaries, geographic realisation or locality. This does not imply that class conflicts have disappeared. In fact, globalization is itself very much class-divided. In the new notions of class, the traditional notion of class as being limited to the first nation-state no longer holds valid. There is now a global class of the very rich which includes robber barons. In developed nations too there is a group or class of people who are getting excluded from the entire process of globalization. Globalization is distinctly class-divided and this class component needs to be debated a little more. Those people who are able to participate in the processes of globalization are also accepting certain notions, images and lifestyles of the global village. There is a shift in the ideology that globalization has engendered which literally sees the poor, not poverty, as something that needs eradication. A quotation from a World Bank official—from a debate in The Economist on the spending of money on AIDS research—reads as follows: 'If AIDS falls disproportionately on the poor people, then the fact that they will die of it will have a positive impact on the economic growth of these nations.' This is the attitude of certain strata of people towards the excluded and marginalized groups. Global culture is a consumer culture.

This implies that the status, identity, social position and other kinds of self-definition are now determined and displayed by what we wear, what we eat, what we buy and how we spend our leisure hours. Those of us who have the money can make the choice to participate in the global cultural consumption patterns, but for those on the wrong side of the global divide, there is also a great cultural divide. Culture, here, is used in the larger sense of the word, to suggest lifestyles and personal preferences. Those who can afford it can talk about being part of a global culture, certain images in advertisements reflect a mode of construction of global culture. There was one commercial television that generated a lot of discussion when it was shown regularly on some of the satellite channels. It was for a company called Allainze, in which a man is shown driving an expensive foreign car from a beautiful sprawling house. This man leaves his little daughter behind at home. The commercial television then has shots of a plane flying over huge wide open spaces, deserts full of solar panels, powerful meetings of high finances, and it ends with the man calling the child, who is dressed in a velvet and lace long-sleeved dress. The entire visual exudes a sense of non-national or transnational luxury and power, in which the definitions of 'luxury' and 'power' are very coded and suggest a global existence for this man and his life. These are the kind of images of global culture that may appeal to a certain section of the society, but these are not the images to which the majority of the population of India can feel any kind of affinity to.

Because this particular form of 'global culture' links together various images and messages and thus conveys several layers of meaning, where riches, luxury, power, global mobility, high technology and consumption are being conflated to create a culture that is desired by some groups of people, this form of 'global culture' is also deeply resented by those who can never, even in their wildest hopes and dreams, aspire to belong to it. For the excluded groups, this form of 'global culture' is equated with a moral deficiency and those people who are part of the globalization are characterised as greedy and consumerist people who have lost the eternal values of a deep rooted culture. The 'global' people are equated with greed, extreme individualism, conspicuous consumption, and a kind of blatant dependency on goods and lifestyles to establish their identities. The 'global' is equated with a kind of moral deficiency. In opposition, we find people falling back on religion and tradition, and using these as alternatives to this consumerist kind of culture that globalization is selling.

Globalization, inevitably leads to a kind of regionalism or going back to indigenous roots, and it is an inevitable response to globalization.

The excluded have been called variously by various theorists. Some claim that these people have created regional tribalism within the global villages. Some other called these excluded people—the 'new barbarians'—and defined them as those population who do not achieve sophistication, without which the global market has little use for them or need of them as the logic of globalisation is consumerism. They do not have the sophistication, education and do not know how to participate in the global market and therefore do not have enough money to participate in the globalised consumer market, and are excluded from the entire process of globalization.

In the present volume an attempt has been made to trace globalization from the historical background, analyse "Why, what and for whom is globalization intended for?"

Not to speak of the uneven benefits of globalization, particularly, to the people of the developing countries, globalization has become equally a nightmare to the marginalized section of the so-called industrially advanced and rich countries of the Western hemisphere. Already the world meltdown has afected the U.S. which is the engine of the world economy followed by the Euro-community which is reeling under the impact of recession that has affected developing countries particularly India. Hence, the retreat of globalization on the western countries have pull down shelters to imports and immigrations.

I am highly thankful to the ICSSR, New Delhi, for awarding me a Senior Fellowship, which enabled me to undertake this post-doctoral research project.

I am highly obliged to Prof. T.Tirupathi Rao, Vice-chanceller, Osmania University and my good friend and long standing, associate Professor V. Ravindra Sastry for extending their good-will and cooperation.

I am equally obliged to the staff of Nehru Memorial Museum and Library, New Delhi, Cannamera Public Library, Chennai, Gokhale Institute of Economics and Politics, Pune, Librarians of Osmania University, Hyderabad, Pune University, Pune, Madras University, Chennai and the Central University, Pondicherry.

Last but not the least my thanks are due to Mr. Shalaj Mittal for bringing out this volume in an elegant format.

V. KRISHNA RAO

Contents

Preface *v*

1. ABC of Globalization 1
2. Why is Globalization Necessary? 20
3. Who Benefits from Globalization? 31
4. The Globalization Syndrome 35
5. Can India Survive Global Competition? 52
6. Marginalisation of the Poor 66
7. Impact of Globalization on Tribal Economy 78
8. Can Market Economy Survive Anti-Globalism? 83
9. Is Capitalism Retreating from Globalization? 90
10. Globalization or Monopolisation? 101
11. Emergence of Electronic Capitalism 110
12. Rise of Mass Media 128
13. Pliant Journalism 146
14. Globalization or Neo-Imperialism? 158
15. Globalization Masks U.S. Imperialism 170
16. Victors Gobble the Sinews of Globalization 179
17. Neo-Imperialism's Hegemonism 212
18. New Resistances to Globalization 219
19. Globalization and Micro Movements 232

Bibliography 247

Index 251

1

A B C of Globalization

Globalization, as a concept, as a process has caught the imagination of many. So much so, today, the views expressed are both for and against globalization. Those who are not in favour of globalization are in a majority. But this majority view is ineffective because they are powerless and weak as well. They represent the underdeveloped and the developing countries whose voice in the field of international economics is unheard. In the international market only the voice of the rich countries is heard. They represent the determing factors.

"Globalization has brought little but good news for those who have brought the products, skills and resources to the world wide market. But does it also work for the world's poor? That is the central question about which the debate over globalization—in essence free trade and free flow of foot loose capital—revolves." (Dani Rodrik: HBS Working Knowledge, 29.7.2004).

Emphasizing on free trade and flow of capital globalization, as understood by many, is only concerned with the integration of world economy. But globalization is not merely an economy. It also means the free exchange of thoughts and ideas and greater mobility of people. Globalization has not been imposed upon us. It is the result of the forces for change that are deeply rooted in human nature—the drive for a broader horizon (Horst Kohler of International Monetary Fund). Kohler further wants us to know that "globalization means a process of increasing international division of labour and the accompanying integration of national economies through the trade of goods and services, cross border corporate investments and financial flows."

Globalization for Whom?

If we consider globalization from the positive point of view we will realize that it conforms with the human instinct for progress, expansion, development, research, mobility, etc. Globalisation, as it is in progress today, is not beneficial to the poor sections of the world. It is not working for the stability of the world economy. It has not brought about a good and healthy environment. Nobel Prize winning economist Joseph Stiglitz considers that "the transition from communism to the market economy was so badly managed that poverty soared in many countries, with the exception of China, Vietnam and a few east European countries" (The Hindu: 06.02.2007). For him, India is certainly a beneficiary of globalization. But despite her important role in the information technology, India's challenge is like any other developing countries to put how the benefits of globalization in a context to the millions of people who are sceptical of the process. The downside of globalization of the Indian economy is that it has lowered the incomes of the poorest in the country. Cotton farmers, for example, found themselves unable to complete in the global market place thanks to the subsidies enjoyed by the farmers of U.S.A. and the European Union. Hence, we regularly receive the news about farmers committing suicides. Same is the case with the workforce of handloom and textile mills. Several hundreds of handloom workers in Andhra Pradesh have committed suicides. Similarly, in Ahmedabad and Mumbai, which were once considered as citadels of textile mills, millions of textile workers today are starving as many as 200 textile mills in the above cities have been closed and their lands have been converted into real estate!

Is Globalization merely an Economic Activity?

But let us not tag globalization to economic activities only. It involves much more than economic processes. It is more complex as it involves economic, social, political and cultural interaction between people living across the world.

During the last five centuries we are experiencing colonization. But today the impact of globalization is more than colonization because the advanced technology and communications have reduced distances considerably. It is going beyond the powers of national governments to control the flow of people, information and resources across the borders. The whole planet is now open to such an extent which was unimaginable a few decades ago. (T. Krishna Murthy: *Globalisation: 2005 P.7*).

NO LEVEL PLAYING FIELD

Each country has to take into account the assets and liabilities before jumping into the bandwagon of globalization. For, despite the hype about the so-called benefits a country derives from globalization, yet globalization does not provide a level playing field—the strong and the resourceful gaining domination over the weak and backward. Farmers of rich countries like the USA, the European Union and Japan are subsidised heavily to the extent of 350 billion dollars annually. The farmers of poor countries like India were not allowed anything beyond subsistence relief so much so that they are not able to compete with others. Hence, their position is deteriorating day by day as the number of their suicides indicate.

Then what is the asset that it can share with the neighbouring needy countries and what it can derive from her neighbours to fulfill her own liabilities or requirements should be given a serious thought. If this is not done with prudence then that country will be the loser. Then there is no point in blaming globalization later.

How Does Globalization Affect India?

Coming to our own country there are certain ground realities which cannot be swept away by the currents of globalization:

1. Rural India is real India. India is not represented by the metropolitan cities—Kolkata, Delhi, Mumbai, Chennai, Bengaluru—but by its villages where nearly 70 percent of the population lives.
2. What India needs is production by the masses' (labour intensive production)—not production by machines. With more than 110 crore population capital intensive production does not solve the problem of mass poverty. Production should generate employment. Then only does employment in turn promotes consumerism. That is what India needs today.
3. And development should be sustainable. Lopsided development—the shining part of India, cities with skyscrapers, flyovers, big bazaars, malls and multiplexes—is of no use. As many as 310 million people are still below the poverty line, while 220 million people in India do not have enough to eat. About 50 percent of the Indian children are under nourished. If the objective of globalization is to find solutions to such problems that India is facing today then why are we unable to solve them? This is what the opponents of globalization are asking.

Many economists are of the opinion that the target of globalization is only to benefit the advanced countries like the U.S.A., European Union, Canada, etc.

Threat to Small Scale Industries

The transition from the era of protection to an era of globalization has posed threats and challenges for small scale industries in the country. Small industries are a source of livelihood for millions of people and labour force. In the absence of generation of employment, the entry of big industrial houses into hitherto manufactured products under small scale industries leave millions of people without any visible means of livelihood. Already multinationals and big industrial houses like TATA and Reliance have entered into agricultural sector. They have purchased vast tracts of agricultural lands cultivating vegetables, fruits and selling them through malls and big bazaars at fairly cheaper rates. This affects the hawkers, street vendors who sell vegetables at higher rates since they get them through the wholesale dealers, middlemen and its paying the high transport costs, which invariably hike the rates at the consumer point.

Globalization for Rich Countries

Globalization has forced all the countries throughout the world to fall in line with it and open up their economies. While the rich and the developed countries are drawing full benefits from globalization, the developing and under-developing countries are facing increased social tensions because of the gap between the haves and the have-nots.

The toughest challenge the world is facing today is, how to improve the quality of life and reduce the incidence of poverty through sustainable growth.

While the project of corporate globalization rips through people's life in India, massive privatisation and labour reforms are pushing people off their land and out of their jobs. Thousands of impoverished farmers are committing suicides. Reports of starvation deaths are being reported from almost all parts of the country (Arundhati Roy: Confronting the Empire: 28th January, 2003). Today imperialism has invaded developing countries like India through corporate globalization with its agents - IMF, WTO and the World Bank.

What is Washington Consensus?

Washington Consensus is synonymous with neo-liberalism. The person who coined this phrase is John Williamson. He used this phrase in 1990, to refer to the lowest common denominator policy advice given by the Washington based institutions, to Latin American countries.

The Washington Consensus is also equated with neo-liberal policies' which caused dissatisfaction among the anti-globalization protesters of both developed as well as developing countries. For globalization has affected equally the developed countries as well. Under the impact of neo-liberal policies many rich countries, the USA, for example, reduced taxes by cutting down the expenditure drastically on welfare programmes, unemployment relief and old age care, etc. This together with the BPO—business process outsourcing—made many Americans not only unemployed but underemployed as well. The number of regular jobs have come down drastically and in its place contract jobs/works are increasing.

Kyoto Protocol

The natural resources of the developing countries are exploited by the rich countries ignoring the adverse affects on nature and mankind due to ecological disaster. This has to be controlled. But the point is who is going to take the lead?

Kyoto Protocol was introduced in 1997. But its implementation is still pending. The U.S. and the European Union want the protocol to be implemented after 2014. This protocol is supposed to encourage the transfer of eco-friendly processes and technologies by developed countries. Although this protocol has the support of many countries, it is only the advanced countries which consume 80 percent of the total energy supplied by the world resources who are opposing and postponing the Kyoto Protocol implementation. Its ratification is delayed mainly because the United States, the world's biggest polluter with 36 percent of green house gas emissions, pulled out of the accord in 2001.

Cultural Globalization

Mahatma Gandhi once said "I do not want my house to be walled on all sides and my windows to be stuffed. I want the culture of all lands to be blown about my house as freely as possible. But I refuse to be blown off my feet by any one of them". (Alternatives to Economic Globalization: Report of the International Forum on Globalization, P.69).

Globalization should enlighten by exposing us to different cultures. But at the same time, no culture should be allowed to dominate one's own culture. What we need is a globalization that promotes cultural pluralism, and tolerance to diversity.

Globalization has touched almost all spheres of our life and has become the central concern of economists, businessmen, sociologists, social science researchers including anthropologists. Even literary studies also have not escaped the impact of globalization.

Globalization, accompanied by the accelerating economic and social processes, has shrunk the globe both in terms of time and distance. Cultural globalization, an offshoot of economic globalization has progressed in two directions—one, it has rapidly uprooted the culture and has visibly separated it from particular areas erasing all cultural territory bindings. Cultural objects like food, clothes, music, dance, etc. changed rapidly. People are no longer interested in classical dances, classical music, traditional forms of entertainment such as stage dramas, concerts, folklore performances, etc. They are replaced by TV channels such as MTV and V channel, which produce 24 hour continuous item numbers, remixes, etc.

Cultural Imperialism

The second direction in which globalization has influenced the culture is what can be called "cultural imperialism."

As a matter of fact globalization should have been a two way traffic—but the flow has been only in one direction—from West to the rest of the world—from developed countries to developing countries, resulting in what is called "cultural homogenisation."

In the earlier centuries, European countries colonized many countries of Asia, Africa and Latin America. But now it is the turn of North America, the USA—and the West to dominate developing countries through imposing their culture on these people through Westernization, Americanization and Macdonaldization (T. Krishna Murthy: *Globalization*: 2005, pp 34-35).

Neo-Economic Liberalism

The "Washington Consensus" was designed to respond to the economic problems faced by Latin America in 1980's and 1990's. Fiscal austerity privatisation and market liberalisation were the pillars on which the neo-economic liberlism was imposed on the developing countries by the Washington consensus through the international organizations—the World Bank and the International Monetary Fund very soon enlarged a third organization—World Trade Organisation to complete the task of spreading neo-liberalism under the garb of globalization.

Fiscal austerity implied a severe cutdown on public expenditure—reduction in public employment, services such as public health and education and social safety measures.

Both the World Bank and the IMF have approached the problem from a narrow capitalist angle—privatisation has to be pursued rapidly. Developing countries like India were forced to practice privatisation in the name of disinvestments in public sector which only compounded the problems. Privatisation became a burden on the customers because of the increased prices of commodities. It also made the workers suffer because of downsizing of the labour force, which only increased unemployment. Not only that, many regular jobs were reduced to "contract" work/part time jobs; with this naturally incomes of many people became reduced drastically. This is what is happening in America where many manufacturing firms such as THE HERSHEY CHOCOLATE. When WAL-MART announced interviews for 325 poorly paid jobs as many as 25,000 people applied for the same (*Frontline*: April, 16, 2007).

Private firms do not bother about the social consequences of unemployment. But they should realize that in the absence of sufficient income the purchasing power of the people will be reduced and they prefer to cater to their needs, instead of wants the corporate sector dins into the ears and eyes of the people through advertising in the media. That is the reason why shops are 'full' with goods while sales are 'nil'! That is the reason why 'Buy one and get two' has become the refrain of malls, Big Bazars and Shopping Centres!

Privatisation's No Panacea

Privatisation cannot be delinked from corruption. Market fundamentalism asserts that privatisation will reduce the 'rent' seeking activity of government officials. I will give you one example of the social consequence of privatisation—that too—in an advanced country like the Great Britain. In Britain some of the railway stations where passengers are very few both alighting as well as getting into the train, the staff were reduced to one Station Maser only who issues tickets as well as gives green signals to the arrival of trains. These stations were handed over to private parties on a contract basis. Then what was the result? Most of these railway stations managed by skeleton staff, soon became abode of antisocial elements—drug peddlers, homosexuals, gamblers and boozers. So much so even those few people who get down or alight stopped travelling in the local trains! If this is the situation due to excessive privatisation in an advanced European country, one can imagine the plight of the people in most populous yet backward countries like India. The entry of Wal-Mart in retail trade in India along with other business giants like Reliance, Tatas, will hit the stomach of crores of retail traders such as fruit, vegetable vendors who are already under-employed. Reliance Retail already controls two Special Economic Zones (SEZs) near the most significant Indian market - Mumbai (*Frontline*: 12.01.07).

Privatisation or Bribarisation?

Privatisation cannot be delinked from corruption. Market fundamentalism asserts that privatisation will reduce the 'rent' seeking activity of government officials. They will either take away the profits of state enterprises by some means or the other or award the contracts to their friends or relatives. "If the government is corrupt there is little evidence that privatisation will solve the problem. After all, the same corrupt government that mismanaged the firm will also handle the privatisation." Privatisation makes the officials to realise that they are no longer needed to be limited to annual profit skimming. By selling a state enterprise below the market price, they could get a significant chunk of the asset value for themselves rather than leaving it for subsequent office holders. In effect they could steal today much of what would have been skimmed off by future politicians." (Joseph E. Stiglitz: Globalisation and its Discontents. P69). Kick-Backs have become a part of dismantling of the state enterprises.

India provides a classic example for the honour of "privatisation at all costs." Privatisation failed to be an effective instrument for growth. It has undermined the confidence in democratic and market institutions.

Liberalisation for Whom?

Liberalization in broad terms means free trade. It means the removal of government interference in financial markets and all barriers to trade.

Trade liberalization is supposed to increase a country's income by forcing the resources to move from less productive uses to more productive uses. But what happens mostly if the resources are moved from low productivity uses to zero productivity uses.

The first impact of liberalisation is the reduction of jobs as inefficient industrial units close down under pressure from international competition. Liberlisation is useful only for the multinationals, which stand to benefit because of the relaxation of rules, which were regulating their activities.

Undue liberlisation puts the world's most powerful corporations against struggling industries of developing countries and removes all regulations which were giving them protection. It leads to more unemployment. That is why it provokes the opposition to decry the hypocrisy behind the pushing for liberalization which has only strengthened the hostility to it. The western countries adopted trade liberalisation for the products they export but continued protection in the sector that might create competition with developing countries. They heavily subsidize domestic industries so that their cost of production becomes so low that they still sell their products at competitive prices which is not just possible for the developing countries whose production is more labour intensive.

The poor countries have no safety net to reduce the impact of recession. Farmers had to pay higher interest rates making it more difficult to buy seeds and fertilisers to earn their bread. The removal of regulations controlling the activities of multinationals, exposes the local communities to abuse and exploit.

Agents of Rich Countries

International organizations that engine globalization—IMF, WTO, World Bank—are functioning in the interest of the advanced countries to reduce the subsidies to farmers, whereas every European cow gets a subsidy of $3 per day, while 40 percent of Africans live on less than $1 a day. The cotton growers in America are paid a subsidy amounting upto 10.7 million dollars a day. And this is more than three times the aid given to sub-Saharan Africa by the USA (Mulloch Brown).

It is not merely Africa but India is also sailing in the same boat with 50% of its population living on less than one dollar a day.

Taiwan and South Korea are often touted as the shining examples of the recipients of the benefits of globalizaton. In fact, they built their international trading strength on the foundation of state subsidies and heavy investment in infrastructure and skills development, which are being protected from competition from overseas firms. On the other hand, there are an increasing number of countries in which full scale trade liberlisation has been applied and it failed to deliver economic growth while allowing domestic markets to be dominated by imports. This often has a devastating effect. (Stephen Byers: *Deccan Herald*: 25th July, 2003).

The U.S. can afford to export lower-skilled bio-tech manufacturing jobs, because cost savings will be ploughed back into higher paid research and development positions back home.

Why B.P.O?

Many U.S. firms in order to cutdown the cost of production are getting the work done in other countries where the labour is cheaper. The total number of persons employed in the U.S. by the bio-technology sector is about 2,00,000. This is very much less than the 3,90,000 jobs already sent offshore by this sector (*Forrestor Research*). This figure may go up to 4 lakhs by 2015.

The Bureau of Labour Statistics of Forrester Research Inc. estimated category wise offshoring figures for eight years ending in 2015. The U.S. offshoring is mostly to India. Hence, it may be appropriate here to reproduce the data.

The U.S. Offshore B.P.O. Estimates

Sector	2004	2005	2006	2007	2008	2010	2015
Management	15,000	34,000	42,000	48,000	67,000	1,06,000	2,59,000
Business	30,000	55,000	91,000	1,05,000	1,20,000	1,36,000	3,56,000
Computer	1,43,000	1,81,000	2,03,000	2,28,000	2,47,000	3,22,000	5,42,000
Architecture	27,000	46,000	54,000	61,000	70,000	93,000	1,91,000
Life Science	2,000	4,000	5,500	6,500	9,000	16,000	39,000
Legal	12,000	20,000	23,000	26,000	29,000	39,000	79,000
Art, Design	4,500	8,000	9,000	10,000	11,000	15,000	30,000
Sales	22,000	38,000	47,000	55,000	67,000	97,000	2,18,000
Office	2,56,000	4,10,000	4,75,000	5,41,000	6,16,000	8,15,000	16,00,000
Total	5,96,500	8,32,000	9,63,500	10,95,500	12,52,000	16,79,000	33,14,000

(Source: *Globalisation* - T. Krishna Murthy, 2005.)

Opposition to B.P.O.

Opposition is growing among the workers in the U.S. for outsourcing/offshoring. Workers are joining unions to fight against offshoring. Slogans like "keep jobs in America" and "off shoring unpatriotic" have become quite common. A worker says: "there is no loyalty anymore. I feel my job was taken away by corporate greed" (San Francisco Chronicle: 9.6.2004). Regular and permanent job is no longer a right but is only a privilege for many all over the world where globalization has affected the economy. India is no exception.

The company Microsoft exported high level of jobs to India. It is having outsourcing contract with Indian companies like Satyam and Infosys. It is said that the routine software programming and testing jobs are susceptible to being grabbed by Indian outsourcing companies, but jobs like devising the blueprints for projects, soft architecture, etc. are retained by American companies for employing its own software engineers. The U.S. companies who entrusted work to Indian companies pay them heavily, i.e. on an average of about $90 an hour per software architect or at an annual rate of $1,80,000. But the Indian companies retain a major portion of it for themselves and pass on a small portion of it as salaries to their software workers which is around $40,000 per annum. Thus, India provides not CHIP LABOUR BUT CHEAP LABOUR. Many technical and professional graduates instead of pursuing their specialized careerss—civil, mechnical, electrical engineering have joined several organisations to work as outsourcing force. Thus robs of their knowledge and expertise in the respective fields which lack professionalism.

BPO for Whose Benefit?

Many products made by the US companies at their overseas sites are in effect the US products. Only assembly line activities are outsourced to developing countries while major project planning and designing are retained and performed mostly by the Americans themselves. Outsourcing is helpful in creating a vital middle class and white collared jobs in traditionally poor countries. The wage levels of the technical workers in India and China are equivalent to the minimum wage level in advanced countries like America. But the American workers cannot be good consumers with what they earn. They cannot buy houses and they cannot afford any expenditure beyond the bare minimum because of the high cost of living. The busting of housing boom in the U.S.A. in recent years made the life of the American middle class much more gloomy than before. Hence, the shifting of routine jobs—offshoring—to Asian countries. B.P.O. not only creates a new middle class often with rich habits, luxurious lifestyle but also finds ready-made consumers of American products.

Why Opposition to Globalization?

On the one hand, the rich capitalist countries engined by the corporate sector strongly in favour of globalization of economy, capital, trade, profits, equally opposition to globalization is also increasing not only from the poor and developing countries but also from a few sections of rich countries. The rich countries and pro-globalists criticise the opponents. Thomas Friedman (the world is flat) calls them "ignorant protectionists." Both in America and Europe they are branded as "spoiled children of the privileged selfish and ill-informed" (T. Krishna Murthy: Globalization: P. 129).

The antagonists of globalization focus their attention the on people and the environment which according to them is threatened while the corporate globalists think that globalization results in the spread of democracy and vibrant market economy, those who oppose it see the power to govern shifting from people and communities to trade speculators and global corporations which are dedicated to profits.

Corporate globalists aspire for a competitive global economy ruled by mega corporations that are not answerable to any person. Joseph E. Stiglitz, the Nobel Prize winner in Economics, in his book *Globalization and its Discontents* is highly critical of the adverse effects of globalization: "The critics of globalization", he says, "are right'. They accuse western countries of hypocrisy. The western countries have pushed poor countries to eliminate trade barriers but kept their own barriers by preventing developing countries from exporting their agricultural products and so depriving them of the desperately needed export income." The U.S.A. was one of the major culprits. But it also cuts the Americans of millions of dollars both as consumers in the higher price they paid and as tax payers to finance the huge agricultural subsidies.

Economic Oppression and Military Pressure

Globalization has not succeeded in reducing poverty or in ensuring stability. Countries like Russia which embraced political democracy and market economy have not obtained any desired results. Economic oppression and military repression are the two sides of the globalization. The economic rape of the poor that accompanies globalization could not stand without the repressive military apparatus that brutalises those who rise upto resist." The fate of Iraq is well known to everyone that hardly needs any detailed narration except to cite as a case in point. However, the American corporations' (17) grabbing of the basic resources such as oil, potable water is being resisted in some of the Latin American countries—the backwardness of North America.

Hirst and Thompson pointout that "globalization is a myth suitable for a world without illusions, but it is also one that robs us of hope leading to the pathology of overdiminished expectations." Globalization is a subterfuge to justify cuts in employment and welfare. In both the developed as well as developing countries workers in declining industries see globalization as an economic threat to their welfare. The same logic applies to the relationship between the state and the recipients of welfare and within states that are potential destinations of migrant workers. Globalization has been particularly hard for organized labour in traditional manufacturing sectors in old industrial countries.

Noam Chomsky has said, "one consequence of liberalisation of capital is rather clear; it undercuts democracy. This is the effect of financial liberalisation and offer measures that have established the "virtual senate" as the dominant force in determining social and economic policy within a country. It means the population does not have control of the decisions taken by their own country." (Noam Chomsky: *Virtual Senate*: *The Dominion*: 12th September, 2003).

Virtual senate means a duplicate senate, which consists of investors and lenders. This is stronger than the real senate of people's representatives.

Globalization is, thus, a system that homogenises global economic activity in which nothing else matters except production and profits. Everything, including culture is to benefit the corporations, it removes power from the communities and handed over to global bureaucracies, marginalises the farmers and workers and renders them homeless.

"Structural adjustments caused economies to fall into a whole wherein low investments, reduced social expenditure, reduced consumption and low output 'interacted to create a vicious circle of growth, rising employment and rising investment as originally conceived by the World Bank-IMF Theory" (Dani Rodrik: Globalization, Good for Whom? *Harward Magazine*: 29th July, 2002).

Even America is of no exception to the adverse effects of globalization, the U.S is considered as a magnet which attracts goods from other countries because it has to fulfill the needs of the nation which has an irrepressible culture of consumption. The trade deficit of USA is helping countries like China to industrialise and join the ranks of developed countries. Asian countries, by keeping their currencies cheap to promote exports making the U.S products costlier which hurts the U.S firms and workers. The goods of China and Japan are cheaper than that of the U.S. which is only widening the U.S trade deficit year by year, though this is beneficial to the US consumer by getting consumer goods at cheaper rates. It is hurting the American worker, as he has to complete with the Asian worker in terms of lower wages.

Growth with Reduced Jobs

The biggest failure of globalization has been its failure to generate job opportunities. The rules of the game of globalization cannot be measured by success in the growth rate. Instead, social protection should be the yardstick of success. The policies of globalization and the institutions that are implementing them have only demonstrated the failures. Its policies and legacy of exclusion and inequality have only resulted in violence, loss of institutional credibility and collapse of inconvenience.

No one stands to benefit more from globalization than the developing countries. Product is now mobile, capital foot loose, technology diffuse (Renato Ruggiera, Former Director, ILO). But for the present generation wealth is not enough. Removal of poverty is not the task of the free trade; but it is the responsibility of the state.

The entire global community should feel happy as the walls that are separating us are falling economically, politically, ideologically and culturally. The entire developing world is jackeyed up by trade and technology.

Globalization is a reality. It cannot be escaped now. If this process cannot be sustained then the cost of returning to protectionism is unbearable. The choice available to us is to either avail the advantage of its immense potential or make a futile attempt to resist its inevitability.

If we are convinced of the advantage of globalization then it becomes our responsibility to work not only at the regional, or national, but at the international level also demanding a level playing field. What is important is the poor people should get access to the expanding and enlarging opportunities in a growing economy. To expect that growth will automatically pull people to gainful employment may not be appropriate. Banks are willing to offer loans to employees to construct houses, buy automobiles at lower interest rates, more than that employees also get tax exemption on housing loans. Whereas poor farmers are denied access to easy loans, even if they get they have to pay higher interest! Sales of automobiles boost the turnover of trans nationals but not the local agricultural produce! Construction of houses enhance the demand for iron and steel, cement, wood and other accessories in which global corporations are interested.

Globalization of the economy has benefitted the countries that took advantage of it by seeking new markets for their exports and by inviting direct foreign investments. The countries that benefitted by globalization are those that took charge of their own destiny and recognised the role the state can play in development rather than relying on the motion of a self regulated market that would fix own problems.

If globalization is to be made more beneficial, it requires certain changes. The question is not just a change in the institutional structure. The mindset on globalization should itself be changed. It is much more than mere integration of national economies into a world economy. What is unavoidable as a result of globalization is urbanization. This undermines the traditional rural societies. This is a threat to cultural values. This problem can be solved to a great extent by disciplining agencies that are subject to globalization by telling them as to what they should do and should not do. The problem is not with globalization, as such, but it is the way in which this process is made use of.

2

Why is Globalization Necessary?

While economists tend to develop empiricist accounts of globalization focused on outcomes, scholars of international relations and international political economy were to be commended for their move towards feminist and post positivist accounts focused on ideas, identities and culture.

While there is considerable diversity in the way globalization is understood, above and beyond this the major international relations and international political economy theories are linked by a certain sociological and political realism.

The task of the researcher is to capture the substance of changes along with foctors such as speed, space, time, territoriality, sovereignty and identity. This may be described as "Global Governmentality." (Wendy Larner and William Walters (ed) *Global Governmentality*, 2004).

Whether theorised as structure, process or epoch, globalization is understood to involve a profound transformation in our social condition. Influential accounts portray globalization as "time-space compression" or as the increasing predominance of "transcontinental or interregional flows and networks of activity, interactions and the exercise of power." Others emphasise human aspects: "the widespread recognition of a worldwide human commonality or of world society as a whole as the framework of human action." Some Marxist accounts stress its neoliberal character. "The main historical thrust of neoliberal economic globalization is to bring about a situation in which private capital and 'the market' alone determine the restructuring of economic political and cultural life, making alternative values or institutions subordinate." Then there are those who focus on "globalization of production" and who are concerned to show how firms, networks, and institutions are being reorganized across the global space.

Seeking to expand the terms of the debate, many post-positivist and feminist accounts exercise caution in their engagement with globalisation. Marchand and Runyan claim that there is agreement that, "capitalism is the defining feature of globalization; that firms and financial actors are its main driving forces; that technology is a key enabling and contributing factor; that neoliberal ideology has played a key role in determining the direction of globalization; and that globalization has implications for social organisation." Their preference is for the term global restructuring, implying that globalization involves a set of multidimensional, multispeed, and disjunctured processes. They identify shifting boundaries and meanings, then emphasise that dominant readings of globalization conceal familiar patterns of economic, racial, and sexual exploitation.

Globalization of "deterritorialisation" implies that as economic activity has become more digital, production more fluid, communication more instantaneous and people more mobile, so, too, has economic, political, and social activity become less bounded.

The geographical territory of the state, the space contained by its frontiers, is only one form of territorialisation. Globalization presupposes (re)territorialisation. (Ash Amin: "Spatialities of Globalisation" in *Environment and Planning*, 2002).

Jessop argues: "Far from globalization being a unitary causal mechanism, it should be understood as the complex, emergent product of many different forces operating on many scales." But what does this pluralisation—from globalization to globalizations—actually tell us? We agree that globalization involves diverse phenomena, we think it is important to the constitutive and creative function of attributing proper names.

Naming is important then, but not just for the reasons that IR social constructivists suppose; that is, as an ideational and legitimately force. Naming also involves assembling singularities out of heterogeneous and diverse phenomena.

Many of the elements now studied as globalization were previously known otherwise: as the "new international division of labour," the "restructing of the welfare state," "transnational interdependence," "deregulation of international finance," and so on.

To focus solely on the transformed territories of globalization is to neglect the question of what it "invisibilizes." Are there not other realities, other objects that we might help to force into existence, but that a focus on globalization would preclude? It is with the question of disclosing other spaces that we turn to a third aspect of "what is globalization?"

As a literature that foregrounds the discursivity and historicity of world order, critical geopolitics represents a valuable intellectual resource for studying globalization as territorialisation. To think of globalization in this way is to place it within a genealogy of the ways of imagining the world. For example, Agnew advances the concept of "civilizational geopolitics" to convey the dominant mode among the Western powers of imagining world space in the nineteenth century (John Agnew: *Geopolitics: Revisioning World*, 1998).

Globalization is also a site of politics. For example, commitment to and preparedness for the global economy is sometimes considered as a measure of a state's fitness—its citizenship within the world community. Who speaks in the name of globalization? Who can pronounce upon its truth?

Typically a globalization discourse tells a story about the transformation of the state system or the growing interconnection of economic activities. By placing the global within the history of geopolitical thought, we might unsettle such evolutionary accounts. We need to construct analytical series and lines that work diagonally across these settled planes.

When did Globalization Begin?

When did globalization begin? This is another question that vexes the commentators. Indeed, accounts of the what of globalization are bound up with the when. Is this a novel period of world history associated with the contemporary crisis of capitalism? Or is globalization simply a new colonial expansion of the seventeenth century? Or even the rise of a world system in the 1500s?

Certainly, an important critique of globalization comes from those who argue that this is an old story that is only now receiving attention because it is being done to "us" as well as "them." Massey suggests that globalization is actually a story about Europe and North America that privileges time over space. Globalization, like civilisation, embodies a claim as to the true or ultimate direction of history, the promise of progress.

Crude accounts of globalization commit a form of teleology, often technologically determined. They find the antecedents of globalization in an ever-receding past and argue that our world is the outcome of the processes bringing human society ever closer together. The past is narrated in terms social and political forms of globalization.

Previous ages did not employ the language of globalization to understand themselves. The mentalities of earlier societies and cultures are effected by this approach. Rather than reading the past formations as antecedents of the present, a genealogy of globalization would seek to grasp the regimes of practices in their own terms.

Genealogy of Globalization

Genealogy implies a different way of answering the when question rather than seeking its origin in a particular set of circumstances or in its distant antecedents, we can be quite empirical and trace the emergence of globalization at the level of forms of knowledge and practice. At what point does the global emerge as a way of knowing and acting on and in the world?

Globalization did not exist in a strong sense until governments, international agencies, corporate actors, scholars, and activists began to name globalization and develop ways to measure its extent and its effects. Even a cursory survey suggests it was not until the early 1990s that the term "globalization" began to gain widespread currency. Scholte, for example, observes that the number of entries for "globalization" in the U.S. Library of Congress multiplied from 34 in 1994 to 693 in 1999 (Jan A. Scholte: *Globalisation: A Critical Introduction*, 2000).

How did it become possible to think in terms of the global? What techniques were required? How are these ideas and techniques transferred in and between organisations? Embodied in what forms of expertise? Answering these questions might involve a genealogy of international indicators, beginning with area-studies typologies that allowed to be clustered together in particular ways; or it might involve looking at how the indicators produced by international organisations such as the OECD or IMF made it possible to think of a space beyond the nation-state. Similarly, how did trade, investment and migration, once understood as transactions between discrete nation-states, come to be understood as measurements of global mobility, flows and networks? How did accountancy come to be rearticulated as a mechanism of global standardisation? Interrogating these reconfigurations of knowledge, technique and space is likely to reveal much about contemporary conceptions of the term global.

Counter-narratives of Globalization

It is not enough merely to problematise how we come to understand ourselves and our time in terms of globalization. To debate globalization is still to engage in a game that keeps it at the centre of academic and public debate to do without globalization? What counter-narratives might displace and dethrone globalization? Rather than emphasising interconnection, why not a history of ways of dividing, segregating, disciplining and allocating territories and population? What ends might be accomplished by making such divisions not supplements or qualifications added on to an already globalised world but primary features in our descriptions?

One could also unsettle "globalization" by calling the concepts it has either displaced or subsumed. How has globalization redescribed and rearticulated a field that was previously mapped as "post," post-modern, post-fordist, post-colonial, post-national, post-cold war, post-Communist? Globalization seems to affirm that we are not merely "after" the past, but more fully caught up in a forward-moving process. One reason for the success of globalization as a concept is that it is more definite and positive than its competitors.

To take a longer-term view, a genealogy of globalization could also relate it to other concepts that may have contained it or, conversely, that it has displaced and reinscribed—modernisation, liberalisation and interdependence. That would not only generate a greater understanding of how and why globalization has the shape that it has, but it would also allow us to appreciate the contingency present in this particular conception of politics.

Where is Globalization?

Much of the discussion on globalization has concentrated on the pressure of "outside' globalization on states. Changes in the organisation of capitalism give rise to transnational economic networks linking spatially discreate organisations and individually. In turn, this challenges nation-state form of politics that assume a unified centre from which politics could occur and give rise to the shift from government to governance. Now there is a sustained speculation about how new forms of the social can be sustained in a globalised, networked, multiscalar world.

However, a number of studies have challenged the notion that globalization is truly "global." Hirst and Thompson highlight the profoundly limited and regional nature of transnational connections. Mann has qualified the talk of globalisation with his idea of "obstracizing imperialism," pointing out that "economic globalization" is mostly Northernisation, integrating the advanced countries but excluding much of the world's poor; and thus widening inequalities." OTuathail points to the uneven access to information and communication technologies as a "functional global apartheid that separates and segregates certain affluent and wired neighbourhoods from other deprived and disconnected zones and neighbourhoods. These interventions pin point the social and political unevenness of the phenomena associated with globalization. But it is possible to go further and question not just the universality or comprehensiveness of globalization but its place.

According to Sassen," to a large extent, global processes materialise in national territories... Many transactions that are a key part of the global economy do not cross borders, or do not do so in ways that investment and trade do, but are located inside the national economies... Even the most digitised global financial market is grounded in a set of very material resources and spaces largely embedded in national territories" (*State and Soverignty in the Global Economy*, 1999, PI59).

This is an argument that many states, or elements of them, are reoriented to guaranteeing the "rights" of global capital. Other studies consider the production and circulation of discourse of globalization in different national settings to show how globalization is far from being a monolithic exterior force; for one thing, it means different things in different places. They challenge the view of globalization as an outside pressure forcing itself upon polities. Instead, we see it as mobilised to legitimate particular domestic policies—some of which were previously justified for other reasons. These efforts to explore the "situatedness" of globalization are an important development. Yet they still assume an underlying common process that manifests itself differently in different contexts.

We need to recognise that globalization is an effect of practices located in time and place. This holds as much for new spaces of power (financial markets, offshore banking centres, electronic transactions and bond-rating agencies) as it did for the old (national currencies, trading posts, telegraphs, banks).

This approach and science and technology studies more generally hold out great potential for a more material analysis of globalization. It is an approach that challenges the tendency to take globalization at its face value, as weightless, or deterritorialised. For it insists that global relations do not proliferate effortlessly. Our attention is drawn to the ways in which knowing of a global scale depends upon diverse and heterogeneous materialities. They participate in the "generation of information, of power relations, of subjectivities and objectives (Law and Hatherington: *Knowledge, Space and Economy*, 2000).

Who are the Subjects of Globalization?

Then, who are the subjects of globalization? Emblematic figures such as cosmopolitans, investors, international students, and entrepreneurs, as well as migrant workers, refugees and asylum seekers can be understood not as self-evident categories but, rather, as performers of the global world. In this context, globalization can be understood as a complex of practices that foster multiple forms of subjectification. Globalization also has many varied effects. Not only is it an economic process, it can also be a rallying cry, a site of community. Globalization some times implies a monolithic force or cause. But it is also an idiom of action, creation and change. In this regard, the question of freedom as the modality of liberal power is central.

Globalizaion is a spatialised and temporalised understanding of who we are. Globalization can be understood in terms of a historical ontology—reflexive moment in the discursive construction of ourselves where a knowledge of the subject is produced in terms of its interconnectivity, mobility and sovereignty. We are produced as global subjects, emerging from a past of nation-state-focused political struggles. Globalization discourse could thus be seen as a moment of reflexivity, a "fold" in which another dimension of human existence is opened up. Less a force that impinges upon the subjects; more a site in the production of particular kinds of subjectivity and experience: "be global!"; "think globally!"

Globalization is not necessarily, then, global and not simply "out there." Rather, globalization is usefully understood as a situated process that involves diverse subjects and objects, including nation-states and socio-technical networks and bodies. Globalization is not so much a new epoch as it is a way of imagining human life. It is a "world in the making," but this "making" is being done through very specific imaginaries, processes and practices. Many are still obsessed with the question of the state, now under global conditions. They seem to want a new theory of it. For example, Sassen rightly seeks to advance the globalization debate beyond the negative conception implied by deregulation, privatisation and liberalisation. She wants to capture "all the ways in which the state participates in setting up the new frameworks through which globalization is furthered" as well as transformations "inside" the state.

For scholars engaged in international studies, the question appears to be: What role will nation-states play in a global world?

In these accounts, nation-states remain preconstituted political actors. To answer this question it is important to avoid projecting familiar conceptual forms onto a different scale (from national civil society to global civil society; from nation-states to global governance). Instead, careful attention needs to be paid to the discourses and practices through which organisations and actors represent themselves and their relations with each other.

Then the question to ask: What sort of a space is the global is? It might be argued that globalization is geo-economic, rather than geopolitical. Rather than the spatial assumptions of nested scales in which city, region, national, and international sit inside of each other, this is a space of multiple flows, networks, and partnerships. It is imagined as a smooth, interconnected space, made up of connections, flows, and hypermobility. But it is also a space of turbulence and self-organisation. Such terms are more than florid. They are idols in the exercise of (geo) political and (geo)economic power (Wendy Larner and William Walters: *Globalisation as Governmentality Alternatives*; 2004).

Politics of Globalization

Globalization assumes particular macro-subjects" (industries, states, regions, firms, networks) with particular attributes and capacities. Then is the question of how globalization sets the terms of political debates. We are told that globalization is unprecedented, novel and unique in human history. It is the dawning of a new epoch.

One problem is that too often the political is understood as local resistence, whereas globalization is transplanetary connectivity, both disembodied and reclified. Oppositional voices are those of women's groups, labour, environmental movement and indigenous people. Similarly, new nationalisms and/or fundamentalisms are seen as responses to globalization. Subversive acts, nonconformists or dissent are seen as resistance to globalization because they happen in a global era. For example, Chin and Mittelman do not seek to discriminate between resistance to globalization and resistance to other issues. We need to get past generalized notions of politics (Chin and Mittelman: In Barry Gill (Ed): *Globalisation and the Politics of Resistance*, 2000).

More generally, the problem with this formulation of politics is that it always places "social forces" as reactive and capital as taking the initiative. Hardt and Negri reverse this assumption, insisting on the active role that counter-cultures played in making the present. At stake is nothing less than the production of "new subjectivities;" "the indexes of the value of the movements—mobility, flexibility, knowledge, communication, cooperation, the affective would define the transformation of capitalist production in the subsequent decades." In their view, capitalism is not that which creates from scratch but a movement of appropriation of cultural form (Hardt and Negri: *Empire* 2000).

Despite the efforts to identify what is novel about globalization as a phenomenon and the search for new analytical inspiration, analysts of gloabalization, along with many other scholars of international relations and international political economy, remain caught in the web of categories and concepts of their disciplines. Broadly recognisable, rather than a unified process, it is more usefully understood as a complex of effects that have shifted the spatial and social imaginaries through consolidation and dispersion, then globalization can be usefully understood as a "global governmentality.

The attempt to identify how globalise a lion involves processes that overwhelm and disrupt each other. By placing the emphasis on difference, disjuncture, and unintended consequences, we aspire to make the universal particular. We aspire to dedramatise globalisation. To set it within a series. To make the familiar looks strange. To relativise our present. The need is to confront globalization and its network of terms—global governance, new regionalism, complexity, networks flows—with dissonance to make it stutter. This is important since globalization is sublime, awe-inspiring, enchanting and terrifying; altogether too big, (Wendy Larner and William Walters, P 511).

3

Who Benefits from Globalization?

Globalization process is, indeed, for a noble cause to bring all the nations together and foster in them healthy relationship through trade and services.

Liberalisation of trade and service is a part of globalization and aims at providing a level playing field for all the participating members to avoid any discrepancy in terms of pricing as noted in sub section (III) of GATT.

Besides such norms to be complied with, our products and services must be saleable in the international market where innumerable brands with outstanding quality, technology and attractive appearances are already available. This is the real catch. If we take our products and services, we stand inferior in the global market. Even our local markets prefer foreign products as compared to our own. In May, 2001 thousands of tonnes of wheat exported to Iraq as per international standards was rejected because it contained stones. Iraq's plea was that they didn't have machines to separate the impurities! (K.C. Agarwal: *Shaping India of Our Dreams*: 2003, P281).

We must endeavour for 'zero tolerance' rather than 'within tolerance' philosophy to compete in all markets and with all buyers.

If we overlook this grave drawback and see only the FDIs or sell our PSUs and private industries to multinationals indiscriminately will only lead to a catastrophe. The developing countries like India who have little to trade will be great losers and eventually fall into a debt trap besides the loss of jobs.

Survival of the Fittest

The ultimate philosophy of WTO boils down to that a country will do only what it can do the best. It is a harsh reality that only the more competent shall survive in the future and not those who lack excellence. What is true with individuals—MIGHT IS RIGHT—equally applies to nations too. Societies and nations that are more affluent and advanced in terms of discipline, work culture, infrastructure, R&D, knowledge and expertise shall excel and outbid others. The noble cause of WTO in reality be so cruel for the rest because they have not come up to that level.

India today looks up at others and works for them rather than be its own master. We lag behind on all fronts and in all faculties. We are not equipped to be a part of WTO. We must first become competent and then only jump into the fire.

'Fittest will survive'—anyway is the punchline of the day.

Is Liberalisation for MNCs?

For India it is already more than 20 years when liberlisation was officially implemented but nothing much is done so far to pay heed to the required safeguards and improve the working conditions. Neither do we foresee any efforts in future in this direction. One cannot build a superstructure on a shaky foundation. Our markets have already opened for others. Imports are now freely flooding our markets, while our exports are yet to enter the US and the European union in a big way. In the present world of common market only the best will sell. Those who are not able to sell shall have to pull their shutters down. Already our industrial base is shrinking, our PSUs are taken over, and large private sector is also going into the hands of the MNCs. While medium industries are crumbling, the service sector is either sold or handed over to them on lease. What then our concern about a bleak future with millions of people going without jobs or means of living should do must be taken seriously.

Who Needs Opportunities Abroad?

People look for jobs outside mostly when their own country is incapable of providing them satisfactory job opportunities because of lack of development; lack of recognition in their own country. When people do not have enough to spend and are unable to support their secondary and tertiary markets then the producers of goods and service providers look for global markets.

While individuals may have surplus money, the manpower engaged in the primary sector in the developed countries is very low. But without alternative secondary markets, the industrial sector that is large and well established and engages a large manpower may go into recession. Exactly this has happened with US and Japan during 2000-2002. Unless, therefore, external markets support their industries they may land into a recession, even when there is no dearth of capital. Therefore, they look for global markets for primary and secondary sectors and also for further extension of their service sector. Here lies the catch. With their idle capacity and surplus money they want to invest in other countries to keep their show going.

A highly affluent society may bubble with money but industries may slacken, giving rise to unemployment. Take examples of TV, fridge or computer. If everybody has these, there will not be much additional need for these items except for replacements. New models and features to attract the consumer and the consumer keeps exchanging the old ones with the new ones. But such gimmicks do not work for long and one has to find additional markets.

Rising Service Sector

More services and recreation avenues may, however, be necessary to cater to such societies. Service sector may boom just not the industries. We can witness people of means touring the world for recreation and fun and spending lavishly— the Japanese coming to India to play golf and the Sheikhs going to the US to gamble in the casinos. But all this cannot engage the industrial sector.

It is easy for the MNC's with their affluence, technology and money power to capture the global markets. The new markets are a bonus for them. They can easily cut down their prices and supply a better quality product.

There is no denying that to grow globalization is the need of the hour. But it does not mean that foreign players will come to our country, sell their products, earn money and go back while our local players will watch them helplessly. If it is so, it is inviting disaster for us. It is like hosting the Olympics where our country's players cannot participate. We must first regain our strength and become capable so that our products are liked by our own people first before they are liked by others. Unless we are able to achieve this, globalization has no meaning and shall be doing us only harm than any good. It calls for a revamping of the whole system and then working relentlessly to achieve excellence in all fields. Without this it is like going to the battlefield without weapons.

Our inadequate infrastructure, poor work culture and bureaucratic hurdles have already caused heavy inflations over the years and have raised domestic prices beyond the competitive level and rendered our quality inferior. Our industries have not failed, they have been made to fail. No cosmetic treatment such as liberalisation will bring any lasting solution to our failures unless the system responsible for all the ills itself is revamped. Without curing the disease a good tonic alone can do no miracle.

In the name of liberalisation bleed the PSUs, bankrupt the nation, drive the people to deprivation, sicken the private sector and then put up a board 'for sale' for PSUs and throw private industries open to face the onslaught of the MNC's.

No nation on earth can ever develop or prosper by undermining its own people. One cannot bask under the strength of others (MNC's) to become stronger or wealthier. One has to be healthier himself to be stronger. With the use of crutches one can only limp and not run.

4

The Globalization Syndrome

"Globalization" is the buzzword of the decade. Journalists, politicians, business executives, academics, and others are using the word to signify that something profound is happening, that the world is changing, that a new world of economic, political and cultural order is emerging. Yet, the term is used in so many different contexts, by so many different people, for so many different purposes, that it is difficult to ascertain what is at stake in the globalization, what function the term serves and what effects it has for contemporary theory, politics, and critical pedagogy (Douglas Kellner: *Globlization and Education*, 2000).

Many social theorists are arguing that today's world is organised by expanding globalization, which is strengthening the dominance of a world capitalist economic system, supplanting the primacy of the nation-state by transnational corporations and organisations and eroding local cultures and traditions through forcing a homogenious global culture. Marxists, Weberians, system theorists, structuralists and functionalists, post-structuralists and many other contemporary theorists are converging on the position that globalization is a distinguishing trend of the present moment. Moreover, advocates of a post-modern break in history argue that developments in transnational capitalism are producing a novel historical configuration of post-Fordism or post-modernism as an emergent cultural logic of capitalism and global culture. In major modern and post-modern social theories globalization is taken as a salient feature of our times.

Multi-Dimentional Concept

Yet, the conceptions of globalization deployed, the purposes for which the concept is used, and the evaluations of the structures and processes described by the concept vary widely. For some, globalization entails Westernisation of the world, while for others it involves a cover for the ascendancy of capitalism. Some see globalization as generating increasing homogeneity, while others see it producing diversity and heterogeneity through increased hybridisation. For business, globalization is a strategy for increasing corporate profits and power; for politicians in power it ensures "kickbacks", for government it is often deployed to promote an increase in state power, while many non-government social organisations see globalization as a lever to produce positive social goods like environmental action, democratisation or empowering hitherto marginalised groups through new technologies and media. Some theorists equate globalization with modernity, while others claim that the "global age" follows and is distinctly different from the "modern age." For many theorists, we live in an age in which globalization is the defining concept, while others find claims for the novelty and centrality of globalization exaggerated (Paul Hirst and Grahame Thomson: *Globalisation in Question*, 1996). In short, globalization today is like a blind man describing a white elephant!

Techno-Capitalism

Part of the "great transformation" to a new stage of techno-capitalism has involved a fundamental restructuring and reorganisation of the world economy, polity, and culture for which the term globalization serves as a codeword. It is bound up with debates over post-Fordism, post-modernism, and a series of other "posts" that themselves signify a fundamental rupture with the past. It is thus centrally involved in debates over the defining features and changes of the present era (Keller: 2000).

A critical theory of globalization overcomes the one-sidedness and ideological biases that permeate most conceptions of this all-embracing and complex phenomenon. While on the one level globalization significantly increases the power of big corporations and big governments, it can also empower groups and individuals who were previously left out of the democratic dialogue and terrain of political struggle.

In a sense, there is no such thing as "globalization" per se. Rather, the term is used as a cover concept for a heterogeneity of processes that needs to be spelled out and articulated. It often serves not only to replace older critical discourses like "imperialism," but also ideological conceptions of "modernisation." As a replacement for imperialism, it could displace focus on domination of underdeveloped countries by the overdeveloped ones, or of national and local economies by transnational corporations. It could serve as a cover for neo-imperialism that serves to obscure the continuing exploitation of much of the world by a few superpowers and giant transnational corporations.

Pro-globalization boosters include champions of the market economy, Bill Gates and *avatars* of the "information superhighway" and new technologies; and other political and economic elites, supported by their academic promoters and sociological theorists who exaggerate the inexorable and irresistible trajectory of globalization while covering over its more troubling aspects.

For its critics, however, globalization is bringing about the devastating destruction of local traditions, the continued subordination of poorer nations and regions by richer ones, environmental destruction and a homogenisation of culture and everyday life.

While Marxists, liberals and multiculturalists, stress the threat to national sovereignty, local traditions and participatory democracy, conservatives see globalization as a threat to national and local cultures and the sanctity of tradition.

Is Globalization a Mask for Neo-Imperialism?

Globalization is not only a replacement term for imperialism and modernisation but is also caught up the modernity/ post-modernity debates as well. Some theorists are claiming that globalization is replacing concepts like modernity and post-modernity as the central theme of contemporary theorizing.

The term globalization is thus a theoretical construct that itself is contested and open for various meanings and inflections. It can be described positively or negatively—to describe highly complex and multidimensional processes in the economy, polity, culture, and everyday life. In order to theorise globalization adequately, it must be seen as a complex and multidimensional phenomenon which involves different levels, tensions and conflicts.

In particular, globalization involves crucial economic, political, and cultural dimensions. A critical theory of globalization must, therefore, theorise each of these levels, how they are interconnected, and how individuals and social movements and groups can intervene to engage critically the different aspects of globalization and reconstruct or inflext its dynamics and forms to serve the interests of democratisation, human well-being, environmental preservation, and other positive values.

A critical theory of globalization attempts to specify the interconnections and interdependencies between different levels such as the economic, political, cultural and psychological, as well as between different flows of products, ideas and information, people and technology.

The term globalization often used as a code word that stands for a tremendous diversity of issues and problems and that serves as a front for a variety of theoretical and political positions. While it serves as a legitimating ideology to cover over and sanitise ugly realities, a critical theory of globalization can also inflict the discourse to point precisely to these phenomena and can elucidate a series of contemporary problems and conflicts. To put it sharply, globlization is an abstract phenomenon. Everyone interpreted to suit his arguments. However, much it is understood and interpreted, whoever be the opposition to it, one thing is certain—THAT GLOBALIZATION IS A REALITY which no one can deny.

While the term can both describe and legitimate capitalist transnationalism and supranational government institutions, a critical theory of globalization does not buy into ideological valorisations and does affirm difference, resistence and democratic self-determination against forms of global domination and subordination.

Culture provides forms of local identities, practices, and modes of everyday life that could serve as a bulwark against the invasion of ideas, identities, and forms of life extraneous to the specific local region in question. Education in turn transmits the skills and materials that enable individuals to participate in their culture in a creative way.

Globalization involves the dissemination of new technologies that have tremendous impact on the economy, polity, society, culture, education, and individual experience. Time-space are overcoming previous boundaries of space and time, creating a global cultural village and dramatic penetration of global forces into every realm of life in every region of the world. New technologies in the labour process displace living labour, make possible more flexible production, and create new labour markets, with some areas undergoing deindustrialisation. While production itself becomes increasingly transnational. The new technologies also create new industries, such as a computer and information industry, and allow transnational media and information to traverse the planet instantaneously. This process has led some to celebrate a new global information superhighway and others to attack the new wave of media and cultural imperialism.

Globalization of Culture

The global flow of culture and rapid spread of new technologies have enormous consequences for education. On the one hand, globalization might entail the imposition of corporate management structures and imperatives on educational institutions, further colonising education by business forces, it might lead to increased commodification of education and rendering quality education only accessible to elites who can afford it. The globalization of education might involve the privileging of Western and particularly English-language and culture in the entire world, as English is emerging as the most preferred language of the elites and the Internet as well.

In relation to education, the possibility of openings for research and communication not previously available earlier to students or teachers who did not have access to major research libraries or institutions. The Internet makes accessible more information and knowledge to more people than any previous institution in history. The Internet enables individuals to participate in discussions and to circulate their ideas and work in ways that were previously denied to individuals who were not connected to the mainstream media of information and communication.

But there are also the dangers that new technologies will be used to downsize the teachers and will be part of a reorganisation of universities along corporate lines. In a globalised economy and culture, "reforms" in one sector or region often spread rapidly to others, frequently without adequate debate and discussion, that the U.S. inspired business models might be imposed upon a wide range of institutions throughout the world.

The new technologies require new literacies and pedagogy that will enable students and citizens to function in a high-tech economy and rapidly changing society and polity. Critical pedagogy has traditionally endeavored to empower individuals to control democratically their own lives and society. In an increasingly globalised world, then, it must engage the new global forces the new technologies and changing social and cultural conditions and the new forms of political struggle in an effort to rethink education in the light of contemporary conditions. This involves empowering individuals to bother to understand and resist globalization.

Hegemony of Capital

To a large extent, globalization represents the triumph of the economy over politics and culture, in which once relatively autonomous spheres are controlled by economic elites and forces. From this perspective, globalization represents the hegemony of capital over all the other domains of life and constitutes an even higher level of capitalist domination than that described by Marx.

A critical theory of globalization recognises the multidimensional, complex, and contradictory reality of globalization, while seeking and promoting conceptions and practices of resistance and struggle that attempt to counter the most destructive aspects of global forces, or that inflect globalization for democratic and locally empowering ends. Very few progressives have attempted to theorise globalization from below, to detect how globalisation can be used to foster a progressive social agenda, and to encourage the project of using globalization to promote emancipation and democratisation.

Against capitalist globalizations from the above, there has been a significant eruption of forces and subcultures of resistance that have attempted to preserve specific forms of culture and society against globalization and homogenisation, thus exhibiting resistance and globalization from below. Most dramatically, peasant and guerrilla movements in Latin America, labour unions, students, and environmentalists throughout the world and a variety of other groups and movements have resisted capitalist globalization and attacks on previous rights and benefits.

Many people these days operate with binary concepts of the global and the local and promote one or the other side of the education as the solution to the world's problems. For globalists, globalization is the solution and underdevelopment, backwardness and provincialism are the problems. For localists, globalization is the problem and localisation is the solution, But, less simplistically, it is the mix that matters and whether global or local solutions depend on the conditions in the distinctive context that one is addressing and the specific solutions and policies being proposed.

Neo-Liberal State

The state has withdrawn from its responsibility to administer public resources to promote social justice. The neo-liberal state, particularly in the developing countries like India is characterised by drastic cutbacks in social spending, rampant environmental destruction, regressive revisions of the tax system, loosened constraints on corporate growth, widespread attacks on organised labour and increased spending on military "infrastructure."

Corporations are becoming so powerful that many are dictating their own terms and conditions to 'soft' states.

The U.S. corporations are spending nearly $40 billion each year, approaching the total annual expenditures of all the U.S. four-year and graduate colleges and universities, to train and educate their current employees.

This process of privatizing the service factor is occurring in the context of new relations and arrangements among nations, characterised by a new global division of labour, economic integration of national economies, the ever increasing concentration of power in supranational organisations and the "internationalisation" of nation-states.

Corporate Chaos

Corporate influence over the nation-state is exercised indirectly, through intellectual leadership, installing in policymakers a new set of values and setting limits on the nation-state's range of options, which is a more effective strategy in changing policy priorities than the explicit threat of punitive sanctions. These new values, aptly reflected in the neo-conservative and neo-liberal agendas promote less state intervention and greater reliance on the free market, and more appeal to individual self-interest than to collective rights. "The internationalisation of production, finance and other economic resources is unquestionably eroding the capacity of any individual state to control its own economic feature... Multinational corporations may have a clear national base, but their interest is above all in global profitability. Country of origin is of little consequence for corporate strategy. In a way they have become a non-national entities in so far as their profit search is concerned.

In summary, there are changes at the economic, political, and cultural levels of society that tend to promote and reinforce a more global perspective on social policy.

McDonaldization of Culture

New patterns of consumption (sometimes termed the "McDonaldisation" of taste—fast, standardised and oriented to convenience over quality), along with new advertising and marketing strategies that promote the "means of consumption" (shopping malls, television buying channels, on-line purchasing, and easy credit). The credit card mania is fast spreading among the Indian middle class which clamour for luxury goods as well as patronise the malls to buy the junkies.

In cultural terms changes in global media (cable, satellite, CNN, the Internet); commercial culture (McDonalds, Nike, the colors of Benneton); increased mobility, with vastly enlarged travel and tourism sectors; changes in communication technologies; worldwide distribution of film, television, and music products; an increased presence and visibility of global religions that change local rituals into transnational ones; or the global world of sports, both in terms of competitive events (and spectacles) like the Olympics or World Cup and also, significantly in terms of sports marketing (Apparel, footwear, equipment), sponsorship/advertising, and global betting and gambling, all show the challenges that confront societies attempting to reconcile their own local and traditional values with the growing globalization of cultures not of their making.

Is Globalization Total?

These undeniable changes not withstanding, however, the effects of globalization are also sometimes exaggerated. The so-called process of globalization is not so global. Vast segments of the world are still untouched by many of these globalization bonanzas. What we are seeing is a segmentation between a globalised culture. For instance, the prevalence of an urban, cosmopolitan habitats, and the rest of the world, which sees few of the benefits (to the extent that there are such) of access to the global market or to cosmopolitan cultures. Likewise, the assertion of something called "globalization" is often used to reinforce its "inevitability" and so to suppress attempts to resist it, yet many attempts to counteract globalization processes are well in place around the world, as in the fields of ecology and resource management, for example.

While globalization may reflect a set of very definite technological, economic, and cultural changes, the shape of its significance and its future trends are far from determined. The historical specificity of this process does not necessarily guarantee a symmetrical or homogeneous impact worldwide.

Certain dualities recur in the literature on this subject. In one widely influential distinction, there are two primary forces at work in the rise of globalization: globalization from above, a process that primarily affects the elites within and across national contexts and globalization from below, a popular process primarily draws from the rank-and-file in a civil society.

Other dualities are between the global and the local; between economic and cultural dimensions of globalization; between globalization viewed as a trend toward homogenisation around Western (or, even more narrowly, around American) norms and culture and globalization viewed as an era of increased contact between diverse cultures, leading to an increase in hybridisation and novelty; and between the material and rhetorical effects of globalization.

The most obvious "evils" of globalization are structural unemployment, the erosion of organised labour as a political and economic force, social exclusion and an increase in the gap between the rich and poor within nations, especially worldwide. Some people associate globalization with an increase in urban insecurity due to the growing urban violence, with the growing presence of extra-territorial, extra-state movements that thwart international development and may pose serious threats to security, peace, stability and development (such as drug trafficking, mafias, merchants of weapons of mass destruction, or terrorist organisations).

Rise of Local Resistance

A number of developing countries, such as China or Malaysia, have become increasingly suspicious of globalization and have tried to find ways to constrain its effects on their national way of life. Yet, at the same time they desire some of the benefits of participation in a global economy and exchange of goods and information. A major question today is the extent to which societies will be able to pick and choose the ways in which they can participate in a global world; or whether, as with other Faustian bargains, there is no halfway alternative.

The rise of local resistance such as against Coco-cola plants in Andhra Pradesh, Kerala and Tamil Nadu and the role of local and international nongovernmental organisations exerting an influence that may be termed counter globalization. In some instances these groups are equally "global" in character (international human rights organisations, such as Amnesty International; environmental organisations such as Greenpeace; or labour organisations such as Save Trees). In other cases they are antiglobalization, profoundly resistant to the economic, political, and cultural interpenetration of different societies and cultures (for example, regionalist and fundamentalist groups of various types). While globalization is clearly happening, its form and shape are being determined by the patterns of resistance, some with more progressive intentions than others. The way in which the crastre corridor project of a Special Economic Zone in Andhra Pradesh was opposed by the local farmers lest they should lose their livelihood in the anti-globalization resistance. Similarly, in West Bengal local people and farmers opposed the projects at Singur. The government cancel all the projects because of stiff oppositions.

National and local economic, political and cultural changes are affected by and actively responding to, globalising trends within a broad range of patterns. Indeed, because education is one of the central arenas in which these adaptations and responses occur, it will be one of the most myriad of institutional contexts. Hence, the answers developed will require a careful analysis of the trends in education, including:

Global Impact on Education

The broader economic effects of globalization tend to force national educational policies into a neo-liberal framework that emphasises lower taxes; shrinking the state sector and "doing more with less"; promoting market approaches to school choice; rational management of school organisations; performance assessment; and deregulation in order to encourage new providers of educational services.

One of the important fallout of globalization, in the context of education, is the sharp decline in the intake of social science and humanities courses. Computer applications, Information Technology, Science and such other courses offered by the UTS (Indian Institute of Technology) and MBA make the youth of the present day "Careerists." This again makes their outlook and perception of life more practical and less ideal. Hence, "Materialism" has totally driven away "idealism". In turn, this has affected "Family Ties" as well. The concept of family is getting diluted increasingly.

Global changes in culture deeply affect the educational policies, practices and institutions, particularly in advanced industrial societies. For instance, the question of "multiculturalism" takes on a special meaning in a global context. With the growing global pressures on local cultures, the question is as how to deal with the terms of local, regional, national, and transnational conflicts, as cultures and traditions whose histories of antagonism may have been held partly in suspension by strong, overarching imperial-states break loose when those institutions lose some of their power and legitimacy?

There is more than that meets the Western eye to globalization in Asia. It is analytically tempting and rhetorically powerful to describe the practices and consequences of globalization principally around the metaphor of the Golden Arches. The signs and wrappers of American McCulture have spread to cosmopolitan areas. With an emergent middle-class Indian appropriations of Western rock and popular culture such a position risks flattening out the one-dimensionalising complex processes of globalization. These processes are not simply uncritical reproductions of Western cultures. Rather, their formation flows out of, (1) a hybridisation and reappropriation of Western cultures; and (2) long-standing incorporations and appropriations of other Asian and regional cultures.

Cultural Hybridisation

Crass "Westernisation," "Hybridity," etc. are not inventions of post-modernism, globalization and post-colonial theory. Rather they are social and cultural formations born out of complex and intersecting histories that often predate direct contact with the industrial and imperial West.

Population mobility is another hallmark of globalization. Travel, displacement and "border crossing" are often cited as indicative aspects of globalization; with population movements across national borders in search of work and improved quality of life.

Another hallmark of globalization is the assumption of Western "capitalocentrism." Yet the flows of power, , and control do not necessarily begin from or end in the West. For example, Asian capitalism, economic power and regional control within their own local, social and economic fields are as pervasive and distinctive in their characteristic configurations and aspirations, hybrid values, identities, and practices as Western capitalism.

No Western product, cultural symbolism, or social practice maps onto blank state indigenous or national cultures. Rather such forces dovetail in unpredictable and unsystematic ways into local histories and relations. Globalization, then, is neither a story of rapacious Western multinationals nor hapless Eastern Victims. Clearly, fat capitalism must contend with local prehistories of other forms of economic activity, other kinds of regional and local exploitation, other fields of class struggle and cultural domination.

Much of the theorising about globalization has come from the West. In this regard, discussions of cultural globalization have tended to be forms of "inside-out" theorising that is, versions of the impact of the extension and articulation of the economic formations and cultural practices of dominant economies and cultures upon regional, diasporic, emergent, smaller and less influential economies and cultures.

Multi-cultural Traffic

Thus far, our focus has been on the cultural politics of the local. An attempt has been made to show, by reference to one local site, the complexity of the multidirectional traffic of "flows," of homogenising and heterogenising forces that are mutually implicated in the dynamics of so-called globalisation. Some of the theoretical issues implicated in what several scholars have identified as the globalisation of discourses of globalisation. The term globalisation has rapidly gained theoretical prominence and intellectual cachet in the last decade, often used to characterise or indeed supplant the equally slippery and catchall term "postmodernism." (*Luke A Luke: A Situated Perspective*).

The most widely accepted definition of globalization is that it is a feature of late capitalism, or the condition of postmodernity, and more important, that it is characterised by the emergence of a world system driven in large part by a global capitalist economy. This "capitalocentric" epistemology is being focused on the economy as the principal force driving cultural, social and educational changes on a global scale, fails to recognise that "economic activity always takes place and is embedded in a culturally constructed context." Such economic determinism drags culture along as a causal outcome, not as a context or broader social field of cultural circuits of signification, identities, and power relations.

As Waters sees it, "globalization is a social process in which the constraints of geography on social and cultural arrangements recede and in which people become increasingly aware that they are receding... a globalized culture is chaotic rather than orderly... it is not centralised nor unified... the meanings of its components are relativised into one another but it is not unified or centralised."

Globalization is isomorphic with a kind of high-tech, multimediated economic and cultural imperialism that in an earlier age might have been termed "Westernisation"—read

Americanisation"—or else a post-modern mutation of colonialism. In that regard, globalization, like its parent term "postmodernism," has pejorative connotations in the sense that the metaphors and images associated with global markets and capital and a global sweep eradicating or at least normalising diversity and difference, paint a picture of a monstrous grotesque of Godzilla—like proportions voraciously gobbling up labour, markets, cultures and traditions. It is "a brakeless train wreaking havoc," a shrinking if not an elimination of time and space and an erosion of "the local" (Harvey: *The Condition*, P8).

The fundamental polarity between local and global, macro and micro, is at the heart of much current debate about globalization in the social sciences. Here the local is cast in a victim narrative, robbed of agency, stripped of authenticity and reduced to nothing more than a hapless consumption machine.

This perspective centres on the proclamation that the West enjoys what is often called a hegemonic position in the world as a whole. Those who maintain that they are representing subaltern or oppressed groups often cast the West as very dominant and thus to conceive of globalization as a form of Westernisation or as imperialism or colonialism in a new guise. In this perspective many non-western societies are regarded as victims without agency and "globalization" becomes simply the pejorative symbol of all things that are allegedly contaminating or disrupting these societies (Robertson and Khondekar: Discourses of Globalization: *International Sociology*, 13, Vol. I 1998).

"Subaltern" is a Western intellectual construct and is not an identity that Asian cultures identify with. Many countries in the region currently undergoing economic and political/social upheaval are using elements of globalization (such as, the "new" financial sector accountability and corporate transparency, and the new global visibility via media and telecommuncations) to challenge "internal" problems.

There is not a homogeneous "West" or "East," or indeed a singular academic, intellectual, or corporate voice on cultural globalization.

But the irrefutable fact is that the United States has the world's largest economy and via the world language of English, its intellectual industries, scientific and military systems and mass media and publishing exert substantial control over dominant modes of representation and communication.

5

Can India Survive Global Competition?

This is the age of global village, global economy, global movement—(Direct Foreign Investment, global shifting of manufacturing units, business process outsourcing (BPO) off shore transactions)—so much so in the opinion of Friedman "the world is flat." But where do we stand? To whom we do look towards for the total transformation of India from "maa baap" tradition to Herbert Spencer's "Survival of the Fittest?" Obviously the youth. But where do our youth stand today? They are rudderless, without any idealism, only interested in promoting, they have individual agenda instead of working for societal interests. This paper seeks to analyse the causes for the failure of the present educational system which is so much politicized with the "Politics of reservations," to inject moral values bereft of the Indian educational system of quality competence and competitiveness.

Do We Need the Degree Malls Selling the Junk?

The judgment of the Supreme Court setting aside the imposition of the quota system in purely unaided (so-called self-finance) private colleges is historic. No doubt, this judgment by the highest court in the country naturally created hickups in the throats of our politicians who never stop from singing the song of welfare of the weaker sections but who never send their children even to the elite managed institutions! This judgement ought to have been delivered at least four decades back. This slapping of the state for its policy of son-in-law distributing the wealth of his mother-in-law! What right does the state have to dictate quotas and fee structures to those educational institutions to which it does not contribute even a single rupee? Already the educational system of India is on the rocks as it specializes only in churning out unemployable graduates and post-graduates of the so-called professional courses, leaving aside those marginalized lot who opt for the touch-me-not conventional courses—B.A., M.A., BOL., MOL., and so on.

Quota vs No-Quota

To quota or not to quota-that is the question to set the debate on higher education with all political parties overwhelmingly pitching for a legislation or constitutional amendment for reservation in unaided private colleges. It is virtually a foregone conclusion that the Supreme Court may have ruled against quotas in such institutions for backward castes, Dalits and tribals but the consensus among the parliamentarians is that one can't do away with reservations, because the beneficiaries of these "quota" constitute a good majority of the so-called VOTE BANK!

Need to Promote Quality Education

But beyond the debate on quotas, there are some equally crucial issues. For whom are those private colleges meant for? And what social obligations do these institutions have? For a vast majority, a five-star education is inaccessible simply because they cannot afford to pay the fees. Merit alone cannot get one into a good position. If money comes before merit, then it is only the minuscule section of our population that can anyway have access to higher education. Issues like these have been glossed over in the furore over the Supreme Court order freeing private unaided educational institutions from state control. The last decade has seen the mushrooming of higher institutes of learning, after the government opened up education to private players.

Unemployable Professionals

A new study claims that only 23 percent of M.B.A. students are of employable quality. A recent report points out that in our country, the business industry requires around 1,28,000 MBAs - 2,000 as CEOs and the rest at other levels. While there are 1,257 B-schools recognized by the All India Council for Technical Education, they only churn out 70,000 MBAs out of which only 23 per cent are of employable quality. The survey has evoked a mixed reaction from industry experts (*Deccan Chronicle*, 4th March, 2007).

While the IIMS, have been kept out of this survey, only 132 B-schools have been rated as "average or better" by the All India Management Association and these produce some 20,000 graduates, who are still not considered top of the league. Professor Rammohan Rao, dean, ISB, believes that students should evaluate their requirements and then choose an institute carefully as there has been a widespread mushrooming of management institutes in the country: "what is lacking is adequate educational infrastructure to groom them. While the numbers of young people seeking professional qualifications have grown dramatically the management institutions have lagged behind."

Industry experts are dissatisfied by the lack of practical training imparted to B-school students. Most of these students are not adequately equipped to deal with corporate demands. Say Venkat Jasti, VC and CEO of Suven Life Sciences Limited, "Colleges may impart the best of theoretical education but of what use is theory alone in the corporate world? What the institutes need to do is to ensure that their students get at least three months of practical training before their transition from classroom to job space." The mushroom growth of professional educational institution, particularly the Andhra Pradesh, has made education a cottage industry, to say the least. Consquently almost in every district there are as many as half a dozen engineering colleges providing shelter to third rate students and busy in distributing degrees and be content in filling up their coffers. So much so professional education in Andhra Pradesh has become a farce.

Jobs Plenty - Competent Hands Few

A Gurgaon-based multinational IT company went headhunting to Nagpur for its high-end specialized processing segment. Why Nagpur? Because almost all metros have been squeezed of available talent. Of 500 applications it screened in two days—300 are B.Tech—but only 60 were found suitable. The rest, though qualified, couldn't speak "manageable English"! Yet, the company was willing to recruit half of them. Why? It had no alternative. So, we have recruits not because they are competent but the organisation needs them! What an irony?

The HR department in a retail major shopper's stop gets at least 8,000 applications every month but hires only about 60 of them. "We need more people. But there is hardly anybody with enough experience in retail or specialized in high-demand jobs like "merchandising and floor management" said the CEO.

In the next seven years an acute shortage of five lakh professionals in IT/BPO companies is the apprehension of market watchers. The health sector wants double that of the present number of five lakh doctors. In retail and telecom, many lakhs are required to fill the empty chairs. In the aviation sector, at least 10 planes fail to take off every day for want of pilots (V. Krishna Rao, *Indian Currents*, 30.10.2005).

Even with all the vacancies, many of the 40 lakh who pass out every year from professional and other colleges will be on the roads searching for a job. In the next eight years, almost a tenth of the population will be unemployed. In the Indian job market, the commodity is skilled labour and the price is salary. But the supply of professionals with the right skills has remained the same.

Indian Education is Incompatible with Global Economy

"The education structure is missing the link with the economy and not evolving with the market. While student intake in premier institutions like IIT and IIM has remained almost the same over the years, school education lacks vocational courses." Most of the syllabus of our professional education is heavily theory-oriented and very practical and skill oriented. Most of our institutions have any tie up with industries. So as to impart practical and working knowledge. Hence the gap between what we learn and how we work.

Many students and their parents do not know which course is useful, they blindly follow others.

An obvious example is India's engineering sector. While there is a surplus of 75,000 mechanical engineers, there is a shortage of 44,000 computer engineers. A study by the National Association of Software and Service Companies (NASSCOM) says that engineers will form a considerable chunk of the estimated shortage of five lakh professionals in the IT and IT-enabled services sectors by 2012 (*The Hindu*: 27.10.2005).

Moreover, with companies in banking, finance and insurance, manufacturing, travel and health set to be major users of IT-enabled services, the demand is only for specialists. Only about two lakh of the 20 lakh graduates are considered "employable" by ITTS. While there is a great demand for specialist/skilled-oriented jobs, the present professionally educated are not fit enough to fill the slot. There is a greater need for diversification courses than in the past.

Breaking the mould is Anusha, 22. While most of her friends went for the usual courses after school, she graduated in tourism from Osmania University's College of Vocational Studies. In a month she got a job at a travel company—Technovate. Hence, product knowledge is important and vocational training helped Anusha in getting the specialization.

But How Many Anushas have this Awareness?

Again, initiatives from students alone won't do, the IIT is not being taught the latest in the market. For three years there has been no change in the syllabus. Students should be made to probe and think. There is no correlation between what they are taught and what they are expected to deliver.

The problem cast a shadow on multinationals like Oracle which came to India to exploit the cost advantage and use the famous brain pool. Its research and development centres in Bengaluru and Hyderabad are the largest, outside the US. But Oracle faces a real crunch in middle level professionals.

High Quantity - Low Quality

The question is not the shortage of quantity but of quality. Then again, there is a shortage of good teachers as well. "Most graduates aspire for a multinational job rather than doing research or teaching." Even IITs face a 30 per cent shortage of teachers, A NASSCOM study says that less than half of the new PhD holders every year opt for a teaching or research job. Last year, the Council of Scientific and Industrial Research could give only four of the 12 scholarships for research because there were no deserving candidates. In many professional colleges the faculty are thus not "first rate but frustrated"!

The biotechnology sector too faces the problem of quality. Hailed as the next to IT, it has an employee strength of 50,000 with the potential to add 10 lakh jobs by 2012. "We have enough pool of B.Sc. and M.Sc. holders. But in specialized areas like pharma engineering there are not even enough to poach," said an HR head at Biocon in Bengaluru.

According to professional services organization Ernst and Young in Hyderabad, India needs 20,000 research professionals and 4,000 investigators by 2010. But currently it has only about 250 trained investigators and 150 research associates. A huge dump of degree-driven, unskilled manpower is not only useless to the industry but also a big social burden to the state.

In the pharma sector, apart from domestic requirement, foreign expansion plans of Indian companies are driving up the demand for specialists. They need people who have set up the plants approved by the US Food and Drug Administration. This includes a wide range of specialists like lawyers, auditors, engineers and quality assurance experts. In the new scenario, even scientists have to be commercially oriented and should have managerial skills. In India, this is a rare commodity.

The health sector is also struggling to get doctors specialized in areas such as cardiac surgery and neurology. The search for quality workmen is on in the manufacturing sector, too. India's biggest car maker, Maruti Udyog, is still dependent on its engineers on the latest design and get them trained in Suzuki's Tokyo labs.

Japan had a similar tie-up with the US 30 years ago. But today, the Japanese Toyota is breathing down the neck of General Motors and Ford. India can do the same but only if we invest in infrastructure and technology. Indian auto sector is already growing by 20 percent, almost 10 times the global rate. Will it be complemented by enough good" engineers?

Why Reservations in this age of Globalization?

The medicos all over India have launched a national stir against the proposed 27% reservations for weaker sections in the "Islands of Excellence" (IITs and IIMs). This apart, they are also very much against reservations in postgraduate medicine courses.

It is hardly relevant today for the protagonists of reservations to demand more space in education and public employment at a time when competition has become the order of the day. In this age of globalization selective discrimination in the name of weaker sections is tantamount to the nations practicing tariffs to give protection to their domestic industries against more foreign competition. This has no relevance in this age of globalization where the operative principle is "survival of the fittest". Therefore, the time has come to throw all our emotions out of the window and debate dispassionately the relevance of reservations in "education and employment."

M. Karunanidhi, Chief Minister of Tamil Nadu said: "Even in races the handicapped are given certain concessions." But this remark is contestable. In this age of globalization, when the left front of government of West Bengal is all for capitalism, why talk of concessions to the weaker sections?

The athletes are given the concessions only at the start but not till the winning post. The protesters are only objecting to reservation in higher education not to the policy as such.

If the conditions of the OBCs have remained abysmal even after 50 years of following the policy of reservation, how will it improve in the future by resorting to it? "Is there any scientific evidence to show that a person's intelligence depends on the community he or she belongs to?

If reservations are treated as a means for achieving social justice, it should not be forgotten that such means also leads people to organize themselves on caste basis, making the caste system stronger. The 27 per cent proposal is a populist measure driven by "vote bank" interests. It is quite disheartening to see thousands of students protesting and many resorting to hunger strikes in the sweltering heart. All they need to do is to go in similar numbers to the polling booth and throw out reservations lock, stock, barrel.

It is absurd to argue that the so-called forward community suppressed others for 3,000 years. Life in India before 1950 was tough and devoid of improved material conditions and institutions.

Any opposition to reservation in the present form which profits mainly the politicians is branded as politically incorrect. This stand is viewed as an apology to the forward castes.

Government and state financed universities are being treated as stepchildren in our so-called "knowledge society." Many have been going steadily downhill for over half-a-century not because they are "government" but because reservation has turned them into captive vote banks, without really educating the deprived communities. Quotas in colleges and universities still admit them with "zero cut-off marks." Without attacking their basic deprivation at the elementary and high school level reservations are only a devaluing of their degrees and diplomas. This has only resulted in the categorization of 'Reserved Services' and Merit Services! How many centuries do they take to get 'reserved' stigma removed? This vote bank approach will only fuel resentful feelings of superiority and inferiority in innocent young minds that have not been given a level playing field to start out with. Hard decisions to improve standards in government schools, attracting talented people as teachers, providing good buildings and facilities, and designing relevant curricula will receive support from an increasingly education-hungry populace.

The rationale behind the decision to increase the total number of seats so as to retain the existing number and the open category is not clear. However, for the first time, the Government has indirectly admitted that the reservation policy will cause a loss to students in the open category.

Reservations destroyment provide lethargy and encourage the weaker section, the so-called the below creamy layer to be parasites of the state and a heavy burden to the tax payer. THE LONG ONE CAN LIVE ON THE CROMBS THROWN AT BY OTHERS?

Government must conduct periodic surveys to ascertain the extent of privileges derived by the beneficiaries and to include genuine, deserving claimants to education and employment excluding those who have already benefitted. The concept of merit and the criterion for reservation have to be constantly redefined so as to reconcile them, keeping in view the growth of the nation and social progress. The current impasse can be resolved by formally recognizing candidates with a strong desire and commitment to serve rural and underserved communities.

Access to Basic Amenities

What the deprived sections need is to access the basic amenities of life-good primary education, and proper employment opportunities. Reservation in professional courses and postgraduate programmes will only improve the position of a minuscule proportion of the underprivileged. They must be taught to catch fish instead of giving them free fish—free bites at the expense of tax payers. This only results in Robbing the Peter and Paying the Paul—quite unscientific policy which only balkanized India into 'we' and 'they' - PC, SC, BC, ST and the Minorities.

The Government can buy the "capitation fee" seats from the private institutions and distribute them to the needy. By this it will satisfy the political agenda, the needs of the rural poor, and of course the commercial interests.

In seeking to implement the reservations scheme, the Government should bear in mind two imperatives. First, if the institutions are to take in additional numbers, it must be serious about strengthening their physical and academic infrastructure, including faculty.

Secondly, the task of strengthening the public school system that caters to the socially and educationally disadvantaged as well as special enrichment programmes that would level the field are equally important and brook no delay. But the mute point is: how can we brainwash our vote bank's greedy politicians who fiddle while the innocent are burning?

Desperate Hunt for Skilled Labour

The desperate hunt for skilled labour has forced companies to tie up with training firms. The result is the emergence of Rs.3,000 crore recruitment and training sector, which is now spreading to smaller cities and education hubs like Nagpur, Kanpur, Kota and Visakhapatnam. Ironically, the training sector itself is facing a crunch of HR managers and trainers. The whole pool is about 4,500. The Government of Andhra Pradesh recently decided to open training centres, one in each district to train the fresh professional graduates. Hence, the need is for an industry centric academic syllabus. We need skills and not degrees. Already 40 percent of the graduates in India are enemployed. It is a terrible waste of resources. There are also increasing calls to introduce courses in soft skills, like communication, in the college curriculum. Hardly a few can communicate in English, despite the mushrooming growth of English medium educational institutions.

An innovative educational system and a pragmatic government are the only hope for better utilization of Indian manpower. The job market is booming and if anybody says I can't get a job, then he ought to be a stupid person. (V. Krishna Rao Expansion of Cultural Imperialism through Globalisation: 2007, P. No. 116).

The Business of Knowledge Capital

We are in the midst of a world economic mini-boom. In the case of India, software services, identified as "high-tech services" account for a significant share of services exports. IT services exports are estimated at around $16 billion currently. What is more, in terms of indicators of technological competitiveness reported by the National Science Foundation of the US, China and India rank well when compared to some European countries and many developing countries.

However, it is necessary to differentiate between knowledge in the production of goods and services and knowledge for the production of goods and services. While knowledge is being applied in production in these countries, the US still monopolizes the control over knowledge. This comes through from evidence of various kinds (Jayati Ghosh: *Deccan Chronicle*: 08.07.2007).

India lag far behind the developed countries in terms of research and development (R&D) expenditure. While the figure is close to 3% in the case of Japan and the US, and between 2 and 2.5% in France and Germany, it stands at 1% or lower in China and India.

In comparision, among the developing economies, total R&D spending exceeded $5 billion only in Brazil, China, the Republic of Korea and Taiwan.

Flood of Sweat Shops

This means that "knowledge" for the production of both high-tech goods and services still emanates from the "North" and from MNCs of the North, and producers in developing countries are dependent upon the transfer of this mostly patented knowledge through licences. In fact, licensing the use of this knowledge ensures significant revenues to firms from the US, far exceeding than that received by other countries.

According to NASSCOM, offshore operations of global IT major accounted for 10-15% of IT services and BPO exports and captive BPO units accounted for 50% of BPO exports. Further, MNC-owned captive units have been scaling up their operations steadily with the headcount forecast to grow by at least 30% this year.

Thus, foreign firms with control over knowledge appear to be exploiting the availability of skilled and educated labour from underdeveloped countries. What is more, there is evidence that the best talent from the developing world is being used to strengthen control over knowledge in the US.

According to the National Science Foundation, out of the approximately 280,000 foreign graduate students enrolled in US universities, 63,013 were from India and 50,796 from China. Further, out of the 37,608 non-US citizens who received doctoral degrees in 2002-2003, 10,089 were from China and 3,238 from India. Two thirds of these students had definite plans to stay back in the US and another 20-25% were considering the possibility of staying back.

Even to the extent that talent remains in the developing countries, there are, signs that through a process of the internationalization of R&D operations, MNCs are exploiting that talent to retain control over knowledge. Currently, MNCs account for around three fourths of global business, R&D.

As of now, more than half of the world's top R&D spenders conduct R&D activities in developing countries.

In India, leading firms like Intel, Microsoft and Adobe have R&D operations within the country. Almost all the global giants in automobile, telecommunication technology, computer, software, machinery, electronics, biotechnology, pharmaceuticals and other major industries have made R&D investments in China.

The problem is that even while such knowledge may be partly created in developing countries like India and China, or by their talent, the fruits of that knowledge are still restricted for producers of these countries. And more stringent patent regimes are making such access to knowledge even more difficult.

All these developments suggest that even while China and India are becoming important based on knowledge bases, production of exportable goods and sources, the largest beneficiaries of this development are MNCs from the developed countries.

An Overview

Apart from quality education which sustains a high degree of global competitiveness among our youth, there is a dire need to promote moral values which are also equally important. In this century of market—economy and rank consumerism, the present educational system is only individual-oriented sans societal development. Such a system only makes our youth steeped into crass consumerism. This is the reason why crime rate is increasing in our country day by day. Therefore, it is high time for the intellectuals, policy makers and social activists to ponder over deeply and come out with a totally rejuvenated educational system which strengthens the competence among the youth and also make them socially responsible citizens.

The Indian economy is growing rapidly and Indian companies are establishing a global reputation as innovators in diverse fields from Information Technology to Biotechnology and pharmaceutical. However, a World Slunk Miuly published last year pointed out that India's demand for highly educated skilled workers was already outstripping supply. While the country would have 2.3 million knowledge professionals by 2010, it could face a deficit of up to 0.5 million workers. Moreover, the number of professionals* engaged in research and development per million population in India compares poorly not just with the developed nations but also with developing countries notably China, Brazil, and Mexico.

In terms of sheer numbers there is no death of technical manpower in the country. India has nearly nine million graduates and two million post graduates in science and 100,000 people with Ph.D. qualifications. Every year two million students enroll for science degrees and another 700,000 for engineering. But as one eminent scientist noted the IT giants are hiring thousands of graduates from abroad while two million science graduates are registered at the country's employment exchanges. The World Bank study estimates that only 10 per cent to 25 per cent of general college graduates are suitable for employment. The key issue is ensuring quality education. Over many years colleges and universities have failed to produce the right kind of human resource. The universities in particular, instead of developing into vibrant centres of high quality education and research able to attract both good faculty and students, have become largely moribund. Overcoming this malady must be given higher national priority than setting up new institutions (*The Hindu*: 09.01.2008).

6

Marginalisation of the Poor

In the wake of economic liberalisation imports were liberalised and global giants were allowed to invade India by successive governments of both right and left hues. Today imports are free from all encumbrances while our industries are gasping for breath.

In the name of reforms we can collect good money through FDIs, selling of PSUs, opening up the stock market to foreign investors and other sources of foreign funds, but let us not forget that all this money will be at the cost of selling our sovereignty and will be consumed once again by our enormously costly and kleptocratic system of governance. They have consumed it in the past, they will consume it now also. Look at the few regular big scams and swindling of public funds coming to light every day practically in every department of the government at the centre or the states.

Marginalisation of the Primary Sector

There is no work in the primary sector as agriculture does not receive much attention in the priorities of the government. Floods, droughts and epidemics reduced subsidies, unremunerative prices, absence of marketing infrastructure remain with their perpetual problems. Hence, their suicides are increasing.

Manufacturing industries such as textile mills are shrinking day by day. Cities of mega textile mills like Mumbai, Ahmedabad which used to employ 15 to 20 lakh workers have closed their mills. These closed factories have become now real estate "bonanzas."

Even in the case of private sector, only those who can collaborate or manage equity participation or can outright sell their establishments to foreign companies may make a fast buck. Some traders may also benefit marketing foreign goods. Some consumers also feel happy in buying them. Plastic money (credit cards) boom and the clamouring for the foreign goods have left the Indian industries marginalised. The decline of local industries have robbed away the livelihood.

For other countries reforms may mean progress and prosperity like in China, Taiwan, Malaysia and Korea or even Indonesia, but for us it means sheer disaster. While the rulers are getting fat the people are groaning. Gradually, our government will handover India to another East India Company - A cartel of MNCs! Already World Bank is ruling India by proxy.

With the galloping deficits because of an exorbitantly costly system of governance and black economy, the deficits shall be on the rise and at a more alarming rate in times ahead, so also the borrowings and the slide of the rupee. This is termed as 'debt trap' and 'bankruptcy' of a nation. We are already neck deep in heavy debts, which we may never be able to repay. We are born under heavy debts and our children will also be born with this burden on their heads.

The country's non-development, high expenses and perpetual deficits are causing unabated inflation. This is an alarm bell indicative of our economic bankruptcy.

Reducing the Rate for Whose Benefit?

The government is gradually reducing the rate of interest on public deposits, basically to provide a level playing ground to all foreign companies, in the guise that it will provide relief to industries and cheaper loans to consumers. This is mischievous because reducing the interest on deposits to a level of 6% or so has already crippled the common man, particularly the senior citizens.

Reduction in the interest rates by the Reserve Bank of India only helps the middle and upper class clients who buy cars, construct houses and buy consumers durables. Interest reduction does not help the poor, the marginalised and the underprivileged as the Bank will offer them loan without any security!

It is no wisdom to bring down our rate of interest to the level of the US or other developed countries who have built an extremely sound economy, infrastructure and various schemes for old age care, whereas we have none. Their allround sound economic base places them on a different platform altogether, compared to our highly crippled and inadequate infrastructure and equally crippled and alarmingly dwindling civic services (power, water, sanitation, hygiene, medical care, roads and others). Moreover, these services too are costly and staff highly corrupt and requires additional expenses to retain these supplies, besides the mental agony, waste of time and disruption in work. Poor roads mean high cost of maintenance of vehicles while erratic power supply and voltage fluctuations damage electric gadgets and demand additional expenses for their repairs and replacements. Such extra expenses add to our cost of living which at present are as high as in affluent societies.

Therefore, people have no income left for saving. A common man has to save for the rainy day and also plan income for his old age through the interest earned on his savings. The diminishing rate of interest has thus further crippled the already suffering common man. Unless we also improve our infrastructure, make civic services available at our doorstep, control inflation and rising cost of living, extend old age pension and medical health care, etc. aping the west is suicidal.

Foreign Direct Investments

FDIs may elevate us for a short while. Money may also appear in the market (printing of equivalent rupees of dollars received), and government can also sit complacent against a comfortable foreign reserve. But all this may prove to be a short-term measure and a long-term catastrophe. If these can initially support our economy by providing some 'seed capital' these may be welcome. But if we invite FDIs and consume them in meeting our unproductive expenses rather than using them for developmental work, it will only add to our liabilities and prove disastrous. We are using these funds to meet our trade deficits and debt servicing. If it is so, it would be defeating its basic purpose and may play havoc with our economy, same as it did with the Mexican economy. Such investments in India are a sort of cover-up to hide our incompetence, excessive government expenditures and consequent galloping deficits. It may mask the actual financial situation of the country with our kind of attitudes and working habits will only deteriorate our condition because easy money given to a spoilt child is spent carelessly instead with prudence and does more harm than good.

Foreign investment money is not ours in the first instance and has to be returned one day in one form or the other. For the time being, however, we may consider it as a loan so long as the business and trade relations with the investing countries remain cordial. Take the example of Enron (Dhabol Power Co., Maharashtra), AES Corp. [Orissa Power Generation Co. (OPGC) and CESCO, Orissa], PSEG [Public Service Enterprises Group Inc.—major share holder in Tanir Bavi, Karnataka and Pillaiperumalnallur (PPN), Tamil Nadu] or Mirant Crop, and CMS energy—all from the US and all in trouble and want to sell their stakes and exit. If they exit we will have to pay back their huge investments in foreign exchange. Therefore, to fatten on somebody else's money beyond a reasonable limit is dangerous. We cannot be ecstatic about short-term gains (deceptive surplus of foreign exchange) and oblivious to the long-term catastrophe (K.C. Agarwal: *Shaping India of Our Dreams*: 2003, P297).

Foreign Participation

Since our economy was in doldrums, we wanted funds to meet our expenses and called the affluent markets of the world to open their shops here or takeover ours since surviving on somebody else's riches is easier than working hard. This is a land of karma not kriya!

They establish successfully and earn for us and themselves. But the question arises, are we so worthless that we can't earn for ourselves that others must do it for us? If they are successful they will repatriate their earnings and bleed us dry @ Rs. 48 to a dollar. It is doubtful that we shall be able to earn enough foreign exchange to meet the heavy imports, pay for profits on their commodities, investments and commissions and debt servicing unless there is a radical change in our work culture. At present if the FDIs fail as we did, they wind up and go and repatriate their dollar investments making India a "banana republic!" Let us remember the crisis experienced by our East Asian Tigers.

If we don't change our work culture, they are bound to fail like we did and chances of failure are more than success. Nobody has a magic wand to make a dead system alive. No one can flog a dead horse into life. What can we do ourselves when others can't do it for us? We all know that we Indians are highly capable, industrious, patriotic and can turn the tide of events only if we are allowed to do so.

Parasitic Culture

We are trying to find out new avenues for collecting money rather than trying to earn. We want free fish, but do not want to catch the fish! In the process we have developed a parasitic culture always depending on other's charity. We all know that we have failed because of poor governance. We, therefore, call upon the countrymen to understand the situation in totality and with more concern to follow and take the right course rather than succumbing to such short-sighted measures such as food for work programmes, free education, free housing, free food, subsidies, free loans, etc. It is high time we remember that no one gives us free lunch.

Road to Serfdom

One day our industries may bow down before multi-nationals. They may either sell-off their business to the foreign giants or to survive become their partners. Gradually, the wealthier and stronger partner will take control of the business as he will bring finances, technology and the global market with him which our Indian partners lack. Our industrialists become their employees. Our younger generation already slaving and slogging at CALL CENTRES, so-called WIPROS, SATYAMS, INFOSYSES, are only running. Cheap centres with cheap workers for their foreign masters. These companies are functioning as cheap labour contractors running SWEAT SHOPS!

Since the market is now open for 100% foreign participation, most of our blue chip companies have gone under their control as already the Union Government is bent upon selling navaratnas for a pittance. Our children are working for them and they becoming our masters once again! Indian constitution has abolished bonded labour but our rulers have global masters!

Job opportunities will also be shrinking because of paperless offices, automation, mechanisation and latest techniques of production adopted by most manufacturers, while we have to support a large force of fresh unemployed youth emerging every year. Automation is good for the west with her low percentage of population but not for india which is world's second largest populated country. The result is markets are full with no buyers!

Private industries and government organisations are already forcing to accept VRS to cut down their flab and to save on cost. It is our everyday experience to see press reports of retrenched employees demanding re-employment while the present employees working, counting their number of days of survival. When new job opportunities are already shrinking where will this surplus staff go? All this will lead to serious repercussions. If the youth remain out of job, their parents are thrown out of jobs and interest rate on deposits is reduced to half, then what will happen? This is the major reason for the increase in violence, crimes and the fast spread of naxal, extremist and ISI activities. These have become alternative sources of livelihood for most of our youth; thanks to globalization.

The continuous dependence on foreign products would lead to rise in the demand for foreign exchange. We have to export our riches (natural resources) to them and be left only with service industries. Already we have permitted MNCs to farm wheat and cereals and flood the markets with consumer durables - squashes, syrups, KFC—bucket chickens, etc. which can be catered and carted by the local manufacturers.

Brand Slaves

The average Indian consumer has already discarded what is Indian and got used to foreign goods. His education, his aspiration, his ethics have been so indoctrinated that he hates everything Indian and embraces everything that is American. His ultimate destination is Dollar land—with this kind of attitude it is only natural for elites to propagate that we develop a global outlook. Container is much more important than the content.

Our exports too, may rise as the foreign participants also establish their manufacturing activities here (mostly assembly of the semi-knocked down (SKD) components that they shall import from their parent units-sort of a screw driver activity in our country). With the dwindling value of rupee, it is not wise for us to have a high level of imports and exports anyway.

MNCs Swallow the Primary Sector

Foreign players also have their eyes on our primary sector, to grow high quality agro-produces. Our present agro yield is far too inferior in quality and much too low in produce. Optimum use of land, hybrid seeds, fertilizers, scientific cultivation and mechanized farming can raise the produce manifold. This is a highly profitable proposition for the foreign players. What we are not able to do they are doing on our soil. They have established large farms and entered into agriculture. They have already captured agrarian sector with seeds, fertilisers, buying crops, financing cultivation and affecting the rural economy.

There are cases of a few foreign contractors who obtained contracts in our country for constructing roads, bridges and flyovers at prices about 60-70% of local contractors and completed the work much in advance and of much better quality because of their systematic planning, working to schedules, importing cement, steel, etc. from Japan, Taiwan, Korea or China at much lower prices than our indigenous expensive products.

The survival of our industries and livelihood of our people is at stake. Whatever we decide today, we should not overlook its consequences of tomorrow, lest in our short-sightedness we make everything go sick and still. Remember, to provide means of living to 120 crore people is the responsibility of the nation and its guardians and no one can absolve himself from this basic responsibility, liberalisation or no liberalaisation, also for that matter reservation or no reservation. Why are the Chinese, Korean and Taiwanian products cheaper than ours?

Poor Work Culture

Continuous inflations over the years have sent our prices soaring. Even at current prices our quality, quantity and work output is much inferior compared to that of the Chinese. The workers there are disciplined and conscientious to adhere to quality norms.

There is an abiding sense of duty amongst all. Back home we lack all this. We demand 'pay' not 'work!' We want 'doles' not 'dignity!' Besides poor work culture there are three more conspicuous reasons for our high prices—high cost of governance, underdevelopment and black economy, resulting in recurring deficit financing, printing of excess currency and heavy dose of internal and external debts and interest on that.

If we count the inefficiency of our labour, power interruptions, old technologies, outdated machinery and other work holdups, delays and holidays, the cost of our products should not be more than 30-35% of what these are.

Many of the entrepreneurs and business houses have already resorted to trading of foreign goods rather than manufacturing them. The purpose of globalization was to have additional global market for our products, rather than opening up our markets for them. This is one reason that has given boost to our service sector. We are gradually becoming importers and traders of their goods and services at the cost of our primary and secondary sectors. It is an assured bankruptcy.

Our present concept of liberalisation aims at collecting money in whatever manner, irrespective of its consequences. It is surprising that we are ready to resort to any kind of compromises, even if it may lead us to slavery, but are not willing to mend our ways of governance responsible for all this. Most surprisingly even our 'comrades' who yell at the top of their voice at American imperialism at the slightest provocation have become mute spectators at this daylight plundering resorted to by our ruling in collaboration with MNCs in the name of globalization!

In fact, the evolution of slavery has already begun, we must have only an eye to see it. Look at large-scale disturbances in many states of the country, Jammu-Kashimr, Northeastern states, Orissa, Andhra Pradesh, Bihar and Gujarat, to name a few killings, kidnappings, suicides and unnatural deaths, tribals eating wild roots and dying of poisonous fevers. Even governments' move to provide mid-day meals to dying farmers, Rural Employment Guarantee schemes, Food for Work Programmes have failed to mitigate the woes of the rural India. They are of no avail as most of their funds are swallowed by corrupt politician-beaurocrat-greedy contractor combine. It is only the elite India that is shining! That too in television channels and "India Today!"

Bubble not Boon

Let us not confuse, the service sector is primarily to support the primary and secondary sectors, by itself it does not generate resources. Unless primary and secondary sectors grow, the gains through service sector are a disguise. The decline in manufacturing activities will negate the gains through services. The country shall lose more than it will gain. Services are welcome but not at the cost of manufacturing industries or agriculture. The growth of services without commensurate growth in industrial and agriculture fronts cannot sustain a large country of our size and its mammoth population. For support, services also call for strong primary and secondary sectors. IT may be the dark horse of the long race and may stay, but then there is a limit to grow and sustain the IT for long on global markets alone unless we also develop our home market. A little slidedown in the US economy and if it crumbles like a pack of cards it will cause a shiver down the IT spine. Then our WIPROS, SATYAMS and their tribe will end up in smoke like a house of wax. Already SATYAM has become Enrou of India!

We must not forget, that the IT sector by itself cannot become a source of large employment. IT cannot cause rains, cannot supply power, cannot produce food. In short IT is not Allauddin's Wonderful Lamp!

Similarly, the telecom and entertainment sectors too will have a limited scope to grow without commensurate growth and well being of its masses particularly the rural sector. The well being of the people is essential to make use of services on a long term basis and that is possible only through the growth of primary and secondary sectors. Service sector doing well may be a short term blessing not a long term boon.

An Overview

Globalization can be compared to our past, when we became slaves about a thousand years ago. At that time our weak and divided rulers in a quest to conquer their rivals requisitioned forces from outside the country to fight for them and then one day fell prey to them only. Arrival of Babar in 1526 and founding of the Mughal empire is one such testimony. Similar is the case of the fall of the great Marathas in 1761 at the hands of Ahmed Shah Abdali. East India Company came here around 1691 and how they conquered and ruled the whole nation is a part of the great Indian history. Then also we had nothing to sell to them and for their merchandise paid them our riches in gold, jewellery and raw material. This time we are wooing MNCs to support our economy. We cannot pay them in dollars and that lead to economic colonialism. In short, MNCs have taken the role of East India Company.

Since reversal from globalization is not possible, the only solution to overcome the present hurdles in the way of our industries, business houses and the common man, is through -

- Evolving industry friendly systems, rules and regulations.
- Inculcating a healthy work culture
- Improving the power position.
- Creating labour intensive jobs for all.
- In the West mechanisation and automation do not create much unemployment since those countries are underpopulated. The same cannot be followed in India with her huge population of 120 crores. Pruning of work

force only results in the raising of a huge unemployed population which is detrimental to an elite aspiring market economy which thrives only on buyers with hefty wallets!

Globalization helped the Indian economy but the poor were hit badly. Benefits of restructuring reached only the rich. An ironical situation prevailed in Indian politics wherein the Congress Government, which wanted to promote integration with global economy, was unable to do so because of the crucial support it required from the Left parties to continue in power. The course of the economy changed in 1990. The public sector, which was considered a white elephant, was done away with wherever possible.

Globalization would have acceptance only when the Government took care of the education and health sectors, especially with regard to the poor. If we want to compete globally we must invest in human capital—education and health—and increase human resources. When the Indian States make efforts in this directions we are sure to be crushed by the merciless march of globalization.

7

Impact of Globalization on the Tribal Economy

This is the age of globalization; whether one likes it or not, the process was set in way back in the early 1990s, particularly after the collapse of the Soviet Union and the Communist regimes of Eastern Europe..

What is Globalization?

Globalization refers to the integration of national economies leading to the nation of a borderless global economy. It can be visualised as an interwoven net of factories, fields and forests, banks, governments, labouring and farming populations, cities and transport spread all over the surface of the earth.

Twin Role of National Economy

A nation tries to organise its economy on a national scale in order to perform a two-sided task. The development of a strong economy to raise the standard of living of its people and to increase the national power in the international arena. If we look at the European history, the birth of 'National Economy' is closely linked with the use of international trade to enhance national power. International trade is frequently interpreted as the continuation of war by other means (Avinash Jha: *Background to Globalization*, 2001 p. 12).

The creation of a strong national economy involves the breakdown of local and regional economic patterns and other replacement by modern national and international economic patterns: Globalization vs. Modernisation

This process is also called modernisation. Modernisation has a connotation of scientific and technological developments; but it is integrally linked with the modernisation of the economy itself. The production of goods has to be organised in a modern way. Original producers and the link between them and the raw materials are disrupted, the sources of finance change. Gone were the days when tribals used to collect raw materials like Reetha, Shikakai and used to sell them for their livelihood. They also used these materials for headbath. But today they collect the same but find few or no buyers. Because they themselves are not using them. Instead they are using shampoos, soaps and talcom powders for personal beauty and skincare. Then again, old raw materials used and processed for new products. For example, trees from the forests are made available (hitherto felled by the tribes for firewood) now to the paper industry at extremely low costs. People who made things from bamboo from forests had to pay high costs for the same.

Roads that Changed the Lives

Thanks to the heavy investment made by the World Bank to modernise the roadways, as part of—hastening the process of "globalization, ' the" lace of villages" in remote tribal areas have undergone a radical change.

Earlier, the remote village Gangapur of Adilabad district of Andhra Pradesh had no access to modernisation. But the village is opening up a whole new world for its people and those in nine surrounding hamlets, thanks to laying down of the roads. Earlier, it used to be a day's travel by bullock cart to reach the town of Pembi, 40 km. away (The Hindu: 10.06.06). It took double time during the rains. But 'all that changed with a 12 km. road connecting Gangapur to the main road and the nearest town of Kadam.

Despite fertile lands and abundant ground water, Gangapur and the surrounding hamlets remained poor; the villagers followed primitive methods of cultivation. Traders and middlemen became fat with the yield while the farmers starved.

Education and healthcare facilities were almost non-existent, officials stayed away from these remote villagers.

The road saved the villagers from the middlemen, who had till then dictated the price of paddy, turmeric, cotton and maize.

The tribals were never paid cash immediately, but only after a fortnight. If money was to be paid immediately, the trader would deduct another two per cent. And so innocent were the tribals that none questioned the re-exploiting practices.

But today the villagers are changed a lot. Some of them go to Kadam town to know the prevailing market prices. In addition to this, they interact with officials and learn the latest farming techniques to 'land and increase the produce.' They now sell Mahua flowers, beedi leaves collected from the forests to Girijan Cooperative Corporation in Kadam.

Trappings of Globalization

Besides the perceptible improvement in income levels, an attitudinal change among the tribals is clearly evident. Education, jobs through reservation quota, particularly supported by the police to counter the influence of the Maoists, have radically changed the lifestyle of the tribal youth.

Corporate 'goodies' have affected their lifestyle significantly. Along with development activity, globalization has ushered in the habits of modern world. There is a great demand for TIKLIES, (Plastic bindis), soft-drinks, mineral water bottles, beer, and gutkha. They are supplied at the three provision shops that have sprang up in the Gangapur. They are flooded with cosmetic items like shampoos, face powder packs, 'bras,' 'panties (under garments) and other beauty aids. Tribal girls no longer wear their traditional dresses except on festive occasions.

Then, in Gangapur alone colour T.Vs with satellite connections have come up in a big way. The entire village is now connected with dish antenas covering around 100 T.V sets. The villagers mostly watch Telugu soap operas and movies on pirated VCDs bought in Kadam. "We have about 70 VCD players in the village," the tribals say (*The Hindu*: 10.06.06).

Transformation of Tribal Life and Economy

Thanks to globalization; a perceptible change is clearly visible in the tribal life and economy of Andhra Pradesh as is evident from the above micro-study of Gangapur village of Adilabad district.

The new generation of the tribals—many of them—have given up their traditional occupation and look to sell their labour to the new producers. Artisans too face the same problem. A new economy has been created and the old economy destroyed. Along-with the old economy, the society and culture have also transformed. They are changed not because of the availability of new products but because the new economy requires the institutionalisation of a different set of motives, skills, activities, social relations which are closely linked with the larger socio-economic patterns of national/international kind (Avinash Jha *Background to Globalization*: 2001 ppl3-14).

The process affects the sections of people in different ways. It depends on who has the power to negotiate the pace and kind of change. For example, Brahmins in the state found it easier to make use of modern educational facilities since they traditionally possessed intellectual skills of a formal kind. The modern economy demands such skills. Artisans belonging to lower castes and tribes have different kinds of knowledge and skills which have become outdated in the modern economy. Hence, they have no choice but to become labourers, unskilled or semi-skilled workers.

An Overview

Globalization is hastening the process of destruction of local production and local markets. Gone were the days of Shikakai,

Reetha, Pulse powders (SUNNI PINDI), neem twigs and Kumkum. Today they are replaced by shampoos, tiklis, toothbrush and toothpaste of hundred and one brands which have swept into the remote villages. Mineral water and knockout beers are available in plenty than potable water in Andhra Pradesh. While drinking water is a scarce commodity liquor is freely available in remote villages like Gangapur of Adilabad district. Even women are visiting bars to sip haywards 5000 beer!

Globalization also brought into the picture the transnational corporations. They jockey with one another and against local interests coconut water is replaced by Cocacola and Thumsups. Carrying mineral water bottles has become not merely a necessity but also a status symbol. Now villagers mouth phrases of modernisation, i.e. pollution, environment, ecology, water contamination through in an incoherent way. Thus, the impact of globalization is very significant on the tribal life and their economy.

8

Can Market Economy Survive Anti-Globalism?

'India Shining;' this slogan of the Bharatiya Janata Party in the 2004 elections irritated people. One has come to the villages and see whether India is shining, and one look into a child's face and see whether India is shining. India is shining only for the glossy magazines and the neo-rich, the hi-techies but if you just go outside Hyderabad you will see that everything about India shining is refuted... In the villages alcoholism is rife and female infanticide and crime are rising. One has to bribe to get electricity, bribe the Revenue Inspector to levy house tax correctly. Yes, the middle and upper classes are taking off, but the seven hundred millions who are left high and dry all only to see gloom and darkness and despair. They are born to fulfill their destiny and have to live this way and die only this way. The only thing that shines for them is the sun and it is hot and unbearable and too many of them die of sun-stroke. The only "mouse" these kids have ever encountered is not one that rests next to a computer but the real thing.

There are thousands of such villages in rural India, China, Africa, and Latin America. That is why it is no wonder that children in the developing world are ten times more likely to die of vaccine-preventable diseases than are children in the developed world. In the worst affected regions of rural southern Africa, a full one-third of pregnant women are HIV-positive. The AIDS epidemic alone is enough to put a whole society into a tailspin. Among the Indian states Andhra Pradesh stands first in AIDS affected population. Without education, young people cannot learn how to protect themselves from HIV/AIDS or other diseases, let alone acquire the life-advancing skills that enable women to gain greater control over their own bodies and sexual partners. The prospect of a full-blown AIDS epidemic in India remains very real, largely because only one-fifth of the people at risk for HIV have access to prevention services.

This apart, many people live disempowered. They are a large group of people who have not been fully encompassed by the globalised world. Disempowered people are those who don't have the tools or the skills or the infrastructure to participate in any meaningful or sustained way. That globalised Indian high-tech sector is accounts for only 0.2 percent of employment in India. Add those Indians involved in manufacturing for export you get a total of only 2 percent of employment in India.

The rest of those other hundreds of millions of people, particularly in rural India, who occasionally benefit from the global world but who are not really living inside it themselves. We saw how much angry this group can be in 2004 general elections, in which the ruling BJP was tossed out of office because of the surge in rural Indian voters with the slow pace of globalization outside the I.T park cities.

Globalization for Whom?

These rural voters—just had to spend a day in any nearby big city to see the benefits of the global world: the cars, the houses, the educational opportunities and the fast spread of shopping malls. "Every time a villager watches the community TV and sees an ad for soap or shampoo, what they notice are not the soap and shampoo but the lifestyle of the people using them—the kind of motorbikes they ride, their dress, and their homes," explained Nayan Chanda, editor of Yale Global Online. "They see a world they want access to. This election result was about envy and anger of those who did not benefit from the so-called globalization. It was a classic case of revolutions happening when things are getting better but not fast enough for many people."

At the same time, these Indian rurals understood, why it was not happening for them: because local governments have become so eaten away by corruption and mismanagement that they cannot deliver to the poor the schools and infrastructure they need to get a fair share of the pie. "They become more religious, more tied to their caste/sub-caste, more radical in their thinking, more willing to snatch than create, view dirty politics as being the only way to get mobility, since economic mobility is stalled," said Vivek Paul of Wipro. India can have the smartest high-tech vanguard in the world, but if it does not find a way to bring along more of those who are unable, disabled, opportunity wise challenged, undereducated and underserved, it will be like a rocket that takes off but quickly falls back to earth for the lack of sustained thrust.

The Congress Party got the message, as to choose as its Prime Minister, Dr. Manmohan Singh, the former Indian Finance Minister, who in 1991 first opened the Indian economy to globalization, placing an emphasis on exports and trade and wholesale reforms. He pledged himself to increase government investments in rural infrastructure.

The world's poor do not resent the rich anywhere nearly as much as the left-wing parties in the developed world imagine. What they resent is not having any pathway to get rich and to join the global world and cross that line into the middle class of our mega cities.

Politics of Anti-Globalism

Therefore, anti-globalism was driven by five disparate forces.

1. One was upper-middle-class American liberal guilt at the incredible wealth and power that America had amassed in the wake of the fall of the Berlin Wall and the dot-com boom.
2. The second force driving it was a rear-guard push by the Old Left-socialists, anarchists and Trotskyites in alliance with protectionist trade unions.
3. The third force was a more amorphous group made up of many people who gave passive support to the antiglobalization movement, as they saw in it some kind of protest against the speed at which the old world was disappearing and becoming flat.
4. The fourth force driving the movement, which was particularly strong in Europe and in the Islamic world, was anti-Americanism. "If America is now touching my life directly or indirectly more than my own government, then I want to have a vote in America's power" was the refrain of the anti-globalists outside America.

Finally, the coalition of very serious, well-meaning and constructive groups—from environmentalists to trade activists to NGOs concerned with governance—who became part of the populist antiglobalization movement in the 1990s in the hopes that they could catalyse a global discussion about how we became global. But in the end they got drowned out by the whether-we-globalise crowd.

After 9/11, many American labour groups did not want to be associated with a movement that appeared to be taken over by the anti-American elements. With the Chinese, Indians and Eastern Europeans, the biggest beneficiaries of globalization, it was no longer possible to claim that this phenomenon was devastating the world's poor. Just the opposite: Millions of Chinese and Indians are entering the world's middle class. Thanks to globalization.

Anti-Americanism Gains Momentum

So as the how-we-globalise forces drifted away, as the number of Third World people benefiting from globalization began to grow and as America under the Bush administration began to exercise more unilateral military power, the anti-American element in the antiglobalization movement began to assume a much louder voice and role. As a result, the movement itself became both more anti-American and more unable and unwilling to play any constructive role in shaping the global debate on how we globalise, precisely when such a role has become even more important as the world has got flatter. As the Hebrew University political theorist Yaron Ezrahi so aptly noted, "The important task of enlisting the people's power to influence globalism—making it more compassionate, fair, and compatible with human dignity—is way too important to be wasted on crass anti-American or left in the hands of only anti-Americans." If a few Latin American countries like Venezula, Bolivia, Brazil could unfurl the flag of revolt against the U.S Imperialism, why not India? Why should India lick the shoe laces of America? And What for? With a strong population of 110 crore and vast amount of natural resources India should be a major economic power.

There is a real role today for a movement that could advance the agenda of how we globalise—not whether we globalise. The best place such a movement could start is rural India (Friedman: *The World is Flat* (2006) p.475).

Protest against the State

"This is not a revolt against the market, it is a protest against the state; this is not a resentment against the gains of liberalisation, but a call for the state to put its house in order through even more reform. The revolt against holders of power is not a revolt of the poor against the rich as ordinary people are far less prone to resent other people's success than intellectuals suppose. It is rather an expression of the fact that the reform of the state has not gone far enough.

This is why the most important forces fighting against poverty in India today, are those NGOs fighting for better local governance, using the Internet and other modern tools of the global world to expose corruption, mismanagement, and the tax evasion; to make it easier for the little men and women to register their land, to start business and to get minimal justice from the legal system; making globalization workable, sustainable, and fair for more people by improving their local governance, so that the money that has already been earmarked for the poor actually goes to them and so that their natural entrepreneurship can get unlocked. It is through local government that people plug into the system and to get to enjoy the benefits of globalization. The average Indian villagers cannot be like the Indian high-tech companies and just circumvent the government by supplying their own electricity, their own water resources, their own security, their own transport and their own satellite dishes. They need the state for that. The market cannot become an alternative for the failure of the state to deliver decent governance.

Allround State Failure

Clients of public education are dissatisfied with its poor quality; whoever can afford to opt out does so. The same goes for health care, given the escalating costs of health care. Ditto for roads, highways, water supply, electricity, sanitation, registration of births and deaths, crematoria, driver's licenses, and so on, wherever the government provides these services, it for the benefit of all citizens. But in fact, in some of these, like water supply and sanitation, the poor are actually not even getting the same basic services as the middle class and the rich. The challenge here is, therefore, universal access.

The activist groups are helping to alleviate poverty; the most are those working at the local village level in rural India to spotlight and fight corruption and to promote accountability, transparency, education, and property rights. The poor have to be helped by making the self-reliant. Help them by getting them the tools and institutions to help themselves. Better teach them how to catch fish rather than providing them free fish.

Market cannot Close its Eyes

Collaboration in poverty alleviation is not just for NGOs but for multinational corporations also. Demand makes simply meaningful and profitable. The rural poor in India represent a huge market, and it is possible to make money there and serve them. One of the most interesting examples of this form of collaboration is a programme run by Hewlett-Packard. HP is not an NGO. It began with a simple question: What do poor people need most that we could sell to them? In order to answer that question, HP created a public-private partnership with the government in Andhra Pradesh. HP noticed that the villagers needed instant digital photos as they require digital photos for identification. Then they went to self-help women groups and said, 'We will train you how to use this equipment.' Gave them two weeks training. Provided them with the camera and supplies. This was no charity. Even after buying all their supplies from HP and sharing some of the revenue with HP, the women in the photography group doubled their family incomes. Less than 50 percent of the pictures they took were for identification the rest were of those wanting pictures of their kids, weddings and for themselves. The poor like family photo albums much as the rich and are ready to pay for them. The local government also made this women's group its official photographers for public works projects, which added to their income. So corporations realize that united with consumers they stand to again, divided they lose.

9

Is Capitalism Retreating from Globalization?

The spending habits of America's 'new rich,' the top one per cent of earners in the wealthiest nation on the planet as ever known has been detailed by Robert Frank in his Richistan: A Journey Through the 21st Century Wealth Boom and the Lives of the New Rich (2007). By 2004, this elite was taking home US $1.35 trillion a year a figure in excess of the take home pay of the whole of France, Italy or Canada. But these people had not just been getting richer. They had been creating for themselves a separate country "a state within the state" closed to those with a net worth under 10 million. Frank calls this country 'Richistan.'

The term "plutonomy" is coined for economies dominated by the spending space, of elites, a relatively new phenomenon resulting from globalization. It is argued that the twentieth century mass democracy was economically supported by the earnings of blue-collar workers, especially those enmassed in mining, manufacturing and transport industries. With their decline and the rise of enterprises employing skilled white collar labour, the economic mass base of democracy weakened, opening the door to oligarchy if not political extremism. Such phenomena are disproportionately skewed in a multi-layered developing economy like India's which ranges from pre-modern agriculture to internationally competitive IT. (Madhuri S. Sondhi: *Deccan Chronicle*: 05.07.07).

CRAS Consumerism

The term "conspicuous consumption" was coined by the late nineteenth century American sociologist, Thorstein Veblen, best remembered for his classic, Theory of the Leisure Class. He criticized not capitalism per se, but the capitalists of his time for seeking social importance through the flamboyant display of wealth. The term now has a wider application, encompassing the neorich with their ostentatious spending, ubiquitous in expanding economies such as those of Russia.

Primitive Capitalism

Primitive capitalist exploitation is a bad business in a globalised world. Veblen himself attacked the "leisure class" for slowing the pace of economic development and immiserating the poor, and pointed to the invidious effects of conspicuous consumption in a democratic society. Although it is true that liberal reforms in India have helped to pull a good number of the erstwhile poor into the middle class, the sheer numbers of their neighbours still outside the reach of the trickle are tinder-box of anger and resentment. It is the marginalized farmers—the displaced and the unemployed—who are agitating against the SEZ (Special Economic Zones) granting of the union and state government to multi-national corporations and industrialists by forcing farmers to sell their lands at a throw away price.

Marginalised Masses

Patwant Singh in his Second Partition Faultlines in India's Democracy (Hay House India 2007) provides a detailed statistical examination of the abyss that separates India's globalised elites and the 300 million marginalised and impoverished "rest" covering ill-health, malnourishment, unemployment, homelessness, and lack of educational opportunities, which aggravate vulnerability to communalism and corruption, etc. Disillusioned with the poor state welfare, Patwant Singh concludes with faith in the possibilities of civic action, for which he has set a personal example with the founding of the Kabliji Hospital in rural India (Madhuri Santanam Sondhi).

If this is the case with India and other developing countries of Asia in particular, the western capitalist elites are giving up globalization and resorting to nationalist strategies of protection and state-backed competition for global markets and global resources, with the U.S. capitalist class leading the way (Waldon Bello: *Frontline*: January 26. 2007).

The Washington Consensus broke with economic strategies involving heavy participation by government and positioned the unfettered market as the driver of development.

Imposed on developing countries in the form of "structural adjustment" programmes funded by the IMF and the World Bank, the Consensus reigned until the kite 1990s, when it became clear that on all key criteria of development sustained growth, poverty reduction and inequality reduction, it simply became ineffective. Still neoliberalism remained the default mode for many high-tech economists and technocrats.

The urgent task is how to manage the retreat of corporate-driven globalization so that it does not bring about the chaos and conflicts that marked its demise in the first era of globalization from 1815 to 1914 (Walden Bello: *Frontline*: 26.01.2007).

The former adherents of the Consensus have gone off in different directions. They realised that market reforms while crucial are not enough. Financial reforms for instance, must be "sequenced" if we are to avoid such debacles as the Asian financial crisis which even the IMF now admits was "because of massive capital inflows into countries that liberalised without strengthening their "financial infrastructure."

Mafia Capitalism

Embarrassed by the Russian entry into the hell of "mafia capitalism" in the market reforms with institutional and legal reforms which enforce private property and contracts have become all the more imperative. Other accompaniments of market reforms are "good governance" and policies to develop "human capital" such as female education. Education and healthcare constitute the core of "human capital" without which no amount of structural adjustment reforms would pull the decadent economies of poor countries such as that of African Sub-Sahara out of morass.

Despite its icing of institutional reforms, the core of the PRSP (Poverty Reduction Strategy Papers) cake remains the same macroeconomic fundamentals of trade liberalization, deregulation, privatisation, and commercialisation of land and resources that were at the heart of the structural adjustment programmers. Community consultation has been limited to well-resourced, liberal non-governmental organizations rather than broad-based social movements.

The PRSPs are simply second-generation structural adjustment programmes that seek to soften the negative impact of reforms. The purpose of institutional reforms is "to make sure that the fruits of growth are widely shared and the poorest people are protected from the costs of adjustment" in order to prevent people from being "tempted to give up on orthodox economic policies and structural reforms."

Retreat of Neo-Liberalism

A second successor to the Washington Consensus is what one might call the "neo-conservative neo-liberalism." This approach is essentially the development policy provided by the famous 2000 report of the U.S. Congressional commission on multilateral institutions which proposed a radical reduction of the role and to provide debt relief by the World Bank for the poorest countries on the grounds that they will not be able to pay the debt and seeks a shift from loans to grants. But the debt relief and grants are conditioned on how government performs in terms of liberalising their markets and privatising their industries, land and natural resources, grants in contrast to loans channelled through the World Bank, "can be tied more effectively to performance in a way that longer-term loans simply cannot." Moreover, grants should pave the way for pro-market reforms and aid policy to be more directly coordinated with Washington's security objectives and with the agenda of U.S. corporations (Walden Bello).

Neo-Structuralism

A third distinctive successor to the Washington Consensus neo-structuralism—moves in a more liberal direction, is an approach associated with the Economic Commission for Latin America (CEPAL) that produced the structuralist theory of underdevelopment in the 1950s. According to neostructuralism, neoliberal policies have simply been too costly and counterproductive. There is no trade-off between growth and equity, as the neoliberals claim, but a "synergy." The neostructuralists propose progressive transfer payment policies that redistribute income in ways that increase the human capital or productivity of the poor including higher spending on health, education and housing programmes. These are a few kinds of programmes associated with the "Good Left" in Latin America, meaning the governments of Brazil and Chile.

Latin America's Forays

Being focused on managing the transfer payments to protect and upgrading the capacity of the poor, the neostructuralist approach does not interfere with market forces in production, unlike the policies of the "Bad Left" (meaning Venezuelan President Hugo Chavez and friends) that intervene in production, markets and wage policies. The neostructuralists also embrace globalization. They say that a key objective of their reforms is to make the country more globalised. Simultaneously they alleviate income disparities, upgrade the capacity of the poor and make the workforce more globally competitive. Neo-structuralist reforms are thus said to hold out the prospect of making globalization more palatable, and less resentful.

Global Social Democracy

"Global social democracy" acknowledges that growth and equity may be in conflict, and it ostentatiously places equity above growth. It also fundamentally questions the central thesis of neoliberalism that for all its problems, trade liberalisation is beneficial in the long run. In the long run, trade liberalisation may, in fact, lead to a situation where the majority of citizens may be worse off.

Moreover, global social democrats demand fundamental changes in the institutions and rules of global governance such as the FA-IF, the World Trade Organization (WTO) and the Trade-Related Aspects of Intellectual Property Rights Agreement (TRIPS).

Global social democrats even see the anti-globalization movement as an ally, for "exposing the hypocrisies and glaring shortcomings of global governance and for ending years of self-congratulation by the rich and powerful." But globalization is where they draw the line. Global social democracy sees globalization as necessary and fundamentally sound and, if managed well as bringing benefits to most.

Is an Enlightened Globalization Possible?

Contrary to an assumption that was gospel truth just a few years ago that globalization was irreversible, global social democrats warn that contemporary globalization is, in fact, in danger of being reversed. The benefits of globalization outstrip the costs, and what the world needs is a social democratic or "enlightened" globalization where global market integration proceeds but is managed fairly and is accompanied by progressive "global social integration." "The aim," as Held puts it, "is to provide the basis for a free, fair and just world economy," where the "values of efficient and effective global economic processes... function in a manner commensurate with self-determination, democracy, human rights and environmental sustainability."

First of all it is questionable that the rapid integration of markets and production that is the essence of globalization can really take place outside a neoliberal framework whose central prescription is the tearing down of the tariff walls and the elimination of investment restrictions.

Slowing down and mitigating this inherently destabilizing process, not reversing it is the global social democratic agenda. Social democratic globalization as the "harnessing (of) the remarkable power of trade and investment while acknowledging and addressing limitations through compensatory collective action (Walden Bello).

Then, it is likewise questionable that, even if one could conceive of a globalization that takes place in a socially equitable framework, this would, in fact, be desirable. Do people really want to be part of a functionally integrated global economy where the barriers between the national and the international have disappeared?

Indeed, the backlash against globalization stems not only from the inequalities and poverty it has created, but also from the sense of people that they have lost all semblance of control over the economy to impersonal international forces. One of the more resonant themes in the anti-globalization movement is its demand for an end to export-oriented growth and the creation of inwardly-oriented development strategies that are guided by the process susceptible to democratic regulation.

Neo-Liberal Globalization's Agenda

Alternative to the Washington Consensus is their failure to root their analyses in the dynamics of capitalism as a mode of production. Thus, they fail to see that "neoliberal globalization is not a new stage of capitalism but a desperate and unsuccessful effort to overcome the crises of over-accumulation, overproduction and stagnation that have overtaken the central capitalist economies since the mid-1970s." By breaking and eliminating national barriers to trade and investment, neoliberal economic policies sought to reverse the long-term squeeze on growth and profitability. This "escape to the global" has taken place against the backdrop of a broader conflict-ridden process marked by renewed inter-imperialist competition among the central capitalist power, the rise of new capitalist centres, environmental destabilization heightened exploitation of the South—what David Harvey has called "accumulation by dispossession"—and rising resistance all around.

Globalization has failed to provide capital an escape route from its accumulating crises. With its failure, we now see capitalist elites giving up on it and resorting to nationalist strategies of protection and stale-backed competition for global markets and global resources, with the U.S. capitalist class leading the way.

Globalization is a spent force and it has evoked tremendous reactions that continue to grow in strength. Today's multiplying economic and political conflicts resemble the period following the end of what historians refer to as the first era of globalization, which extended from 1815 to the eruption of the First World War in 1914. "Our urgent task is not to engage in the futile task of steering corporate-driven globalization" in a "social democratic" direction by reforming the WTO and the IMF and promoting "corporate social responsibility" but "to manage its retreat so that it does not bring about the same chaos and runaway conflicts that marked its demise in that earlier era" (Waldex Bello).

Is a Benign Globalization Possible?

That is one challenge. The next big challenge is not to be waylaid into promoting a "benign globalization" but to transcend it that is, to create a truly equitable international order of independent national societies where domestic and local economies will be revived along with the transformation of class relations and the achievement of a healthy balance between the community and the environment.

In this connection, the radical initiatives in Latin America—initiatives moving in a regional or national rather than global direction take us more decisively in the right path than the enlightened globalization alternative proposed by the global social democrats. Long exploited by foreign energy giants, Bolivia has nationalized its energy resources.

Argentina gave an example of how a developing country governments can face down finance capital when she forced northern bond holders to accept only 25 cents of every dollar Argentina owed them. President Hector Ecuador took the bold decision of keeping the oil in the ground rather than exploiting it for short-term gains, thus showing how a Third World country can contribute creatively to addressing global warming.

For many of those in the anti-globalisation movement, the Hungarian thinker Karl Polanyi has seized as a great inspiration. Polanyi talked about "capitalism being a process of disembedding the market from its social matrix and eventually making it the force that drives the society. Globalization has been the climaxtic point in this process of disembedding the market. "The task is to re-embed the market in to the over reaching goals of justice, equality, solidarity' and not to forget national sovereignty'" (Polanyi).

Resistance from Latin America

The resistance from Latin America, particularly from Venezuela of neoliberal globalization and U.S. foreign policy, regard the U.S. as the leading terrorist state in the world for the first time since the Spanish conquests. South America is not only moving towards greater independence but also integrating to some extent. Even if one's motives are the promotion of democracy, the use of bloodshed as intimidation makes it very difficult to predict how one's enemies will react. (Noam Chomsky: *Hegemony or Survival: America's Quest for Global Dom,* Nance: 2007).

Whether it is Asia or Latin America, the motives are the same. The operation of ideological hegemony to maintain power over public opinion has been largely responsible for the brainwashing of a majority of Americans as well as millions around the world into believing that Iraq had amassed weapons of mass destruction.

"Manufacturing of Consent"

Hegemony, thus, operates through mechanisms including the media, education systems and newspeak with the primary function of maintaining public support for the dominant socio-economic system in the U.S. and sometimes, if need be, force is employed to make nations and people fall in line (Chomsky: 2007).

The elite decision-making reinforces the hegemonic repressive rule of the state. Since in open societies, brutal force cannot be tolerated by the masses and thus subtle means of ideological state apparatus begin to be strategically employed to control opinions and attitudes. Such self-righteousness of the state is visible within the state or outside it when powerful nations, in the name of democracy, intervene or resort to military action for self-promoting agendas. Walter Lippman's notion of the "manufacturing of consent" is thereby vindicated in the state machinery's success in casting a network of false consciousness over the public. American altruism is only a sham. The media-elite nexus concentrates on the common interests of the media and the corporate world. The New York Times, a right-wing paper, allows adverse opinion only as an eyewash. The truth is that not a statement made by Edward Said or Chomsky in the post-9/11 months found any space in The New York, Times a rightwing paper that allows opinion only as eye wash.

All intellectuals in the West have supported the war on terrorism, but any questions that involve the terrorism of the state are conveniently kept out. The media are instruments used for the naturalization of power relations, to bestow ideological validation onto a range of social disparities and thus setting out to create a world to make believe impartiality. Antonio Gramsc explains this phenomenon of power dynamics in our society' as a "spontaneous" consent given by the great masses of the population to the general direction imposed on social life by the dominant fundamental group.

Corporate interests dominate the shaping of the U.S. foreign policy. National Security' is only an excuse to promote the U.S. military—industrial interests, bulldoze any opponent, be it Afghanistan, Iraq or Somalia.

The hypocritical strategies followed by the American State in its blatant dismissal of elementary human rights, evident in the Abu Ghraib and Guantanamo Bay debacles, and its simultaneous support for democracy and human rights. The U.S. inches towards becoming the most powerful state in the history by using military and economic policies that were anything but democratic. Globalization is another means to boost up American capitalism.

10

Globalization or Monopolisation?

The word *'Globalization' is intended to cover the economic imperialism of the west,* particularly the *United States of America* whose economy is under the scanner.

In the U.S. manufacturing sector has been almost marginalized with the rise of the service sector—the IT industry. This is the course that led to growing poverty, unemployment, unrest among the middle class. Resorting to business outsourcing methods by the U.S. multi-nationals put the American capitalism in the dock.

Joesph Stiglitz's *Globalization and its Discontents* (2002), notes that contemporary capitalism is marked by an ever-increasing interdependence, that is by economic globalization. Capital 'flows' much more readily looking for the optimum conditions to reproduce itself and in turn accumulate greater capital. Businesses look around the world for greater profit. Contemporary capitalism is marked by the pre-eminence of transnational corporations which in terms of their size and power are able to take advantage of all opportunities to lower the costs of production by shifting the manufacturing units from wealthier to relatively poorer countries, or through consolidation, mergers or 'takeovers.' Finally, contemporary capitalism takes place within a regime of global governance that seeks to accommodate both the particular interests of nation-states (rich and poor) and the needs of transnational capital, which seeks access to open markets and cheaper resources.

Capitalist Concept of Freedom

To the early liberals the rise of capitalism or 'mercantalism' represented a great advance on the hitherto existing society. For them precapitalist society meant feudal and pre-feudal forms in which most of the population was held in some form of subjugation. The emergence of capitalism meant the emergence of the individual from a world in which his 'opportunities' were limited by the fact of birth. Under the feudal conditions to be born a serf meant to die a serf, irrespective of one's talents, capacities or worth. Under capitalist conditions, however, many of us are in a situation where we lack a master. Being thrust into the world without a master was the very quality celebrated by early liberal theorists and enshrined in the idea of the 'rights of man.' And what are these rights? To the seventeenth-century philosopher John Locke, they were the right to 'life, liberty and property.' We are free: free to work for whomsoever we please, or not. Free to take our own chances, to set ourselves up, to try something novel or profitable. It is also a freedom to fail, a 'freedom' to find oneself homeless and unemployed. Capitalism celebrates such freedom as the essence of its own creation. 'Freedom' is 'freedom from arbitrary interference; from other people's plans; from government meddling; from clerics and priests; from people one has not chosen to be with. As a system built on the right of private property, capitalism conforms to and fully embraces this notion of freedom.

According to this conception of freedom, individuals are free to earn whatever they can. If one turns down another's offer of 50 rupees a day, then he has exercised his rights not to be 'exploited.' But this still leaves him looking for money. Similarly, someone is prepared to pay Sachin Tendulkar a 'lot of money to play a festival match, because they think he is worth that. Sports is big business and successful sportsmen and women can command huge fees because a lot of people want to watch them play, buy shirts with their name or posters to put on their walls.

For many liberals this is what freedom is like: some will win, and many will lose; but whether one wins or loses is not arbitrary. That is, it is not based on the whim of a tyrant, a king or a priest, as it was in the past. It is based on what you are worth to others or what others will willingly give you. An important point in this context is that what goes for individuals, goes for countries too. Western countries, particularly the US and Britain are lucky because they are blessed with hard-working entrepreneurial individuals, important natural resources, good trading links, and a long history of settled institutional development. Other countries are not so lucky. It is for this reason that they are much poorer. They are not poor because the latter two are rich.

Is Capitalism a Justification of Freedom?

Hayek and Milton Friedman argued that a (capitalist) market society is not only free society, it is also a productive society. It works, and in working it provides employment, dynamism, and opportunity. Goods are getting cheaper—DVDs, digital cameras, cars, holidays, indeed bicycles—because of competition, lowering costs, opening markets and increasing productivity due to enhanced use of technology. All that outsourcing, downsizing, flexibilising is at one level for 'is,' as shoppers. The capitalist is doing us a personal service: he wants to make a profit, and in doing so he is benefitting us, making our lives easier, cheaper, more fun, more mobile, more creative and more whatever.

The 'happiness' is not confined simply to the consumer end of the scale, for, what a competitive market system encourages at the producers end is risk-taking and entrepreneurship which in turn leads to job creation, employment opportunities, and thus to personal and collective wealth. As Adam Smith famously noted, all this happens by the operation of the 'invisible hand,' which is to say that it is not even an intended outcome of the acts of individual capitalists. One's desire for money, wealth, glory, self-satisfaction leads him to set up a business which in turn requires the labour of others. From such desires come opportunities and employment for others. Self-interest is the motor that drives economic progress and which leads to highly dynamic societies. Where self-interest is curbed by state intervention, economic stagnation follows.

This is an entrepreneurial society, not a society based on dependence—on the state, on the tax payer, on charity, on good Samaritans. So the justification for capitalism is that it promotes economic growth and dynamism as well as, in turn, the economic well-being of individuals, of society, and by extension the world. And to do this we need a free market, a market that is, with the fewest possible encumbrances, tariffs, taxes, obstacles to overcome, hurdles to clear, bars to jump over.

Transferring to the global debate, what we are describing is what is known by pro- and anti-globalisers as the 'trickle down' theory of development. Capitalists are going to get rich in a free market, but in enriching themselves they will provide opportunities, employment, goods for the rest of us. The logic is that countries that are poor today will be better off tomorrow through the action of free trade and capital mobility.

End of History?

Neoliberalism is basically a restatement of the classical strands of liberalism. There is nothing very novel about neoliberal ideas as such. What is novel, however, is the sense in which they have gained a purchase on the minds of political and economic elites across the world. During the last century, these classical statements of liberty had declined into virtual unimportance. A cursory survey of political discourse over the period from 1929 (the period of the Wall Street Crash) to the late 1960s and early 1970s reveals the degree to which it was social, democratic, Keynesian and welfarist arguments that held sway in the advanced industrial countries, even in the US. The elites had accepted that part of the task of government was to provide for citizens from 'cradle to grave.' People needed to be housed, educated, cared for when they were sick, given pensions, and social facilities. This is what 'progress' meant, even more so 'progressive polities.' It was for this reason that the tone of a work like Hayek's *The Road to Serfdom* (published in 1944), which argued against planning and welfare state, is so shrill. Indeed, his work is infused with a sense of defeat, the defeat of liberal 'orthodoxies,' of 'individualism' of freedom. Libertarian liberals lost the key arguments. They had failed to stem the tide of 'collectivism' that threatened civilisation itself. Bolshevism and Nazism being in his view mere exaggerations of the collectivist tendencies he attacked in the nascent welfare states of Europe and America.

Oil Crisis—The Cut off Point?

All this changed with the Oil Crisis of 1973. The major oil-producing countries of the Middle East embargoed the West, quadrupling oil prices and sending elites into a frenzy of recrimination concerning the costs of economic growth, the ever-mounting burdens on business, and the suffocating cost of social democratic measures. This is starting point to intimate the debate on the 'crisis of the welfare state,' the 'overloaded state,' 'dependency culture' and so on.

Birth of Neo-Liberalism

There is nothing like a crisis to provoke a serious introspection on any issue. In the US, Robert Nozick's *Anarchy-State* and Sir. Thomas More's Utopia published in 1974, brilliantly restated the case for an ultra-minimal, ultra-libertarian politics, the rhetoric of what became 'Reaganomics.' In the UK, Hayek became the court philosopher to Keith Joseph, in turn the principal architect of Thatcherism.' Both stood for minimal state, the state should do less, a lot less. If it did less, we would be freer and we would also benefit from the entrepreneurial forces unleashed in the wake of the 'rolling back of government.' So what did neoliberalism imply in terms of policies?

Return of the Market Economy

The main thrust of the return of the market has been in terms of privatisation of economic activity, particularly as regards state-run or state-owned industries. This is less a factor in the US where the state had little to privatise, but in Europe, Latin America and Asia privatisation has significantly altered the balance between the private and the public sectors, 'rolling back' the decade's long process of nationalisation. Nationalised industries are 'inefficient,' 'unwieldy,' they inhibit 'risk-taking' and 'entrepreneurial activity.' They had to go. But neoliberalism demands much more than competition between businesses; it also demands competition within businesses. Thus, one of the novelties of neoliberalism is the penetration of the market into every aspect of the functioning of the enterprise, which is now itself reconstructed as a series of sub-markets. Units within the same firm compete against each other for the same work. Workers within the same firm are expected to see each other as 'resources' or competitors, encouraging the individualisation of work and, in turn, of rewards.

The neoliberal revolution also implies a shift from supply-side economic management, as opposed to the demand-side economics that typified the Keynesian model approaches of the 'post-war consensus.' Government could no longer create demand by embarking on large scale public works which would in turn soak up unemployment, but instead had to adopt 'fiscally prudent' measures for money supply, public borrowing and the control of inflation.

The task of government was to create an environment in which capital could prosper; it was not to displace, moderate or 'interfere' with capital, but to comply with the 'austerity measures,' 'structural adjustment' policies and drastic cuts to public expenditure.

Finally, under the neo-liberal regime, services that remain in the public sector have to be compelled to run themselves as if they are private enterprises, even if they aren't. Thus, schools should be made to compete for pupils, hospitals to compete for patients, public and leisure' services to compete for 'customers.' Neoliberals insisted that there is no separate 'public life' outside the market, only for competition. Manufactured goods, agricultural goods, services like education, healthcare, everything is marketed and nothing is made available exgratis by the state. In short, neo-liberalism is nothing but rolling back to Police State.

Police State

One of the more disturbing facets of neoliberalism has been the encouragement to regard the whole of life as a resource for corporate profit.

To the neoliberals, there is only one rational way of measuring the value, and that is in the market-place. Any answer that departs from the formula whatever he/she/it is worth in the market' has to be arbitrary, that is, based on the bureaucrat's notion of what something is worth.

Genesis of Anti-Capitalism

In a ptolemical essay published in 1989 entitled "The End of History?" ("The End of History?" The National Interest, 1989, pp3-18). Francis Fukuyama suggested that with the fall of the Berlin Wall history had in some important sense come to an 'end.' What he meant was not that history as 'the passing of time' had ceased or that important events would somehow be prevented from happening. What he wanted to suggest was rather that Hegelian notion of history as having an end or goal was about to be vindicated in political terms. Fukuyama insisted that with the fall of the last great ideological crusade, communism, there merged a consensus that liberal democracy with market economy was the 'best' or 'most desirable' political system. Liberal democracy had emerged victorious from the Cold War, from the more fundamental clash of ideologies that characterised the post-enlightenment world. Ideological conflict was a thing of the past. We were all liberal-democrats now.

Liberal Democracy Sans Liberalism

The qualities attributed to liberal-democracy by thinkers such as Fukuyama are those most under threat by these macro-economic developments. "Indeed, it is little exaggeration to say that if anything triumphed in 1989 it was not 'liberal-democracy' but global capitalism" (Simon Tormey: Anti-Capitalism, 2006 P.40). This is to say that it was not politics that triumphed over economics, as implied in Fukuyama's analysis. It was a case of economic triumphing over the political. The anti-capitalist 'battle of Seattle' represented 'a return of the political,' a return of ethics, morality and values in place of the vacuum created by the 'departure' of politics from the global scene.

With the battle of Seattle, it is evident that we are witnessing a crisis of liberal democratic politics. The emergence of a global anti-capitalist movement is a symptom of that crisis. In particular, it is a sign concerned individuals that political actors are capable of influencing, let alone controlling, economic actors. This is not the same as saying that the nation-state itself is in crisis, which is implied in much of the commentary on globalization. Rather, nation states are all too often taken hostage by forces, principally transnational corporations that are able to apply considerable pressure to ensure that their every whim is catered for.

Problems begin when the community has little or no control over its own affairs, when it is unable to govern itself in accordance with its own wishes. Liberal-democratic thinkers like to describe liberal-democratic politics as, in essence, one of self-government.

Capitalism of the major corporations is conducted beyond or outside the direct control or influence of the nation-state. The major corporations conduct themselves in a 'state-like' manner, acting upon their own self-interest as opposed to the interests of the nation associated with the company or brand. In 2002, when the US giant Ford chose to announce 35,000 job cuts as part of a plan to become 'competitive,' it of course, 'consulted' politicians. That is it told them it was cutting jobs' but it was Ford that decided how and where the jobs were to be cut. The process propelling us towards economic globalization has not hitherto been matched by a process of political globalization (Simon Tormey: P.42).

The institutions of global governance are at present subject to corporate needs and interests rather than the other way round. Then, those political bodies that do claim quasi-sovereign character, such as the UN, are without the means of controlling the activities of global economic actors, let alone those states who choose to ignore the decisions of the UN unless it suits them to do otherwise. The net result is that while the domain of political authority has remained at the nation-state level, the domain of economic activity has increasingly shifted to the global level. There is no global state and there is no effective mechanism of accountability for those actors who operate at the global level, such as global corporations.

End of the State?

The economic domain has become even more detached from political control and thus that the relevance of the state as a primary site for democratic decision-making is becoming diminished by the day. It is in this context the 'death of the nation-state' thesis emerged at a time when Fukuyama wrote so glowingly of the 'triumph' of liberal-democracy. The capital that became transnational, created a political vacuum which is felt today in a number of ways that can help explain the emergence of a global anti-capitalist movement. These can be seen in the decline of ideological polarisation and a steep fall in democratic participation.

11

Emergence of Electronic Capitalism

Electronic capitalism has a media mind. As a result, it is at times dangerously mindless, a social order suffering from a collective attention deficit disorder the media absorption of culture and information. But there is no escaping in the fact that we are all affected. Our view of the world is constructed by what we see and hear, and what we see and hear more and more of the time is media. The media are so central to the functioning and structure of today's society that it is no exaggeration to say that they are at once the driving force of our economy, the core of our culture, and the sine qua non of all successful politics and politicians. Daniel Bell's The Coming of Post–industrial Society was simply a "service society" or a "knowledge society," but he did argue that while energy was the central technology of industrial society, information was the central technology of post-industrial society. (*Democracy's Delemma*: Robert C.Paehlke, Mit Press London-2003).

Electronic capitalism, as a conceptualization of the contemporary society, differs from Bell's post-industrial society in at least three ways. First, both are models of a society in which knowledge economic sector is not finance, but media, second, a particular form and structuring of information and the key means of social organization, communication, value formation, and sociopolitical control. Third, information has become a mass-marketed product.

In electronic capitalism, both the means of production and the products are increasingly electronic. So too are the means of economic, cultural, ideological, and political communication and organization. In dollar terms, the most significant export from the United States to the rest of the world is not automobiles or airplanes, but Hollywood films. This "weightless" product results in export earnings in excess of $30 billion annually. These films are on the whole ideologically loaded, both, North American consumption habits and products—and, in general, violence.

Computer software and video games are equally important as products. They are typically more violent and mindless. The Internet promise to only accelerate the extent to which the commercial values predominate. In electronic capitalism, many actual physical products are more electronic image content than physical content. A clothing item produced in Southeast Asia or Central America or the Caribbean may be manufactured for 10 percent or less of its sale price. A far larger proportion of the price will go to the producers and conveyors of photographic and television advertisements as well as to media figures such as athletes successful to display logos on their clothing. Much of the rest of the cost goes to in-store presentation and to profit for "manufacturers" (of the image and brand) and retailers. The actual (subcontracted) "manufacturer" operates on modest margins, and the workers who make the items are fortunate if they earn enough to live in a dorm and have enough to eat. They almost never can afford the products they produce. The broad point here is that an ever increasing proportion of all physical products are information. Those images are not knowledge and are often, in fact, literally wordless.

Media Dominance

Media dominance has created a society that is increasingly becoming one unidimensional. Contemporary media have many physical forms (radio, television, film, Internet, magazines, newspapers, books, and recordings). Yet in many ways the media as a whole speak with one predominant voice. This is in part because one form of media overwhelms all the others—television is far and away the most influential contemporary form of communication. More important, most media are directed to a dominant objective to increase, influence, and organize commercial transactions through advertising. Also, virtually all media are now owned by large private, for profit corporations.

Communications through the electronic media have certain characteristics. The seemingly endless varieties of visual and sound images are similarly framed. Some of this media framing is technically determined; some is ideologically determined. In either case, this framing shapes the way most people see the world most of the time. The largely technically determined rules of electronic media framing include the following: (1) entertainment must predominate and ratings are the central goal; (2) for television, nothing is newsworthy if there are no visuals; (3) complex analysis is presumed to be beyond most viewers and listeners and likely to be impossible in any case; (4) a story cannot go on air without a good sound bite and almost no story is worth more than a few minutes air time in total; and (5) every story must be "news" there must be a new hook and some kind of story line with broad appeal. Taken tighter these aspects of framing help to create what might be termed a sense of "false immediacy."

Ideological Determinants

The ideological determinants of framing are hardly necessary, given the power and effect of the technical determinants. Television news has been largely replaced by infotainment "news" about media "personalities." The so-called hard news has been increasingly dominated by a succession of real-life soap operas. All this can be seen to be a conscious ideology of critical silence regarding any deeper changes or potential issues in modern life and society. Its way, however, be more a reflection of the technical limits of the electronic media and the uncritical outlook of the wealthy creators and purveyors of media content. A survey in the Columbia Journalism Review reported that 40 percent of journalists admitted to "practicing self-censorship by not covering stories that might offend advertisers or the owners of their news organization." Fifty-two percent avoided stories that were "too complex" and 77 percent did not pursue stories that were "important but dull."

There are at least two clear ideological dimensions to the framing of most media images and presentations, especially those delivered any large commercial organizations do not offend any very large or powerful organizations or definable groups, and never question the desirability of growing prosperity, the importance and fundamental usefulness of most products, or the unlimited linkage between happiness and consumption there are occasional exceptions to these rules, but these exceptions rarely survive in the media unsolicited junk mail, a form of advertising not beneath the dignity of many large corporations that also advertise on television.

Hypersaturation of the Culture of Hype

The primary focus and central purpose of, virtually, all media is advertising. This reality has evolved to the point where advertising is so pervasive that it arguably is the essence of contemporary culture. Iconographic product images had become the central and dominant images of contemporary life. Art can but replicate them. Our age seems to celebrate promotion and commercial image making icons and corporate logos permeate the visible, thus far earthbound universe. There are fewer and fewer noncommercial spaces of significance. Noted celebrities will have corporate logos tattooed onto the exposed portions of their bodies and both church sermons and university lectures will have corporate sponsors (if they do not already). Most live performances have corporate sponsors, even when the commercial is entering the public school classrooms. And, in the United States, seventeen billion catalogues (sixty-four for every man, woman, and child) are mailed each year, equal to the total waste produced by 521, 000 American households.

Motion pictures have a long tradition of hidden commercials for smoking and any number of brand-name products. Motion pictures shown in theaters have added slightly sexed-up, TV-style commercials to the previews.

The board point is that commercialization is more and more pervasive and invasive in today's society. Most North American children will be exposed to more than 100, 000 TV ads before high school graduation. Typical North Americans are exposed to 50 to 100 ads each morning before 9:00. What are the effects of this level of exposure? In terms of intentional effects, advertising expands the size of the economy and results in the sale of considerably more goods and service than might otherwise be sold.

Why is this important? One can have ethical doubts about the extent of advertising from three possible vantage points: environmental, social, and cultural. Environmentally, one need not to demonstrate that zero economic growth is, or ever will prove to be, essential or warranted to question on environmental grounds the desirability of a continuous stimulation of consumption by any and all means. Economic activity typically carries a considerable environmental price. Even if a particular good or service carries only a small environmental price, its creation and sale may serve as a multiplier of less benign economic activity. Both the high proportion of newsprint devoted to advertising and the induced purchases of products where no real need exists exact real and measurable environmental costs.

Social Effciency of Consumption

One also might be concerned about what might be called the "social efficiency of consumption." That is, to what extent does advertising determine whether the mix of goods and services produced and sold is socially the best mix of goods and services? The central underlying assumption in contemporary consumerist ideology is the view that advertising stimulates the economy and thereby increases the likelihood that all will benefit, that all (at least on average) will improve their prospects of satisfaction within the market consumption is increasingly inefficient socially. Indonesian families more often go hungry while North American families are induced by both relentless advertising and declining prices to hang clothes in their closets that they will rarely wear. The efficiency of production, in combination with advertising, promotes the "inefficiency" of inequitable consumption.

As regards the notion of socially inefficient consumption, one does not need to assume that the capacity to consume (wealth and income essentially) should be equal or anything like equal. One need only to accept that electric lights are somehow a more "meaningful" use of electricity than electric toothbrushes, and a meal for a hungry child is more important than a larger-than-necessary meal for someone who is already overweight. The combination of environmental and social inefficiency of consumption is what is particularly problematic in ethical terms. Both the consumption and the costs of consumption are shared unequally. It is this combination exists that renders advertising underlying assumption morally reprehensible. That twofold assumption is that all consumption is essentially of equal value and all additional consumption is good.

The core of the cultural argument against excessive advertising is that it can, through implicit repetition of particular messages, elevate this assumption to a status of central cultural precept. In effect, if a significant proportion of consumption is both socially and environmentally inefficient, then there is, in electronic capitalism, an ongoing and massive denial and moral silence.

That silence is primarily an act of omission, an overwhelming of such considerations through the sheer repetition and volume of the all-consumption-is-equally-good message. It is also a function of the dominance of media forms that do not lend themselves readily to ethical debate ethics is not easily rendered as a news bulletin, a form of entertainment, or a no tedious visual image.

A number of analysts discussing the development and evolution of the market economy observe that "the greater randomness of individual choices is not unstructured, for the cohesiveness of the whole is maintained through the ruling socialization pattern which encourages persons to interpret their needs solely as needs for commodities." That ruling socialization pattern is, increasingly, delivered electronically. Even the satisfaction provided by the commodities themselves is diminished in this process.

"The individual must become increasingly indifferent to the fine shadings and nuances of both wants and the objects he pursues in the search for satisfaction." Why? Our complex needs themselves are all increasingly commodified, even when they cannot be really satisfied with commodities. Moreover, the need for continuous production and replacement of goods requires a decreasing attachment to particular and particularly enduring goods. This indifference to the qualities of objects, and the slightness of our attachment to them as we so readily replace them with 'new, improved' versions, is merely the other side of the developing shallowness and triviality in our articulation of our needs themselves."

The source of this inherently unsatisfying quest lies in the transformation of industrial society through the rise of advertising. The commodity market parodied the patterns of 'conspicuous consumption among the rich capitalists and middle-class imitators at the turn of the century, this time 'democratized' on a mass scale.

The mass marketing of television carried the consumer imagery into the back corners of home life." Ideological consumerization as a deliberate substitute for the discontents of work in modern factories and the weakening of the bonds of rural family life. The family as a consumption unit was sold as a replacement for the family as a production unit. Nonetheless, television and consumerism have survived all such disruptions and "television," "became the common synonym for mass communications: a futuristic analogue to the hearth. Situated in the midst of the American household, TV became a vehicle for a consumerist mentality."

While a consumption-defined middle-class existence was preferred in shows and bolstered by the flashy beginnings of modern television advertising, working-class life was characterized chiefly by the laughable boorishness of the family breadwinner (men) could hardly make it through the day. The normalcy of consumerism was defined and writ large in the living rooms of the American populace.

Commodification

Several analysts have attempted to relate the psychology of satisfaction and measure of happiness to be issued having to do with commodification and the environmental costs thereof. Drawing "psychological data from several nations confirm that the satisfaction derived from money does not come from simply having it. It comes from having more of it than others do, and from having more of it than last year. Thus, the bulk of the survey data reveals that the upper classes in any society are more satisfied with their lives than the lower classes are, but they are no more satisfied than the upper classes of much poorer countries than the upper classes were in the less affluent past." "Most psychological data show that the main determinants of happiness in life are not related to consumption at all," "above the poverty level the relationship between income and happiness is really small." "Expectations, fuelled by advertising and social pressures, rise with income, but satisfactions do not. So there is always an element of dissatisfaction which increased income cannot cure." Many Americans were unhappy because they sought to meet nonmaterial needs with material goods each has an insight similar to this finding based on survey data of social psychology. Hirsch's classic *The Social Limits to Growth* links the dissatisfactions of prosperity to the declining utility of positional goods, goods but a few, or at least not a majority of individuals. This psychological quirk, of course, lies at the heart of advertising and marketing. It is inevitably, however, a source of frustration and accounts for why individuals will pay double or even tenfold what they need to pay for goods as long as those goods are visibly branded and known to all. It is worth mentioning. But having one very expensive watch or automobile rather than five or ten ordinary ones will impose less ecological damage.

For the most part, advertising, consumerism, and the exploitation of inherent dissatisfaction carry a considerable social, spiritual, and environmental price. "The ideology of human domination over nature is the most extreme version of this attitude. Its practical expression is the sort of pursuit of human goals in production and consumption activities that remains utterly indifferent to the impact of those activities on the viability of other life forms; the most extreme version is the social practice based on the doctrine of the insatiability of human material needs. In this social practice nonhuman nature is regarded as nothing but a means for human satisfaction." "Work-and-spend," insatiability of human material needs, it is 'human nature' always to want more, to want the kind of consumer goods we seem to find irresistible, and to resent taxes and other efforts to direct our resources toward communal needs and the needs of the less advantaged rather than toward private gain. "Psychoanalytic insights into our vulnerability to anxieties about our bodies and our social selves reveal starkly the manipulations employed in advertising messages." Individuals are led by the imposed need for the rising levels of consumption to misinterpret the nature of their needs for the rising levels of consumption to misinterpret the nature of their needs and to misunderstand the ways their needs may be satisfied. The dominance of contemporary social life by advertising and the values and attitudes on which it is for the most part based. Many, if not most, citizens are also generally irritated by the ever-increasing intrusiveness of advertising. Yet advertising expenditures continues to grow by some 6 percent per year, easily double the rate of growth of the GDP. There is little restraint on the quantity or the content of ads, Governments have taken an ever more hands-off role, in part because those in office are themselves highly dependent on both advertising and media. For the most part they don't choose to regulate either in terms of content or quantity. There is no longer even any restraint of the ever more centralized ownership of media outlets, an outcome that arguably poses as great a threat to liberal democratic values and practices as does governmental control.

Newspapers are now part of large print media chains. Virtually all owners of media have one thing in common: they are very wealthy individuals or (often tightly held) corporations, and are in any case beholden to large corporate advertisers. Electronic capitalism is characterized by an ever-increasing concentration of all industries on a world scale, and the media are no exception. In the United States by the end of the 1980s the control of almost all national media was in the hands of twenty-three corporations. This trend toward consolidation, growing cross-media ownership, and ownership concentration has continued or intensified. A few giant firms now control vast media empires vision, film, books, videos, and a significant Internet presence. The media "products" of these firms are also increasingly marketed globally. In recent decades, media firms have, through merger or purchase, become ever more global in organizational structure and scope.

Chain Papers

More than 80 percent of U. S. newspaper circulation is in the hands of chains. Only a few highly influential papers like the New York Times and Washington Post remain outside the control of major chains. Other aspects of media are also highly concentrated, including magazine ownership book and magazine distribution, and increasingly in recent years book publishing and book retailing. One of the few shifts toward voice and control multiplication is in cable television. Cable channels are, however, in many cases affiliated with each other or with major media organizations. In the United States, public television reaches a limited audience and, given stringent limitations on public funding, is generally sponsored by corporations as a public service. Other than the public broadcasting networks, what the multiplicity of cable channels almost never present is current affairs programming that raises fundamental questions about the nature and quality of contemporary society. Most local television news emphasizes crime reporting, accidents, sports, and weather.

Business and Business only

Business news is reported constantly on many stations simultaneously. "Every evening, network news shows faithfully the report of stock-exchange averages, but stories deemed important to organized labour are scarcely ever touched upon. Reporters seldom enlist labour's views on national questions. Unions are usually noticed only when they go on strike, but the issues behind the strike, such as occupational health and safety or loss of benefits, are rarely acknowledged." From the perspective of media decision makers, however, the matter of ideological perspective in many cases may never have rise to the level of consciousness. Business news has a prosperous audience that commands a lineup of prospective advertisers for every available advertising time slot. At present, labour figures are almost never seen other than when there are labour problems, and environmentalists are only ever asked to comment on particular and suddenly visible environmental issues, narrowly defined. This selectivity is not unrelated to the effective demise of the labour movement in some wealthy nations. The selectivity is also an essential source of "economism" of electronic capitalism (Robert C. Paehlke).

Many questions are only rarely asked and almost never answered in the media world. It is not so much that there are things that cannot be said on television, but that many important matters are rarely considered seriously in any forum, electronic or otherwise. All interests are taken to be "particular" interests, more pejoratively "special" interests. Discussing the economy, is seen by all to be the prerogative of economists, politicians, and business people. Everyone involved in the discussion, therefore, agrees on virtually all the questions that matter. There are scripted disagreements, to be sure, but fundamental or value-based disagreements are almost never aired with regard to economic matters. There are occasional "don't forget about giving us our share" assertions, but no serious discussions about possible public priorities or governmental interventions.

Serious Questions Ignored

Some questions that are almost never seriously engaged in media discussions include the following: Has the increase in global trade and investment provoked a race to the bottom in terms of wages (especially among poorer nations), social policy, taxations, and/or environmental protections? Is economic growth always beneficial or worth the cost? Are the remuneration levels of the upper corporate management excessive? Does climate warming carry any non-technical implications with regard to the processes and patterns of production and consumption? In what ways is the distribution of wealth in the world shifting, and what can be done about it? Do some societies get more (or less) social benefit from their level of wealth than others? Which societies distribute wealth most equitably?

These questions are difficult and not readily dealt within the terms of sound bites. Moreover, many people do not have the time or inclination to think about such matters. That is the point. To the extent that our society is media driven and our culture is now defined by electronic media, such questions will not easily enter the broad public discourse.

Revenue is of Primary Importance

The best hope of breaking the media-advertising cultural monolith is the creative imagination devoted to debunking advertisements, especially for tobacco, pesticides, automobiles, military weapons, and handguns. The pseudo ads produced are as slick as, and harder hitting than, "real" ads. Some are brilliant. Many are not shy about appropriating and manipulating carefully cultivated brand images. Most are very visually oriented. This group has also produced "anti-ads" for televisions, but despite efforts to buy airtime, few if any ads have been broadcast. The best response to the slick smoothness of consumerist unidimensionality may be slickly smooth alternative and noncommercial rejoinders. Other efforts of interest here include award nights for the least truthful corporate ad campaigns or public pronouncements of a sort that has come to be called "green washing." Such events may not be reported extensively but could gain cult credibility precisely because they are not the society as a whole is now even more thoroughly immersed in and saturated by media and those media are, more centrally controlled. Those whose job it is to influence media interpretations of events have many more tools and skills at their disposal. Pollution is no longer visible to a majority without effective media coverage, in part because some of the most visible impacts have been partially ameliorated.

The most important potential competing (alternative) values routinely fail to generate issues of political and policy significance, or to keep what issues they do generate in the public eye long enough to see through anything more than minor adjustments, social equity and environmental sustainability are potential competing values to the central thrusts of electronic capitalism unimpeded consumption and increasingly concentrated wealth. The pursuit of these latter objectives is so single-minded that it is rarely noted that they themselves are probably contradictory.

Reasons for such a lack of balance are advanced in McKibben's *The Age of Missing Information*. A media-saturated, highly educated, post-agricultural, post-industrial society is, missing a great deal of fundamental information. The greatest loss, however, comes from what we do not do either at work or while watching television three to four hours a day on average.

Deliberate Deception

The problem with television and other contemporary media is not a matter of deliberate deception. The problem is oversimplification of a complex world. It is an inability to convey anything very interesting about the world's two most significant problems: climate warming, which moves at an excruciatingly slow and uneven pace and for the most part lacks visuals, and poverty, which simply is not news, since it is there, it has always been there, it seemingly always will be there. The failure here is rooted, in television's relentless dailiness.

Television can cover most natural disasters, accidents, and arrests very effectively, but against not the two that matter most climate change and world wise poverty. "The worst disaster move much more slowly, and thereby sneak past the cameras." There is a glacial slowness about the evolution of climate change and a relentless daily sameness about poverty. Those who produce news programmes recognize the seriousness of these problems, but television fails to communicate their importance. Television is utterly unable even to make them widely understand our dependence on electronic media is central to our seeming inability to come to grips with sustainability issues: the retreat from nature, the rapid globalization, the loss of skills needed for self-sufficiency and so on all came to full blossom in this period. By some estimates, for example, human beings have used more natural resources since the end of World War II than in all the rest of human civilization.

Networks do not Cover Civic Participation

The political implications of this reality are more fully understood in a brief return to one of the most important social scientific revelations of the last decade, declining social capital. The crucial role of civic participation and social networks of a strong and active society civic interaction has declined through four decades since the 1960s. Involvement with organizations as diverse as women's clubs, civic organizations, churches and church-related organizations, labour unions, literary societies, and bowling leagues has also declined significantly. His membership in some types of organizations has increased, but these expanding organizations do not engage members in face-to-face interaction of a civic character reasons for the decline in civic life. He offers five contributory explanations: the shift of women into the labour force, residential instability, shifts in the character of contemporary families (more divorces, fewer children), a decline in community-based enterprises, and the increased role of electronic media (which Putnam describes as the technological transformation of leisure). Each of these is related in some way to our model of electronic capitalism, deep-seated technological trends are radically 'privatizing' or 'individualizing' our use of leisure time and thus disrupting many opportunities for social-capital formation. The most obvious and probably most powerful instrument of this revolutions is television; "television has made our communities wider and shallower. In the language of economics, electronic technology enables individual tastes to be satisfied more fully, but at the cost of the positive social externalities associated with more primitive forms of entertainment. The same logic applies to the replacement of movies by the VCR." It also applies to the Internet. The Internet is perhaps the ultimate in wide communications, the technological transformation of leisure has all but undone effective civic and democratic involvement. Meaningful civil engagement by, or even civic interaction among, the majority of citizens is in sharp decline.

The Internet is highly multicentred, because an input presence (website) can still be obtained at relatively low cost, with reasonable quality production affordable to non-wealthy individuals and small groups. The Internet is far and away the cheapest way to communicate on a worldwide basis for those who have access to a computer. It help to avoid commercial domination. There remains, however, a considerable danger that the Internet will evolve from being principally a multicentred information source to being principally yet another means of commercial advertising and/or goods acquisition.

Politics of Internet

In effect, it could become much like commercial television, but with difference the commercials will be integrated into the programmes and there will be no need to venture out to a shopping mall. One will just click a box on the screen using the remote in one's hand. Order what you see while you see it, with no need to pick up the phone and no need to continuously enter and reenter a credit or debit card number. The clothes or jewellery that the personality on the screen is wearing or the furnishings in the room can be yours; just point and click and your set-top box will transfer the precleared access to your bank account. Given the time taken up by increased hours of work and twenty or more hours per week of media absorption, there might be precious little time to shop. "Zap and get" is the answer to a question no one has asked. The Internet has the potential to be a significant and positive step away from media unidimensionality. The Internet is the only communication medium, other than books and small magazines, where the centralization of power and wealth could be challenged in any significant and consistent way. The Internet is an island of hope within the smoothly mindless and commercial, ideologically unidimensional, monolith of modern media.

The Internet is already a significant weapon against explicit political and religious repression outside the liberal-democratic nations. It is significant new means of getting information and opinion both into and out of repressive authoritarian regimes. There is also little prospect of preventing undetected electronic eavesdropping in the long run if that is the intent of the government.

The Internet could also become a new means by which to invade non-commercial privacy, including political privacy.

Globally, the advantage of the Internet may be even more disproportionate. Those in large, rich, and well-established firms and nations have an overwhelming advantage. Selling globally on the Internet requires global brand recognition and that is not easily achieved over the Internet alone it is achieved primarily through the power of television, film, the paid endorsements and to a lesser extent through the print media and other, but also expensive means. A website only brings that part of the world to your door that knows where that door is and is willing to trust the assertions and products available. The Internet remains the only electronic media from where ideas can have an autonomous presence and can compete outside the direct control of large-scale commercial interests. It is also the only electronic medium where ideas have a degree of autonomy from commercial objective.

Many questions regarding the impact of the Internet remain. How important will the noncommercial functions of the Internet be in people's everyday lives? What proportion of the population will acquire effective ongoing access? Will the Internet be truly significant in the realms of ideas and politics? It clearly has the potential to bypass corporate-dominated media gatekeepers. It opens a discrete and effective channel for the socially ostracized, including dangerous voices such as pornographers and racists. But the Internet is also a helpful channel for less dangerous voices, such as those of greens, labour or the lift, which are also relatively powerless and invisible in the wider world of electronic media.

12

Rise of Mass Media

Thanks to globalization; both the print and electronic media became an integral part of man. Hitherto, T.V. and dailies and periodicals were part of the living room of the middle and upper middle class people. But today, woman are fed with news channels, entertainment channels by the electronic media.

Today, media serves not the common man, but the corporate giants. This chapter deals with the evolution of the electronic media and discusses how it serves the commercial interests of the multinationals.

Evolution of the Electronic Media

Television was initiated in India to promote education and information and as a means of development communication. In the initial phase, the target audiences of Indian television were the poor, the illiterate, and the deprived masses, but in the course of time, that agenda got eroded. The television industry underwent a massive transformation, from a tiny monopolised government controlled propagondistic establishment to a highly market-centric, investment oriented one feeding on advertising revenues. Television programmes originated from its popularity rating by an 'audience' that represented the Indian consumer market. Most of it catered to the intellectual appetite of a section of the urban and semi-urban elite and middle class, leaving the poor and the illiterate, mainly residing in the rural areas, untouched. Moreover, under the new state policy of privatisation and globalization, all the early objectives lost fundamental relevance (Ranajit Chakravarthy, Mugdha Sengupta, Social Change, September, 2004).

Original Agenda

Television was expected to fulfill the following objectives in the country;

- Act as a catalyst for social change;
- Promote national integration;
- Stimulate scientific temper in the minds of the people;
- Disseminate the message of family planning as a means of population control and family welfare;
- Provide essential information and knowledge in order to stimulate greater agricultural production;
- Promote and help to preserve the environment and ecological balance;
- Highlight the need for social welfare measures including welfare of women, children and the less privileged;
- Promote interest in games and sports;
- Create values of appraisal of art and our cultural heritage (Doordarshan; 1997, New Delhi, Audience Research Unit).

In August 1965, entertainment and information programmes were introduced and the medium was re-defined as sources of education, information and entertainment. An all-new medium in this country, TV had to obtain social legitimacy in an orthodox traditional society, and became geared to promote a nationalistic outlook. In the same year, from January 1, 1976, advertising on television ('commercials') was introduced.

Development Communication

When television was still in its infancy in India, there was a need to supplement educational broadcasts with other programmes that would provide a lighter mood for the television viewers. Film and film-based programmes were the easiest way to achieve this objective. Weekend Hindi and regional language films, film-based programmes, quiz programmes were introduced. The only soap operas shown on Doordarshan were borrowed from foreign television, such as American popular shows like *I Love Lucy, Star Trek*, British shows like *To the Manor Born, Sorry or Some Mothers Do Love them* or German television game shows, telematches and detective serials like *The Fox, Indian Programmes* that proved popular were quiz shows like *What's the Good Word*? talk shows by Kamleshwar and Tabassum (Phool Khile Hai Gulshan Gulshan) and sports programmes. Doordarshan programmes had been classified by audience, industrialists and even by Doordarshan authorities themselves as educational and entertainment. As a result, staging of a discussion programme meant promoting education and showing a feature film meant entertainment. It took 25 years for Doordarshan to conceive that education and entertainment might be converged in development communication. In 1984, it came up with the first Indian soap opera *Humlog*.

Soap Operas

Humlog is considered a milestone in Indian television for many reasons. Soap opera did not enter into Indian television as a means of commerce, i.e. to earn revenue. The prime objective was to handle social issues related to development communication. Indian television was inspired by the success of Mexico's Televisa,' a private commercial network producing popular melodramatic series such as *Ven Conmigo*' (Come with me), which aimed to promote family planning, adult literacy, health and sanitation.

Sponsored Serials

Humlog was the first honest attempt to communicate development messages through entertainment. It was based on a story of ups and downs of a north-Indian middle class family with agrarian roots, emphasising issues related to political corruption, underworld activities, Indian joint family values, women's problems, unemployment and smuggling, and family planning. Producer Sobha Doctor, who was from an advertising background and had a fair degree of knowledge in promotion management, prompted the idea of sponsorship. Doctor's concept of advertising originated the concept of sponsored serials, beginning with *Humlog*. Maggi Noodles, a product of the Nestle subsidiary, Food Specialties Limited, are launched in the Indian market in 1983, sponsored *Humlog* and became a popular food product in India overnight (Ranjit Chakravarthi and Mugdha Sengupta).

Flow of Tele Revenue

'If Mrs. Indira Gandhi's Government had not decided to expand the television network to cover 70% of the Indian population, launched its own satellite INSAT IB and started colour telecast in 1982, it is extremely doubtful if many of today's products would have seen the light of day in the Indian market. As an example, Maggi Noodles wouldn't have been so successful'.

Maggi, from a brand name of noodles, became a brand name for Nestle, serving as a springboard for it to launch its other food products. The fact that *Humlog* contributed significantly to the success of Maggi Noodles opened the eyes of Indian advertisers to the potential of promotional communication. Prior to *Humlog*, Indian advertisers were not much convinced about television as an advertising medium.

Serials Selling Brands

As in the case of product marketing, where a vigorous market research is conducted to identify what the consumer wants. In developing the plot of *Humlog,* it was kept thoroughly abreast of what the viewers wanted to see. This paid off—*Humlog* turned out to be a brand, a 'serial' that was not to be missed. Moreover, *Humlog* made 'serials' a best selling brand for Indian television industry by establishing itself among the viewers as a most popular programme in prime time. The revenue from advertising of Doordarshan *soared.* In 1982-83, before *Humlog* was telecast, Doordarshan revenue was Rs. 15,88,74,060. This doubled in 1984-85 (Rs. 31,43,45,326) during the *Humlog* telecast, and further shot up to Rs. 136,30,00,000 in 1987-88, after *Humlog,* an Indian indigenous soap opera, displayed its immense strength to reach the Indian audience.

Humlog opened the floodgates for sponsored indigenous soap operas and sitcoms, heralding the coming of an age of the 'serial,' which, for the Indian audience meant both soap opera and sitcom. Doordarshan increased its advertising rate by 15.0 percent in three years after Humlog. Advertising revenue grew by an average of 62.5 percent over a period of eight years, to Rs. 361 crores in 1992-93.

By 1987, more than 40 serials had been telecast, such as *Buniyad, Khandaan, Yeh Jo Hain Jindegi,* etc. On an average, two were shown every evening at prime time. By this time the basic objective of introducing television in this country was forgotten.

Joshi Committee

The Joshi Committee report clearly argued that the audiovisual mode of communication had the potential of serving as the most powerful promoter of growth with equity in an illiterate and inequity stricken society. The committee warned the urban middle class not to monopolise the medium, which was originally meant for the illiterate, underdeveloped rural people, and projected possibilities of the medium becoming a propaganda tool for the short term gain of politicians.

Ironically, popular soap operas like *Rajani, Kakaji Kahen or Nukkad* proved that the electronic medium could easily be the mouthpiece of common people. Basu Chatterjee's *Rajani,* where Priya Tendulkar played the lead role, became a popular soap. Rajani was an outspoken middle class woman, very straightforward, who always spoke of her mind and stood for the right things.

Similarly, the *Nukkad,* it was shown that the 'citizens' of a slum called *Nukkad,* represented only a working class, irrespective of any caste or religion, and had to stand united to fight for their survival, as they shared similar interests. These serials were the indications of the great potentiality of Doordarshan in bringing a change in people's attitude, creating an environment for development and arousing a consciousness among the deprived population. But, as the Joshi Committee observed, Doordarshan ignored this ground reality and promoted a non-development corpus of commercialised programmes in the area of entertainment.

As the number of soap operas increased, the plot, set, characterisation and story became more diversified. DD2, the Metro Channel was started in the mid-eighties. Viewers became more selective and fragmented. With advertising costs eroding the advertiser's budget, they became more demanding and wanted returns on their every penny's worth.

Television Rating Point

The Television Rating Point (TRP) of IMRB was the first attempt at TV viewership monitoring. They became more dependent on TV viewership monitoring. Indian advertisers became more dependent on TRP for the media planning as they could readily grasp the TV viewing habits of people by glancing through the TRP. As the TV serial producers tried their utmost to climb up the

TRP chart, Doordarshan shifted from being a best selling brand serial to a best selling branded serial.

Era of Mega Serials

As Indian advertisers grid their loins for the battle of the brands, vying with each other to climb the TRP chart, there emerged the concept of 'mega serial,' with the big commercial box-office filmmakers of Bollywood, who recognised the revenue potential of the small screen. Ramanand Sagar and B.R. Chopra produced religious serials on Indian mythology, the *Ramayana* and the *Mahabharata* ignited religious emotion among the millions of Hindus. Reports published in newspapers showed that many villagers worshiped and offered *Pujas* (prayer) to television sets while the programme was on the air. Arun Govil became a branded Ram, and Dipika became a branded Sita for many Hindus. This time, not the businessmen, but politicians and Hindu fundamentalists took advantage of such branding. Arun and Dipika dressed in Ram and Sita costumes participated in political rallies and campaigned for a political party with close ties to Hindu fundamental groups. These super mega serials, though based on Hindu Epics, were viewed by millions of people of other religious denominations throughout the country. During the telecast period all roads virtually remained deserted as everyone remained indoors.

B.R. Chopra's *Mahabharata* became such a super hit branded mega serial that streets were deserted on Sunday mornings when the programme was telecast. It scored the highest audience rating among all other television programmes till 1990. In his contextual analysis of how the *Mahabharata* fit into Indian popular culture in 1993, Ananda Mitra mentions that nearly 92% of total television viewers had watched the serial. Many replica of arms and weapons of ancient India, as shown in *Ramayana* and *Mahabharata*, appeared in children toy stores at street corners. Monkey masks, crowns of kings, teeth of *rakshasa* (demons), posters, stickers,

Mahabharata diaries and other specialty items were brought into the market. The word *Mahabharata* also came to be incorporated into the linguistic orthodoxy of Indian advertising. Products were labelled as Maha, for example, Maha Strong (Amrutanjan Balm), Maha cola (Coca-Cola), Maha Shakti (Rin), Maha Coil (Mortein) along with many 'Maha Chut,' 'Maha Chad,' 'Maha Offer' or ' Maha Pack,' ' Maha Movies' and so on. *Mahabharata* influenced people's lives in a Maha (great) way.

Entry of Giant Channels

In winter, 1991, in the wake of the Gulf War, Cable News Network (CNN) of Atlanta, Georgia made its presence felt in India through its telecast of the air attacks on Iraq. This particular coverage made such a difference in the attitude among viewers towards the news channels that it inspired other news companies to enter the Indian market. BBC (the British Broadcasting Company) was incorporated in Star TV on October 14, 1991 as the news channel of star network. These two global giants in international news services and the closest competitors too, received immense acceptance among the Indian viewers due to their technical and professional superiority in news presentation and coverage (Ranajit Chakravarthy and Mugdha Sengupta).

Film Based Programmes

Film based programmes, particularly film songs have been much popular from the very beginning of Indian television till today. They remained one of the most popular shows for the Indian audience. The film song in television was, in fact, a desi version of the music video of the West. One film-based programme that held its brand equity substantially over more than a decade was *Chitrahar*. No other television programme has remained so popular for such a long period of time.

As the number of channels increased after the satellite TV invaded this country, there emerged immense competition among all television channels in India. Doordarshan lost its crown to the satellite channels. In response, Doordarshan went by the old adage: 'If you can't beat them, join them'. Doordarshan pushed forward DD metro and other original channels, telecast more film-based entertaining programme such as *House Full*, *Hello Bombay*, and *Mirch Masala* and the TRP of the metro channel went up again. The advertising rates for regional channels were trimmed, and discounts were offered depending on the slots and the number of times the same advertisement was shown. Thus, in the face of competition, Doordarshan promoted more film song-based programmes. This was criticised by the Joshi Committee, on the ground that primary objectives were lost sight of.

These programmes fulfilled the intellectual appetite of a section of the urban and semi-urban elite and middle class, leaving the larger section of the population, the poor and the illiterate, mainly residing in the rural areas, untouched. For the poor and the backward sections of the population, films and film-based programmes, and serials remained most popular. Programmes on classical music and dance remained a classy affair of the urban elite. There was no special drive to popularise such programmes among the common audience. In that sense, once again, it revealed the monopolistic control over the medium by the urban people.

The development of major areas of programme genres can be viewed in the light of increasing influence of the market mechanism in India. Apparently, this is a normal development of the media market. The very objective of using the electronic medium as an instrument of development communication got reversed in the ocean of promotional communication of Indian business. Further, commercial rewards out of such market demand received primary consideration. After the satellite channels invaded the country, concentrating on the market share through generating popular mass culture became more acute with the increasing privately owned cable channels, privatisation and globalization.

Thus, instead of promoting a scientific attitude among the people or taking a proper social accounting of the children of a developing nation, Indian Television is promoting medieval values through mega (epic) serials and western culture through the clockwise programmes of MTV, V and Fashion Channels. These are the channels owned by the corporate sector whose primary objective is to rake in enormous profits by cashing on hedonistic weakness of the viewers. In this mad race for profits all channels—be they national or regional—function alike.

Mass Media Ignores Masses?

We cannot describe our country as the world's largest democracy, but for the existence of an independent media—independent of the state but depend on the support of a small but powerful corporate sector.

Large sections of the corporate media in the country have become totally commercial, focusing almost entirely on enhancing the advertising revenues and catering to small wealthy influential elites.

Media's main thrust is on entertainment, spreading consumerism, making people rush towards malls and Big Bazaars forcing their impulsive purchases of junk of all sorts. In short, the media now-a-days is catering to the wants of the craving population.

Even as much of the mainstream, media in India dumbs down its readers, viewers and listeners, a narrow segment still believes that it is possible for the print and electronic media to not just entertainment and inform but also educate and empower.

Over the past decade and half the print media all over the world is facing a tough competition from the electronic media—the T.V. Channels. India is the only country to have more than three dozen 24 hour news channels and current affairs, barely a quarter century after the world's first 24 hour TV news Channel (CNN) started in 1980. Till 1991 T.V. viewers in India could see only Door Darshan and 2-News Channel was the first private news channel started in 1984. At present India is the only country in the world where cable T.V. subscriber for an amount varying between the equivalent of $ 2 and $ 6 to receive anywhere from 30 to 100 channels, in most of the languages one is unable to understand! Till the end of July 2006 the Union Ministry for Information and Broadcasting allowed 185 private satellite channels to be uplinked from India and 65 channels had been allowed to officially downlink in India.

The cinema industry in India continues to be prolific producing around 800 feature films a year. It is in this larger context that the role of the electronic media, the only medium (NEWS MEDIA) that combines mass communication with inter-personal communication, namely, the internet or world-wide website, should be looked at. (G. Anantha Krishnan: The Challenge of Growth for News Media: The Hindu: April 23, 2007).

While there is more than one TV Set for every 10 Indians and one mobile phone for every 10 citizens, there are less than two personal computers for every 100 Indians. These statistics indicate the long distance that has to be covered before the Internet as a medium makes a discernible impact on Indian society.

While the expansion of the 'old' media has gone beyond urban areas and is fast spreading across the length and breadth of rural India, the growth of the 'new' media (the Internet) has become dependent on technology penetration and the development of the telecommunication infrastructure.

India's telecom industries have expanded at an incredibly rapid space in recent years; the number of fixed and wireless telephone connections has doubled between 2004 and 2006 to exceed 150 million. We hardly have a remote village in India today which does not have a STD shop. Though potable water is still a distant dream for many rural areas STD booths have mushroomed in all nooks and corners of our great country! On an average, five million new mobile phone connections are being added each month. Indians are at present enjoying the lowest call rates anywhere in the world. At present, the overwhelming majority of the users of Internet in India is not merely educated but also belongs to the social elite that speak, read, write and think in English (The Hindu: August 16.2.2006).

Access to Internet

Public access to the Internet is becoming relatively easy through cyber cafes and educational institutions. A small town called Suryapet in the district Nalgonda of Andhra Pradesh has more than 20 cyber cafes, not to speak of 11 degree colleges and one engineering college. Many schools today offer computer science as a subject.

At the same time traditional media is expanding despite being impacted by the Internet. The power and potential of the media for not just disseminating information but also for imparting knowledge is infinite. The corporate commercial media cannot dominate the entire diverse and plural media environment in the country. With millions of illiterate young desperately wanting to read and write, the small elitist commercial media with its narrow constituency cannot dominate the vast, diverse and plural Indian society.

Impact on Youth

The standard media image of the youth is that of trendy, gadget wielding, metropolitan boys and girls. A nation wide survey conducted by the Hindu-CNN-IBN reminds us of that one out of ten has a personal mobile phone or a two-wheeler—the two most coveted percent have an internet consumer goods. Only three connections at home (The Hindu: 25.8.06).

The media in our country is unique in more than one way. It is the one sector which has consistently outperformed the rate of growth of gross domestic product in India in the entertainment and media services sector. This sector, as per the estimate of the approach paper to the Eleventh Five Year Plan that started on April 1, 2007, is expected to grow at a Compound Average Annual Growth Rate (CAGR) of 19 percent till the year 2010 and beyond, or twice as fast as the rest of the Economy. The approach paper has put out estimates of the growth rates of TV around 42 percent, followed by print 31 percent, films 19 percent, advertising 3 percent while music and live entertainment 2 percent and radio 1 percent.

Top Priority to Commercial Values

The print media in the last one and half decade is facing a tough competition from the T.V. Several surveys reveal a sharp decline in the paid circulation of the newspapers and periodicals. Hence, today print media's main thrust is based on entertainment anatomising the woman's body much to cater the crass cravings of the average leader. Radio too is facing the popularity crisis. Surprisingly, the Internet's popularity is fast gaining the ground not to speak of video games. Whenever circulation dips, it has became quite common for the English Weeklies—OUTLOOK and INDIA TODAY—to undertake sex surveys, extra marital relations and on pre-marital sex to boost up the popularity of the periodical.

While some newspapers are mired in the old habits of thought that they serve a public cause. Many, particularly the Times of India, boldly proclaims its exclusive devotion to commercial values. The TOI succeeded in not merely squezing out the last rupee of advertising revenue yield but even sharply boosting circulation and profitability. It has become the role model for the rest of the Indian newspapers in the age of globalization. At a time when the relevance of media to its traditional constituencies has itself been called into question, the TOI not merely remained relevant, it has created new constituencies along with lifestyle paradigms it has propagated.

As a case study, the TOI is important for understanding the media as a social and political institution in the new world order. The BCCL (Bennett Coleman and Company Ltd) that owns the newspaper is replicating what has been done by mainstream medial—the subordination of journalism to the whims of advertisers. Advertiser is the king and the readership a distant abstraction that did not have any immediacy to the newspaper except a burden to be borne.

Soft Porn—The Staple Diet of Media

The print industry for long mired in romantic recollection of its contribution to the Indian freedom struggle, deluded in the belief that it had a role in underwriting the quality of the public discourse was shaken out of its reverie by the TOI by using "simple marketing principles" and good business sense to transform a down-in-the dumps publishing company into a profit machine. The editorial content has been made to meet the needs of the advertiser. Fashion, lifestyles and entertainment became the main focus of the newspaper—political discourse and public causes have taken a back seat. Sensational celebrities, crime reporting, anatomy of woman, photos often straying into the territory of soft porn has become a staple diet of the print media in this age of globalization to survive the onslaughts of the electronic media—TV and the Internet. While the older generation is disgusted with the pimping role of the media, the print media is attracting the patronage of the unexplored demographic segments such as the youth and the high purchasing power strata.

Decline of Editorial Priorities

This transformation of the newspaper in the advertisement and circulation aspects relegated editorial department and elevated the advertising department. Pro- friendly advertiser attitude has overtaken editorial ethics. Earlier editorial priorities, which bore a relationship to the world that the majority of people actually, lived in, had to yield before the demands of fostering the entertainment and celebrity lifestyles.

Today the editorial page has neither any agenda, nor any purpose other than drawing the attention of the political and bureaucratic elite which needed little education in any case and contributed little to the financial fortunes of the print media. Only those who were prepared to abandon the conceit that they could make a difference to the quality of the public discourse need to entertain any ambition of joining the mainstream media. The same is the case with regional media—with devastating effects. Reporters are paid for the amount of advertisements they book rather than how many columns of news they file. Gone were the days when a newspaper is known through its editor—Frank Moraes, Shamlals, Girilal Jains, Kasa Subba Rao. Today print media rivals in showing on the front, last, nay, almost all pages except perhaps classified advertisement pages in displaying a buxom woman with skimpy clothing around her torso or a pretty lass dressed to the barest minimum. The new refrain of the media is:

IF CREDIBILITY IS LOST NOTHING IS LOST

IF CIRCULATION IS LOST SOMETHING IS LOST

IF ADVERTISING IS LOST EVERYTHING IS LOST

Regional Media Reeks with Sensational Trivia

The regional media -"both the print as well as the T.V. channels is not far behind when it comes to sensationalise the trivia involving very often celebrities. Incidents involving the murder attempt on a film producer at actor Balakrishna's residence. The murder of his watchman, the suicide attempts of actress Aarti Agarwal all received the full attention of the media for quite sometime while several miseries suffered by the ordinary people did not touch any 'human interest' sense of the media!

Almost all Telugu T.V. channels invariably telecast regular programmes lasting half-an hour or so exclusive only crime reporting attention of the regional channels. Almost on daily basis sting operations mostly involving bribing petty officials in local government offices are telecast on a regular basis. But mostly these reportings are confined to petty officials only while the big sharks remain untouched. They try to popularize these programmes by inviting information from the viewers and justify their Peeping Tom activities in the name of discharging their social responsibility as sentinels of public morality.

In recent years journalism, whether of print or electronic media, has become hundred and one percent commercial. Often journalists are recruited not on the basis of their ability to observe and write but on the sole consideration of their public relations! But why ? Public relations fetch advertising revenue. Press too cares less for reporting and more for revenue. Revenue in the form advertising/special supplements yield more money than the sale of the copies of the daily/weekly/fortnightly/ monthly, etc. Same is the case with the electronic media. That is the reason why they sensationalise trivia and cater to the libido psyche of the bored reader/viewer of the media. It is no wonder when Chief Justice of the High Court of Andhra Pradesh while hearing arguments in one case commented on the quality and content of the regional media and wondered whether anyone seriously reads Telugu dailies (Andhra Jyothi 30.03.2006). This critical comment itself is enough to indicate the poor quality of regional media. Very often news is spiked or insignificant news is reported only to shift the attention of the reader to commercial advertisements. (*P. Sainath : The Hindu*, 1.4.2006)

Spread of Free-for-All Culture

There is a free-for-all in the media today. Some newspapers are consumed by page three while TV channels appeal to the lowest common denominator. The mushrooming of TV channels meant that the profession was no longer seen as a mission; it was now a cut-throat business where everyone was chasing the holy grail of the "breaking news" story. The "grab all and anything" culture can be traced to globalization and the opening up of the economy. "The great excuse is that the readers want it, the younger generation wants it. Hence, we have to appeal to the lowest common multiple." The media which caters to the big metros is particularly guilty of dumping down news because it is easier to report a salacious titbit than cover a serious story. Thus, 'minis' are hyped and magnified as 'mega events' and the clippings are repeatedly telecast. This way our T.V. Channels are copycats of GOBBLES! Aping each other in the name of "breaking the news" has become quite routine. This trend is very much evident in the channels which proclaim as the purveyors of round the clock 'news' suppliers.

This trend is only part of a larger process of voyeurism in which the public is often a willing participant. A man invited cameras into his bedroom because he claimed his wife regularly beat him. Viewers tuned in a Star News faithfully telecast "Mujhe Meri Biwi Se Bachao." Was this news or puerile peeping? Sociologist Shiv Visvanathan says, "the question is not whether you are trivialising news. I would say news is often equally trivial. The sad part is that you are trivialising pain.' Does India then have its own paparazzi now? "It's a fake paparazzi. An imitation. It's hardwork in the West where they pursue celebrities for weeks. Here you just peep in or turn your camera on some painful reality" (*Outlook*: 06.02.2006).

Spread the Stench

Privacy is not an issue for the hypocrite public official. They should be exposed. Spying on those in public life has always been the business of journalists. The means and doings have become more sophisticated. A journalist is justified in using whatever means he can to expose those who profess one thing and do something entirely different. There is far too much skull duggery going on and it is the duty of journalists to expose it. It needn't be just politicians but anyone—civil servants, holy men and women. Of course, the criterion is that the journalist must be strictly above board.

Journalists have been playing a very positive role whether it is exposing Sanjay Joshi whom they caught with his pants down or the Kanchipuram seer making passes at women despite his vows of celibacy. They had to be exposed for the sake of public morality. Think of it: the MPs who were caught red-handed taking money for questions would never have been exposed except for this new sophisticated technology.

It's not just the technology that has changed, it's also the attitude of the news media. Even if a newspaper or magazine editor had access to these sophisticated means few would have dared to publish the results. It meant taking a huge risk which no proprietor would be willing to take. But it's quite a different matter in these days of dozens of TV channels and newspapers all vying with each other for scoops. In these circulation-conscious times few editors would think of self-censorship, except a conservative newspaper like The Hindu. And that is as it should be. After all exposing people who deserve to be exposed because their pretensions don't match their practices.

Every citizen has the right to privacy and anyone who invades it deserves to be punished. Thus, the use of hidden cameras in hotel rooms and bridal suites should be punished by cancelling the hotelier's licence, heavy fine and jail. However, a distinction should be drawn between a private citizen and a person in public life like politicians, civil servants, defence personnel, members of the judiciary leaders of religious organisations and others who preach public morality. If what they profess in public does not tally with what they indulge in private they should be exposed. One should remember the old adage: *Public Men (Women* too for that matter) do not have any private life—at least as far as India is concerned as we tend to worship and idolise our leaders as holy cows.

13

Pliant Journalism

"A newspaper particularly on its front page, daily presents a view of reality. In fact, this reality is totally relative and highly subjective. The front page of a Mumbai newspaper will portray a 'reality' very different from that of a newspaper published in Chennai. Even events with global repercussions such as 9/11 or the December 2004 tsunami will get very different places. For instance, in India, the casualty figures of Indian citizens involved would take precedence over other nationalities."

Reporting about a local problem alone would be done only if a newspaper is a specialized city gazette.

Rajdeep Sardesai, owner-editor of CNN-IBN had this to say: "Traditionally we've been structured to put bad news first. Journalists are always at loggerheads with the establishment. So, of course, there's negativity."

News has to be something extraordinary that the public would find worth reading or viewing/listening to. It need not be bad at all. If India wins the ICC Champions Trophy, it will be the lead in print and electronic media despite the fact that many who were interested in the game would have watched it live (*Indian Currents*: 22 October, 2006).

Santosh Desai, the President of the advertising firm McCann-Erikson India is of the opinion that advertisers must have a say on 'matter that gets printed between the ads.' Desai says,

"Journalists have an implicit bias for bad news since it seems more substantial. But the feeling one gets is that the world is a miserable place. Good news, on the other hand, renews our faith. A sting operation always shows the guys who took the bribe but what about showing the two who refused to be bribed? That's the kind of news that would renew our belief in the goodness of human nature."

Someone like Bangaru Laxman accepting bribe will not be telecast in Desai's channel because he wants to tell us what a wonderful world it is because there is one among several people he offered a bribe refused it.

Also, unprecedented anxiety is a sign that grips somebody who has a lot to lose. A beggar on the street will never be bothered if somebody tells him about an earthquake that has destroyed many lives because he is in a worse condition.

The chief of Doordarshan news criticized private channels for their coverage of Amitabh Bachchan's illness. Head of DD news, Amitabh Chakrabarti, said: "The ferocity with which these channels raise hypes—perhaps with an eye on Television Rating Points—goes close to the culture of tabloid journalism. T.V. channels had dramatized the event, compare BBC and CNN's coverage of Diana's funeral (not death) with the coverage of Bachchan's illness. Bachchan is an icon, bigger than Sachin Tendulkar.

People would definitely want to know about his illness and how well he is recovering. But to post a big crew in front of Lilavati Hospital for that purpose and cover events like somebody having a *havan* for Bachchan's recovery was definitely an overreaction by private news channels.

Private channels were angry at DD's plainspeak. Star News CEO Uday Shankar retorted: "Bachchan is the biggest entertainment personality in the history of India and when he is unwell, the concern is immense and the people want to know more about him (Indian Currents: December, 2005).

That sounds excellent except the private channels are always influenced by a consideration called rating points. But the Star News' CEO was perhaps unaware of Amar Singh's allegation. Doordarshan, over a week, had Bachchan's illness covered in 63 bulletins.

Does Media Need Ethical Restraint?

There is the need to evolve a self-imposed code of ethics for the media to report truthfully and without any bias.

Only a credible media report has the potential to win the confidence of the people. Times are changing fast and the media needs to prepare a road map, carving out its role in the changed scenario and be able to mirror the wider, more fundamental concerns facing the nation.

Can the media extend its support to the task of improving governance and generate people's will to make any public programme like universal literacy, population stabilization, building a strong secular web, protection of environment and heritage conservation a success?

Key issues of governance that needed sustained focused media attention include making governance in democracy inclusive of managing the welfare of the poor. Other issues include rural development and rejuvenating the agriculture, electoral reforms and combating the malice of corruption.

Powerful Role

The media had a powerful role to play in democracy. An informed public opinion is needed and that is what the media can mould. Media needed to play a greater role to solve societal problems.

Print Media

The traditional newspaper, which is facing competition from different media, can only compete with them in terms of quality, says Mathias Mass, Deputy Editor-in-Chief of the German newspaper Die Zeit (*The Hindu*: 17.01.2004).

"A newspaper today is a slow medium. We cannot compete in terms of speed with television or the internet. That is why we have to keep our standards high." The veteran journalist said in his address on "Globalisation and its effect on media." In New Delhi even when there was pressure on circulation during a difficult economic environment, there should be no compromise on the quality to gain a few new readers.

"You would risk alienating your core readership. They want a paper that invests in good journalism, good writing, extensive research and international coverage. They expect in-depth analysis and background stories that they do not get from the electronic media. They want food for thought."

In addition to the challenge, from the Internet and television, there is competition from free papers, whose circulation had crossed that of the quality newspapers.

Was the Fourth Estate, once a solid pillar of western democracy, crumbling and which section had contributed to this? Nass quoted a German publisher for the answer. "The printed world has an enemy and that is the young people." One way, all the major papers were trying to cope with the internet challenges was setting up online editions: some were attracting more readers or 'users' than their parent papers.

(All the traditional quality standards readers are used to something which they expect from their paper and at the same time offer them electronically an alternative that is faster, much more flexible, open for experiments. Cooperation between the journalists and managers is helpful but the editorial side should stay independent. There can be no compromise here. Compromising editorial independence for commercial interests would be putting the axe at the root of the profession. "Never hurt the credibility of the paper. It is your most precious good."

Media Reaches the Masses

There has been an increase in the reach of the press, television, radio and the Internet. Cinema generally recorded a decline in audiences, the findings of the National Readership Study 2006 (NRS 2006) reveal. In India dailies had a total readership of 203.6 million, adding 12.6 million readers during the year. The print media, i.e. dailies and periodicals combined, had a readership of 222 million. The study says that urban readers spend 44 minutes a day on newspapers and rural readers, 35 minutes.

The National Readership Studies Council, an autonomous division of the Audit Bureau of Circulation, released the findings of NRS 2006 (The Hindu, 30.8.06) with the following findings: -

The Times of India is the most read English daily with 7.4 million readers. The Hindu is second with 4.05 million readers. It has overtaken Hindustan Times, which stands third with an estimated readership of 3.85 million. Television now reaches 112 million homes, including 68 million households with access to cable and satellite TV. Radio too showed a resurgence, with its reach increasing from 23 percent to 27 percent of the population on an average in a week.

The number of Internet users logging on every week grew from 7.2 million to 9.4 million, with faster growth in the urban areas (*The Hindu*: 30.08.06).

Lack of Cultural Policy

Lack of a declared cultural policy was exposing the hollowness of the ruling parties, leaders of Janasakthi, a left-wing literacy organisation, observed.

The cultural policy being followed by successive governments had been the combination of local feudalistic culture and foreign imperialistic culture which is being imposed on the society. While the urbanites are fed with western inputs leading to deculturalisation of the Indian society, the rural areas are still under the grip of feudalism which has taken the form of higher castes exploiting the lower castes politically, economically, socially and culturally.

Continuation of courses on *Vaasthu* and astrology in universities was also part of the undeclared cultural policy of the Government, they alleged (The Hindu: 23.12.06). Allowing half naked dances in discotheque, bars and clubs, turning a blind eye on the organized prostitution in the name of development of tourism, depiction of women as sex symbols in television serials and feature films were also part of the feudalistic and imperialistic cultural policy.

Comparing the present education system with the two-tier system in villages, *Janasakthi* alleged that while government schools were for the poor and downtrodden, residential schools were available for the rich and middle class.

Governments were not making the people to understand the adverse effects of imperialistic globalization.

Biased Programmes

The mushrooming growth of private television channels has "unfortunately" not been conducive to social harmony or a serious appraisal of issues, was the gist of a resolution passed at the Dalit-Minority International Conference which was held in 2006 in New Delhi.

The resolution noted that in the present stage of the nation's socio economic evolution, the role of the electronic (TV radio, print and Internet) media has become critical. But the growth of private TV channels has been in direct proportion to the rise of the caste and communal temperature. This has been the opinion of many left-wing cultural organizations in Andhra Pradesh.

Anti-Rural Bias

The perspective of most programmes betrays a caste, anti-rural bias. Conceding that there were many exceptions, it felt that these exceptions were buffeted by market interest and television rating points.

When Britain and the U.S. surrendered their media to the market, they had reached an adequate level of egalitarianism and narrowed the gap between the rich and the poor.

"We are still an evolving society, mediating economic, caste, communal political differences in myriads of complex ways through the ballot box. We (India) are a power of the future, in need of a purposive public service. TV, by remaining equidistant from the state and the market—a truly independent media—free of all bias should be responsive to the needs of the society."

Is the New Media Responsible for the Decline of Newspapers and Television?

With new media platforms emerging, newspapers and broadcast television in developed countries are on the decline (Editor-in-Chief of The Hindu). Narrow cast technology, niche audience and specialised channels are gaining the ground. There was gloom in mature media markets with the spread of the new media in the form of the Internet (*The Hindu*: 19.09.06).

The spread of newspapers had reached saturation levels in the developed countries whereas in India it was a picture of growth, though with a very low base of 65 copies per 1,000 population, against 800 in Scandinavian countries (J. Ram: *The Hindu*: 19.09.06).

Migration of Readers

On the other hand, India's Internet users are only 11 million as against 123 million in China and 220 million in the United States. There are fears that the Internet was eroding the base of the newspapers, radio and broadcast TV.

"The readers are migrating depending upon the access to Internet and broadband and it will have a big impact on how news is covered and what the readers' preferences are" (The Hindu: 19.09.2006).

An important function of newspapers was to provide credible information by accurately sourcing it.

Media should influence agenda-building to promote discussion on issues that matter without dumping them down. The real future of the media lies in creating a template for discussion. While keeping in view the plurality of the country, N. Ram said truth-telling, factuality, accuracy and careful analysis should be given priority in reporting.

Declining Credibility of Regional Media

Whether we like it or not media—both print as well as the electronic—has become a part and parcel of daily life. It is the media that guides a majority of people in forming an opinion about several aspects of public life—political, economic, social and even cultural—not to speak of influencing our lifestyle through catering to the requirements of the advertiser the so-called promoter of hundred and one sponsored programmes that our private T.V. Channels telecast everyday. But the odd part of it is that though the media has become a sine quo non of our daily life yet neither the viewers/readers/nor the journalists T.V. channel people know about the role of the media nor its function properly.

Whenever we think of electronic media today, our attention is drawn to the 24 hour news channels. Only these are the channels that din into our ears and strain our eyes with the same news/same video pictures repeated in almost all hourly bulletins. However, it is the print media that gathers the news about what is happening there and what people think of the same. Despite the galore and the visual presence of a galaxy of personalities on the T.V. screen it is the print media which has a lasting effect on the mind and memory of the people. Therefore, despite the spread and continuously increasing popularity of the electronic media the presence of print media can never be underestimated. Regional media in Andhra Pradesh, be it print or electronic has reached the nadir. It is full of stench which stickens the average reader/viewer to say the learned. Highly partisan, totally biased Telugu India have thrown all ethical values in to gutters.

What We Expect from Media?

The purpose of media is to educate the people about various issues involving governance, civil society and the problems faced by the country, besides keeping a continuous vigil on the functioning of the Government. In democracy media happens to be the fourth pillar of the system. Democracy without a free and fearless media is like a morgue. Many people depend on the media not only for information, to know what is happening around the world, they also depend on the media to form an opinion about various aspects touching the public life and public affairs.

Such being the onerous role that the media is expected to perform, it is only natural that it should remain free from the control, interference and influence of the state, the people who control the machinery of the government. Hence, it should be managed by the private enterprise.

Mass Media Sans Mass Interests

However, independent a privately run media would like to be, it cannot ignore the investors interests—it cannot ignore the commercial interests of the owners of the media—be it a newspaper or a.T.V. Channel. In India the connection between media and commercial interests are too well known to many that hardly needs any detailed elaboration. Many of the newspapers and T.V. Channels are owned by the corporate sector. This is a fact not only at the national level but also in the state of Andhra Pradesh.

Proprietorial interests, the political inclinations of those who manage and run the media play an important role in the quality as well as the way a newspaper/T.V. channel functions. This happens particularly when the society is dominated by the clash between different ideological, political and organisational competition among the different sections. In such a situation a newspaper takes up a position among the ideological/political contestations often supporting one as against the others.

Until 1983 such a situation did not arise in Andhra Pradesh, as the state political scene was overwhelmingly dominated by the Congress Party and its various factions. But in 1983 a situation developed wherein the famous Telugu film actor N.T. Rama Rao floated a regional party—the Telugu Desam—contested all but four seats in the State Assembly elections of 1983, offering an alternative to the age-old corrupt, and faction-ridden Congress party's uninterrupted rule.

This opportunity was seized by the regional media, particularly by a leading Telugu daily newspaper (EENADU). This paper played no less an important role not only by pointing out at the inefficient corrupt Congress rule of the State but also ceaselessly campaigned in favour of the Telugu Desam. This newspaper's campaign strengthened the already determined Telugu voter to dislodge the Congress and put the Telugu Desam on the seat of power.

The success of Telugu Desam made the media to believe in its own ability to dislodge the party from the seat of power and put another one of its choice at the helm of affairs. Hence, it has taken the role of creating public opinion as it 'wanted' and decided what is good for the people. This slowly made the media to keep distance from the people. Added to this is the commercial interests of the media barons who own several other enterprises which include film studios, pickle manufacturing units not to speak saree and jewellery emporiums. This naturally makes the media to serve private agenda, throwing the main interests on the roadside.

Media Mania

Hence, the media keeping in view the proprietorial interests began to set its own agenda independent of the public interest, with the result that both the print as well as the electronic media have lost their credibility. Earlier people used to follow the newspaper to formulate their opinion. Today they know which paper writes what, supports whom. When the attitude and the views of the media and the people are the same, media used to create an impact on the public mind as it happened in the Andhra Pradesh in the 1983 Assembly elections. But when the public decide differently no amount of the campaign by the media can influence it as it was amply demonstrated by the 2004 State Assembly elections when the majority of the print and electronic media were directly or indirectly controlled/influenced by the then Chief Minister, Chandrababu Naidu.

Unfortunately, today be it print or electronic, the media in general has become totally partisan—either serving the interests of a particular political party or catering to the commercial interests of the proprietors. Consequently, Telugu print media particularly has been reduced to one of the pamphleteering. Gone were those days when people used to buy a particular paper because it was edited by Narla Venkateswar Rao (Andhra Prabha), Frank Moraes (Indian Express), Khasa Subba Rao (Swatantra). Today hardly few people know which paper is edited by whom.

Large sections of the corporate media in the country have become namely crassly commercial, focusing almost entirely on catering to small wealthy influential elites.

Media's main thrust is on entertainment. People rush towards malls, and big bazaars forcing their impulsive purchases of junk of all sorts. In short, the media now-a-days is catering to the baser needs of the craving population. Media's single agenda is to force people to convert their 'wants' into needs' which are most often the 'branded' products.

14

Globalization or Neo-Imperialism?

Globalization, theoretically speaking, has been the key concept of the 1990s, instrumental in comprehending the changes that have encompassed the socio-cultural and politico-economic spheres of the life at local, national and global levels and continues in the present. Once it acquired academic significance, along with other conceptual frameworks like post-industrialism, post-modernism, post-liberalism and post-Marxism by the mid-1980s, it has occupied centre-stage in the mainstream of socio-political analysis. The global impact of globalization in both theory and practice is evident in its overbearing omnipresence, overshadowing all other components of socio-cultural and politico-economic life. It is perceived as an anathema in some quarters and irresistible in others.

In our view, it is a conceptual error to think of globalization as a new phenomenon or as an inevitable process or even as the ultimate and irreversible phase of capitalism. In fact, the movement towards the international integration of national economies is as old as the history of capitalism itself. Globalization may be seen as ' beginning in late 15th century with the rise of capitalism and its overseas expansion: the conquest and exploitation of Asia, Africa and Latin America and the white colony settlements in North Africa and Australia were all instances of globalization.' In other words, globalization was from the outset associated with imperialism (the global linkage was based on European capitalist accumulation through the exploitation of the third world) and its impetus was always centred around the imperial state institutions, specific class configurations, extracting resources from the domestic economy to finance overseas conquests and private accumulation, exploitation of the third world, inter-imperial trade, trading companies integrating and appropriating resources and exploiting cheap labour and international exchange (on unequal terms) of commodities. Essentially then, globalisation is hardly a new phenomenon: it is merely a new name, subcode for capitalism, that subsumes diverse socio-political and economic processes. The imperial historical origins have remained embedded in a matrix in which new states and actors compete for privileged access to networks and state support. The principal agencies today, the multinational corporations, fulfil the roles played earlier by the trading companies (integrating and appropriating the resources and exploiting the cheap labour) while the imperial states extract domestic resources to finance overseas expansion and to secure the conditions for the reproduction of global capital accumulation (J.A. Scholote: *International Affairs*, 1997).

Globalization-A New Avatar of Imperialism

Globalization is not synonymous with globalism, although the professed aim of globalization, as delineated by its advocates is creation of a 'global village' (or global metropolis!) by means of unhindered trade flows, capital flows and technology flows across national frontiers. The idea that is propagated is that the world is coming closer and is getting united, but the consequential reality presents a contrary picture and, in fact, threatens the prospects of integral globalism.

As revealed by historical evidence, the imperialist nations drained out the resources from the colonised nations and thrived at their expenses. In the Indian context, a major part of the Indian freedom beginning with the nineteenth-century-liberal economic nationalism through the militant strategies of *Swadeshi* and boycott in the first two decades of the twentieth century, to Gandhi's crusade for *Swaraj* in the subsequent decades. The anti-imperialist struggle was, thus, also anti-globalization. (Asha Kaushik: *Globalization, Democracy & Culture*, 2002).

The first imprints of the globalising process were admittedly felt in the economic arena but soon it expanded into the political and the cultural terrains, as a clearcut ideological move, as it were those who trace globalization to the dawn of civilization miss the point of the exploitative core of the current phenomenon of globalization based on the liberal-capitalist logic of inequalities as intrinsic to the very organization and development of capitalism. The arguments are also mistaken in synonymising globalism and globalisation. The two are not synonymous, but distinguishable through adherence to an ideological agenda in case of the latter and an ideal, harmonised, interactive international cooperation in the case of the former. Not only this, globalism is not incompatible with the sovereign-independence of the nation-states, whereas globalization threatens the same. In this sense, both Marx and Gandhi would qualify as proponents of globalism and not of globalization, in contrast to the liberal-capitalists who celebrate freedom of the market as the freedom of the human race.

Drawing on Lenin's analysis of imperialism as the highest stage of capitalism, the dependency theorists, notably Frank and Amin argued that monopoly-capitalist imperialism has survived by perpetuating underdevelopment as a pattern of dependency between the developed capitalist centre, the colonialist and the underdeveloped periphery, the colonized. Amin also takes of the social democratic alliance' that links the central bourgeoisie to the affluent working class on the one hand and to the satellite (comparador) bourgeoisie on the other. By acting together these three groups can maintain the status quo (Rajani Kothari: *Footsteps into the Culture*, 1974 PP 110-11).

In contrast to the 'dependency theorists,' analysis of world economy as world capitalism, Wallerstein emphasises the state structure as the focal point of world economy. He differentiates three types of states—core states, with strong developmental structures integrated with a national culture, peripheral areas, with weak governmental structures and invaded cultures and semi peripheral areas, with moderately strong governmental structures. There is division of labour between the states in each of these regions: tasks requiring higher levels of skill and greater capitalisation are reserved for higher ranking areas (Joan Bondurant: *Conquest of Violence*, 1965, PP 225-26).

The preceding pre-emptive analyses of a globalising world are theoretically significant to get a proper perspective of the current phenomenon of globalization, but the distinguishing feature of contemporary globalization is the emergence and the decisive role of transnational practices and relationships in the global arena. Perhaps, a more significant reference point is the global capitalist system, based on a variegated global capitalist class, which unquestionably dictates economic transnational practices and is the most important single force in the struggle to dominate political and cultural-ideological transnational practices.

Undoubtedly, then globalization is a calculated imperialist design of hegemonisation in economic, political, ecological and cultural terrains, threatening the underdeveloped countries of the loss of economic self-reliance and political sovereignty, erosion of democratic structures and damaging of their plural cultural identities.

Culmination of Multinational Capitalism

As a culmination of the unbridled, unrestrained multinational capitalism, globalization leaves the poorer countries behind in global competition, as the clear objective of capital mobility is profit, prestige and power for its owners and not the well-being of the people at large. As investment capital has moved and modernised, it has also, in the process, exploited people and natural resources and often left behind pollution, poverty, inequality, injustice, crime, corruption and a general degradation of environment—a record not much different from the imperialist history of aggressive capitalism, obsessed with growth and profit.

The myth of MNCs building technological capabilities for the LDCs is being widely exploded. Possibilities of recolonisation of agriculture, especially in the Indian context are also apprehended. Threatening the prospects of production/real economy replaced by finance capital, technology, scientific knowledge, information network, communication network and propaganda as new determinants, are increasing.

The most important political fall-out of globalization is the decline of the nation-state. David Held rightly argues that forces of globalization are undermining the nation state. He holds that increasing economic and cultural connections reduce the power and effectiveness of governments at the nation state level—they can no longer control the flow of ideas and economic items at their borders and thus their internal policy instruments become ineffective. State power is further reduced because transnational processes grow in scale as well as in number. TNCs are often larger and more powerful than many governments. (David Held: *Political Theory Today*, 1991 PP 197-235).

Cultural Homogenisation

Cultural homogenisation or de-differentiation of culture in the form of Western cultural imperialism is the most serious fall-out of globalization, popularly understood as Americanisation or Cococolanisation. Featherstone has developed a comprehensive theory of consumer culture explaining this phenomenon. As he explains, consumer culture is more than the mere fact of consumption. In consumer culture, customers are encouraged to want more than they need. The consumption items do not just remain material objects but assume a symbolic value and a status-sign. Consumption becomes a form of self-expression and the chief source of identity. Consumer culture implies that both the material and the non-material items become commodified. In other words, their value is assessed by the context of their exchange rather than by the context of their production or use. In its advanced stages, consumer culture results in what has been aptly called "hypercommodification." This is decisively medicated by advertising and simulated, even 'hypersimulated' as Baudrillard would say, by mass media (Feather Stone: *Consumer Culture and Post Modernism*, 1991).

Growing concentration of economic resources and political power has also aggravated social schisms and conflicts. Plural cultural identities and normative structures are under severe attack, by what has been described as the "Cultural invasion from the skies" that is, by the satellite channels, owned by the globalised "culture industry," propping up not only a hybrid culture of newfangled consumerism, commodity fetishism and one dimensional consciousness but also hyper-simulated conditions and transmission of the culture-ideology of consumerism from the centre to the periphery of the world-system.

Thus, in the age of globalization, the nation-state is the 'spatial reference point' in the global capitalist system, based on a variegated global capitalist class, which unquestionably dictates economic transnational practices and is the most important single force in the struggle to dominate political and cultural ideological practices. Evidently then, globalization is a totalising process in terms of both hegemonisation and homogenisation, an extended and subtler American version of European colonial/imperialist ambitions of dominating, expropriating and transforming the world in its own conceptualisations of progress and derivative of the earlier conceptualisations of progress and modernisation, premised on the U.S. centric view of civilization, materialism and economism, glorification of the 'invisible hand' of the market, growth—obsessed industrialism, objectification of nature and an instrumental treatment of humanity.

The era of globalization is seen as opening numerous opportunities for millions of people around the world through increased trade, new technologies, foreign investments, expanding media and internet connections. Global markets, global technology and global ideas are seen as symbolising enormous potential to change the world through "more wealth" than at anytime before. It is also argued that contemporary globalization is not only expansive and encompassing but is being operated by new actors, new rules, new tools and newer markets.

However, we would insist that the point missed in the zeal to portray globalization as a 'new' and 'different' phenomenon, is the underlining core of inegalitarianism, injustice and exploitative practices inherent in the capitalistic-imperialistic-hegemonising trait of the neo-liberal ideology of globalization.

Who are the Beneficiaries?

Admittedly, the world moves forward with commendable advancement of science and technology and expansion of opportunities in the new global order of borderless economy, culture and even politics. But the basic question, remains pertinent as ever—the question of who are actually benefitted by the stupendous infrastructure of growth, development and the rhetoric of advancement? Attempted answers to this question, by proponents and defenders of globalization remain unsettling, especially if the 'basic question' is taken as the major criterion of assessing the impact of the impressive advancement in macro cumulative terms on the common people and the nations that are still at the periphery of the globalising world (Asha Kaushik: P 56).

Across the world, as reported by the Human Development Report, 2001, unacceptable levels of deprivations in people's lives are visible. Of the 4.6 billion people in the developing countries, more than 850 million are illiterate, nearly a billion lack access to improved water sources and 2.4 billion lack access to basic sanitation. Nearly 325 million boys and girls are out of school. And 11 million children under the age of five die each year from preventable causes—equivalent to more than 30,000 a day. Around 1.2 billion people live on less than one dollar a day (1993 PPP US$) and 2.8 billion on less than two dollars a day.

The figures that appear in the Human Development Report, 1999 underline the point: the income gap between the richest fifth of the world's population and the poorest fifth stood at around 3:1 in 1820, 11:1 in 1913, 30:1 in 1970, 60:1 in 1990 and 86:1 by the end of the 20th century. By 1997 the top 20 per cent of the global population living in high-income countries earned 86 per cent of world GDP and the bottom 20 per cent just one per cent. It is also stated that the assets of the three richest people are more than the combined GNP of all least developed countries. The assets of the 200 richest people are more than the combined income of 41% of the world population. And the annual contribution of one per cent of the wealth of the 200 richest people could provide universal access to primary education for all ($7-8 billion).

More often than not, the openness of economy is hailed as enhancing economic growth and economic growth as reducing poverty. None of the propositions, however, is acceptable as an unqualified generalisation. It is also argued that trade and investment bring exposure to new ideas and techniques used in foreign countries. Foreign direct investment (FDI), in particular, is lauded as a vehicle of technology transfer. But, quite often what is brought in as new technology is not really new technology but only new brand names.

Inegalitarian Global Order

It is true that globalization connects the global and the local through a number of politico-economic, technological structures. On its face value, connectivity is welcome, as it broadens the horizons of the local ideas, perceptions and capabilities through innovative techniques and technologies. In its deeper dimensions, the professed connectivity/integration/unification of the local and the global is a camouflage for the inegalitarian, hegemonic politico-economic global order, transgressing the borders of honourable identity, dignity and autonomy of the people and the nation-states, that are on the periphery of the global order. The neo-liberal march towards growth, abundance and development has not been able to abate poverty, inequity and injustice either within the nation-states or at the global level. In an important sense, even the democratic order, more importantly, the democratic values stand threatened in the face of the globalising politico-econo-technological forces. Truly, therefore, there is no alternative to it. A highly undemocratic presumption on the part of those who swear by the ideals of democracy! All are equal, but some are more equal than others!

Globalization is a network of transnational practices operating on the economic, political and cultural levels, with finance capital, technology, scientific knowledge, information network, communication network and propaganda as the new determinants. As confirmed by the recent empirical evidence, one third of the global trade conducted by the MNCs is instrumental in liquidating national economies. In the political sphere, the nation-states find themselves increasingly constrained, as new centres of power emerge to delimit political sovereignty in terms of foreign aid, IMF loans, deregulation, etc. Growing concentration of economic resources and political power has also aggravated social schisms at national levels and conflicts at global levels. Plural cultural identities and normative structures are under severe attack, by what has been described as the "Cultural invasion from the skies" and transmission of the 'culture-ideology of consumerism' from the developed centre to the developing periphery of the global system. The escapable impact of policies favouring globalization on intra-system functioning of the nation-states is also evident, in terms of receding welfarist agenda and fragmentation of political commitments. Guided by the politico-economic transnational practices, globalization has emerged as a totalising process in terms of both hegemonic structures and homogenising cultural traits deliberately transforming the world in its own image. Ideologically, it is derivative of the earlier conceptualisations of 'progress' and 'modernisation,' premised on the West-centric view of civilization, materialism and economism, glorification of the 'invisible hand' of the market, growth-obsessed industrialism, objectification of nature and an instrumental treatment of humanity (Asha Kaushik, PP 150-51).

The growth-modernisation model may have to its credit, enormous acquisitive attainments. But ironically, the betterment of life, in terms of rising material standards of living, has often resulted in eroding the foundations of good life, through a lopsided emphasis on material accomplishments and hedonism. Extending to the politico-economic and cultural spheres, the phenomenon has been instrumental in creating structures of domination, with both hegemonising and homogenising traits. "Increasing rationality," as Habermas notes, has not enhanced understanding of the "self and others, because as Marcuse argues, it has been 'one dimensional.' Likewise, increasing materialism in Gandhi's view, is no indication of human well-being. Gandhi's strong recommendation of moral reasoning should be taken as a necessary corrective to the obsession with economism and crass materialism.

Many question the utilitarian calculus of liberal political theory and its glorification of atomistic individualism, "not founded upon the relations between man and man but rather upon the separation of man from man," as Marx argues. Conflicting economic interests converted into a political economy of oppression and exploitation, have been primarily instrumental in separation of man from man and of nation from nation. This separation/antagonism has resulted not only in politico-economic disjuncture but also in moral schizophrenia.

As history provides ample evidence, oppression, inequity and injustice do not remain unchallenged for long. Globalization too is being protested through numerous fora around the globe. It is possible to see common opposition to the capitalist state and globalization. Majority of protest movements exist today in the US and Mexico against NAFTA. In Europe, the movement toward economic and monetary union is under severe attack. And throughout the Latin America peasant movements are moving to the forefront of the struggle against globalization. Similar trends are visible in other countries as well, including India. In India, particularly in Andhra Pradesh, the common people are still to know the adverse effects of the globalization, as they are still expecting 'bonanzas' from the state in the form of 'free power,' free education,' 'free housing' and of course freedom to do anything without fearing the consequences.

More recently anti-capitalist, anti-globalization protests have become a major movement or mass campaign of our times, having mobilised over three million grassroots activists or delegates in several countries. Globally, the movement has fired the imagination of socially concerned young people as never before—including in elite campuses in the US, for the first time since the Vietnam fiasco.

Grass-roots movements in India and other parts of the world are also notable. Besides organised movements by the left parties, People's Science Movement, Azadi Bachao Andolan (Save Independence Movement), Chipko Andolan ("hug the trees" movement) among several others in India and Movements for Alternative Technology and Green Peace Movements all over the World deserve special mention in the context. The way in which in Nandigram, Singur of West Bengal struggles who waged against the handling over of thousands of hectors of fertile agricultural lands to multi-nationalists in the name of setting up of Special Economic Zones (V.KRISHNA RAO, paper presented at the national seminar on Special Economic Zones, organised by the Indian Institute of Advanced Study, Shimla, 21-23 September 2008) is a clear indication of local peoples opposition. This establishes the fear that the ruling elites in India do not care for the names.

15

Globalization Masks U.S. Imperialism

'The motive for globalization lies with the imperialist economic interests of the Western powers (with US imperialism at the centre). Increasingly, questions are being raised by many intellectuals, not all from the left fold about the motive and ideology of globalization.

The present state of international capitalist development is the allround globalization of the economy. 'What is this phenomenon of globalization'that has been subject, at the same time, to such vilification and such praise?' asks Joseph Stiglitz. He answers: "To understand what went wrong, it's important to look at the three main institutions that govern globalisation—the IMF, the World Bank, and the WTO. The IMF and World Bank both originated in the World War II as a result of the UN Monetary and Financial Conference at Bretton Woods. The most dramatic change in these institutions occurred in the 1980s, the era when Ronald Reagan and Margaret Thatcher preached free market ideology in the United States and the United Kingdom. The IMF and World Bank became the new missionary institutions, through which these ideas were pushed on the reluctant poor countries that often badly needed their loans and grants (Joseph Stilgledge 1999).

Did Bretton Woods Propel Globalization?

A growing divide between the haves and the have nots has left the increasing numbers in the Third World in dire poverty, living on less than a dollar a day. Despite repeated promises of poverty reduction made over the last decade of the twentieth century, the number of people living in poverty has actually increased by almost 100 million. This occurred at the same time that world income actually increased by an average of 2.5 per cent annually. If globalization has not succeeded in reducing poverty, neither has it succeeded in ensuring stability. Crises in Asia and Latin America have threatened the economies and stability of all developing countries.

Often even the best-intentioned projects have backfired, leaving the poor more vulnerable than ever. 'When projects, whether agriculture or infrastructure, recommended by the West, designed with the advice of Western advisers and financed by World Bank or others have failed, unless there is some form of debt forgiveness, the poor in the developing world still must repay the loans.' Social dissolution and conflicts have followed in such situations; the benefits of globalization have been less than its advocate's claim, the price paid has been greater as the corrupted and the rapid pace of change, has not allowed countries, time for cultural adaptation. The crises that have brought in their wake massive unemployment have, in turn, been followed by longer-term problem of social dissolution from urban violence in Latin America to ethnic conflicts in other parts of the world, such as Indonesia.'

Adverse Environmental Impact

"The World Bank," according to Wendt, received a great deal of criticism for the adverse environmental impact of the projects, including the numerous dams they have financed and ill-conceived mining and logging projects. International environmental groups and other "green" activists are highly critical of the Bank's record on the environment and its rhetoric on the issue.'

It is the industrialised nations that produced by the far most toxic and nuclear waste, which is increasingly being exported to the developing nations where storage and treatment regulations are either non-existent or ignored. Because wages and standard of living are lower in developing countries than in more developed countries, the costs of polluting are lower. They will not complain or protest especially if there is a chance of a job.' The World Bank uses 'transfer of technology' loan or credit to help finance the movement of older and outdated production system and product manufacturing to the developing countries from the countries where these items are no longer in use. These are usually the heavy polluting industries that would face stricter regulations, thus high costs; in more industrialised countries, or have to be disposed of in highly expensive procedures.

Plight of the Small Farmers

World Bank projects encourage small farmers to substitute food production for cash crops often in areas that are ill-suited for the farming of those crops resulting in farmers suicides as is evidenced in Andhra Pradesh, Karnataka and Maharashtra. This has disastrous consequences.

This cash-crop production reduces food availability for consumption and leads to further depletion, increased use of fertilisers and pesticides and eventually, financial difficulties for the poor farmers who are no longer growing their traditional crops. Poor farmers rarely, receive the irrigation benefits from large dam projects or power from huge power projects (financed by the World Bank). If the water does reach the small farmer, the World Bank and/or the national governments of project countries will fully ignore inherent flaws in the design of corruption surrounding the projects only to blame the 'ignorant peasants' when the project fails to meet expectations (Sukomal Sen : *The Marxist*, Jan-March 2003).

Violation of Human Rights

Some of the strongest criticisms of Bretton Wood Institutions have been in the area of human rights. The BWIs were lending to countries that have records of mistreating their own citizens. BWIs prefer to work in the authoritarian rather than with democratically elected leaders. For example, in the late 1970s, countries such as Chile, Uruguay, Argentina and the Philippines received hundreds of billions of dollars in loans, despite the onslaught of torture and repression by the governments. Critics respond that by approving loans to repressive regimes, the BWIs free up other resources that can be used to harm the nation's own citizens or pay for expensive military equipment purpose.

Women's Woes

Women, especially poor women, have had to pay a disproportionate share of the costs of development. Women comprise over fifty per cent of the world population, but earn only one per cent of the world's income and own less than one per cent of property. Despite these statistics, the World Bank did not treat women as a separate group in reports on world's poorest groups. A major problem relates to the efforts to improve the productivity and output of women. When the statisticians (of World Bank) measure productivity levels of women and conclude that they have increased, they mean that women have secured 'a job' usually outside the home. This ignores the fact that those women still have to perform all their traditional duties at home as well.

Social Costs of Reduced Services

'Structural adjustment' programmes, frequently result in harsh economic adjustments which the "developing countries have to make in order to receive funds from the IMF and the World Bank.'

The adjustments typically include (i) devaluation of a country's economy making the currency worth less in relation to other currencies, (ii) cuts in government spending and subsidies, including spending for social programmes; (iii) reductions in the money supply, which may result in high interest rates; (iv) privatisation of state-owned entities, which may result in the loss of jobs. During the crisis of the 1980s, many debtor countries implemented these measures and vulnerable groups, such as the poor and women were hit the hardest by the adjustments. Indeed, most of the statistics show that during the debt crisis, poverty increased and the gap between the rich and the poor widened. This led observers to label the 1980s, the 'lost decade' meaning a decade during which the debtor countries lost all opportunities to grow and develop (Sukomal Sen).

Consequently, the poor and other vulnerable groups are hit the hardest for several reasons. The most obvious reason is that the poor segment of the population are the ones who need the most government assistance in terms of schooling, healthcare and other social welfare programmes. The poor are also the hardest hit when the food prices rise. Many countries reduce or eliminate food subsidies and increasingly larger percentage of a family income goes towards food. At the same time, that income is shrinking, and when times are bad it is the poor whose incomes get stuck first and fastest.

To sum up, the globalization is clearly harming the poor, the third world countries while nakedly benefiting the rich, the profit hankering of the MNCs, monopolists, the elites of the third world countries and above all the imperialist interests.

Privatisation or Briberisation?

Austerity, privatisation and market liberalisation were the three pillars of Washington Consensus advice throughout the 1980s and 1990s. But privatisation to what end? The IMF argues that it is far more important to privatise quickly; one can deal with the issues of competition and regulation later. But the danger here is that a vested interest has been created; it has an incentive and the money, to maintain its monopoly position, squelching regulation and competition, and dictating the political process along the way. Whether the privileged monopolies are more efficient in production than the government, they were often more efficient in exploiting their monopoly position; consumers suffered as a result' (Joseph Stiglitz). He expresses his concern for the workers and unemployment:

"Privatisation has also come not just at the expense of consumers but at the expense of workers as well. The impact on employment has perhaps been both the major argument for and against privatisation, with advocates arguing that only through privatisation can unproductive workers be shed and critics arguing that job cuts occur with no sensitivity to the social costs. Privatisation often turns state enterprises from losses to profits by trimming the pay roll. Economists, however, are supposed to focus on overall efficiency. There are social costs associated with employment which private firms simply do not take into account" (ibid).

All credit to Stiglitz that he mercilessly unmasks the disastrous effects of privatisation on the workers in the developing countries. In industrialised countries, the pain of lay offs is acknowledged and ameliorated by the safety net of unemployment insurances. In less undeveloped countries, the unemployed workers typically do not become a public charge, since there are seldom unemployment insurance schemes. There can be a large social cost nonetheless—manifested in its worst forms, by urban violence, increased crime, and social and political unrest. Huge cost of unemployment include widespread anxiety even among the workers who have managed to keep their jobs, a broader sense of alienation, additional financial burdens on family members who manage to remain employed and the withdrawal of children from school to help support the family. These kinds of social costs endure long past the immediate loss of a job. They are often, especially, apparent in the case when a firm is sold to foreigners. Domestic firms may at least be attuned to the social context and be reluctant to fire workers if they know there are no alternative jobs available. Foreign owners, on the other hand, may feel a greater obligation to their share holders to maximise the stock market value by reducing the costs and less of an obligation to what they will refer to as an overbloated labour force'.

Privatisation for Kickbacks

But Stiglitz makes the most devastating criticism of privatisation when he deals with corruption associated with privatisation:- "Perhaps the most serious concern with privatisation, as it so often been practised is corruption. The rhetoric of market fundamentalism asserts that privatisation will reduce what economists call the "rent seeking" activity of government officials who either skim off the profits of governing enterprises or award contracts and jobs to their friends. Privatisation has made matters so much worse that today privatisation is jokingly referred to be as 'briberisation.' If the government is corrupt, there is little evidence that privatisation will solve the problem. After all, the same corrupt government that mismanaged the firm will also handle the privatisation. Government officials have realised that privatisation meant that they no longer needed to be limited to annual profit skimming. By selling a government enterprise at below market price, they could get a significant crunch of the asset value for themselves rather than leaving it for subsequent shareholders. In fact, they could steal today much of what would have been skimmed off by the future politicians. Not surprisingly the rigged privatisation process was designed to maximise the amount the ministers could appropriate for themselves, not the amount that would accrue to the government treasury, let alone the overall efficiency of the economy.

Today privatisation is carried out under the orders of imperialists-controlled 'international' bank, by imperial-funded consultants and government agencies that devise programmes, decide on prices and identify potential buyers. The time frame and scope for privatisation is dictated by the imperial super-powers, whose priority is to ram through the transfers of property that will make the transition to neo-liberal capitalism irreversible.

The privatisation strategy of the imperial centre is in the first instance to homogenise every region of the world economy subject to its penetration, while differentiating access to the world market according to the productive capacities of each region. The process of privatisation is thus not principally a means of taking over enterprises and penetrating markets so much as it is a means of eliminating alternative structures of production which could compete or challenge an imperially dominated world.

The advance of privatisation is thus located within a global strategy of empire-building during a period of counter-revolution in the third world and collapse of communism in the East. The strategy of privatisation is thus an imperialist-impelled strategy with a view to penetrating the productive forces of the concerned region.

Large-scale movements of impoverished workers and peasants back and forth between urban and rural economies, the cheapening of industrial production and a decline in well paid jobs in the advanced capitalist countries, the growth of poorly paid service-jobs only add to the world-wide crisis of living standards for labour. Technological innovations, largely related to the processing of information will lead to the growth of relatively small elite of well paid software engineers and executive and a mass of poorly paid 'information processors'—the new proletariat. The outsourcing of labour intensive computer work to low wage areas is already a growing social phenomenon. Thus, the centrality of wage labour will greatly increase even as it is impoverished.

The social and political implications of the change are momentous. For one thing, it will generate a radically different social structure and system of relations. For another, it highlights the strategic position of labour. Combined with the growth of huge industrial reserve army and its depressant effect on the wages of the employed, the change wrought in the labour force and the social structure of society will undermine and weaken the capacity of capital to discipline labour and to stimulate the accumulation process.

16

Victors Gobble the Sinews of Globalization

"Globalization" is perhaps the most contested and debated concept of present times. A critical analysis to debunk some of the popular myths being propagated in the mainstream media and even academic circles in favour of the present wave of globalization needs to be attempted so as to dispel the illusions of political economic elites of developing countries like India. Time has come to demonstrate that these popular notions are over simplifications at best and often motivated by the objective of perpetuating the privileges of the existing elite (Kavaljit Singh: *Questioning Globalisation*: 2005).

The proposition that financial liberalization leads to efficiency, economic growth and development by bringing in foreign investment and technical know-how needs to be examined carefully. Financial liberalization means implementing policies like deregulation of interest rates, removal of credit controls, privatization of government-owned banks, liberalization of restrictions on the entry of the private sector and/or foreign institutions into domestic financial markets. It may culminate in the removal of all restrictions on the movement of capital beyond the borders of the country. Kavaljit Singh finds that while almost all the developing countries have carried out financial liberalization, only a handful have actually received foreign direct investment (FDI) – only 14 countries account for over 85 per cent of the private flows to developing countries. Moreover, financial liberalization may not always lead to an inflow; the outflow of capital has been a more common experience across the developing countries—in sub-Saharan Africa, an estimated net transfer (negative) of $ 20 billion was recorded in the 1990s. Kavaljit Singh brings out how it is a complex set of internal and external factors—the institutions like market and state, infrastructure, geopolitical factors—that guarantee a combination of competitive returns and security to the capital which together ensure capital inflow but not through were liberalization (Rahul Varman: *Economic and Political Weekly*: July 21, 2007).

Besides, there is little to suggest a connection between financial liberalization and economic growth—the International Monetary Fund (IMF) estimates an average annual world output growth in the 1990s to be only 3.1 per cent, much below the 4.4 per cent rate in the 1970s. South Korea, in the 1970s and 1980s and China in the 1990s demonstrated that growth per se has little to do with financial liberalization alone. In spite of all the capital mobility, the US continues to absorb two-thirds of the world's surplus savings despite its low rates.

Growing liberalization has only contributed to financial crises in many countries and regions and states are left with little control over such crises resulting in the pauperization of the multitudes—Mexico, East Asia and Turkey being were more talked about instances. Finance is only one of the inputs required by a poor country and thus can at best be only one of the factors and not the be-all as a development instrument. Industrially developed countries are demanding a comprehensive investment agreement, which includes provisions such as foreign capital being treated at par with national capital and the most favoured nation treatment that bans performance requirements like technology transfer, local content requirement and export obligations. Though there has been tremendous resistance to such rules from the third world, it would be native to think that this threat has receded either at the global level or even at local level. In the form of bilateral agreements and arm twisting by developed nations through multilateral agreements like the North American Free Trade Agreements, developing countries are put at a disadvantage level. Checks on the practices of transnational corporations (TNCs) are required to curb the malpractices and exploitation of weak institutions in the third world of which there is so much of evidence. Even amongst the developed countries, issues like national treatment faced resistance in the 1970s and 1980s and they used many such measures. Not too long back, the US used a variety of performance requirements like ban on employment of foreign workers by foreign companies; Italy imposed 75 per cent local content rule on Mitsubishi, the US imposed the same rule on Toyota and so on. In developing countries, states and institutions are so weak that TNCs have broken their commitments with impunity. For instance, Pepsico never complied with the performance requirements that it made in 1989 while entering the Indian market but now they want such restrictions to not exist even on paper.

There is little evidence to say that even such one-sided and unfavourable agreements for developing countries bring any investment to them. FDI flows declined from $ 19 billion in 2001 to $ 11 billion in 2002 despite 78 new investment agreements signed by the African countries. In fact, FDI itself is no cure at all even when it pours in. It can crowd out domestic investment, may not bring any technology and lead to the takeover of domestic modesty by foreign capital through mergers and acquisitions, resulting in a drain due to transfer, pricing and import of technology.

Proponents of globalization not only claim that it is correlated to democracy but it also makes us to believe that the former brings the latter. The neoliberal project has not only an economic agenda to free capital from the restrictions of the state and host society but to make the extent that globalization riding piggyback on pliant third world states. The project also has a strong political component, which peddled through multilateral institutions in the name of democracy and "good governance." This is what is generally touted as "second generation reforms." Failure of economic reforms—the "first generation reforms," is now blamed at the doorsteps of the victims themselves in the form of lack of appropriate institutions and predicated upon the "second generation reforms" of the state and its institutions—to bring them in line with the logic of international capital and first world irrespective of their specific, immediate and historical context. What about the US own record (and that of the rest of the first world) in bringing Iraq-style "democracy" in so many places across the globe? Then there is the question of the dimension of concentration of power in the hands of corporations and its implications for democracy, especially in the third world. Indeed, the biggest threat to any notions of democracy is the rapidly rising inequality across the globe. Moreover, "one size fits all" global policies are taking common citizens further away from any say in decisions that affect them instead of bringing them any closer to democratic governance.

Since 1996, the World Bank has launched over 600 governance-related programmes and initiatives in 95 countries and is currently involved in several governance and public sector reforms in over 50 countries. For instance, IMF's 1997 programme for Indonesia had 48 governance-related clauses out of a total of 81 conditions. In recent years, aid packages have been suspended on account of "poor governance" and since 1999 the Bank has been regularly carrying out institutional and governance reviews. In fact, the Bank pledged more aid for those countries that carry out political and legal, besides economic reforms. International financial institutions normally should proclaim political neutrality and they are only "to set the prices right." But the wholesale failure of economic reforms in the 1980s and also the changed international political scenario in the 1990s have led them to bring in the political agenda (of neo-liberalism, this time it is packed in the technical language of "good governance." There has been a major shift in the priorities of global agencies "from getting the prices right." But there is something fundamentally to "getting the institutions" paradoxical in this whole idea of constructing institutions from the top at the gunpoint of dollars. In the West, institutions evolved organically over centuries with the development of capitalism. Hence, it is naïve to expect such institutions to be put in place overnight only because global agencies are providing a few dollars. Institutions cannot be brought in from nowhere riding roughshod over the existing political realities. Often aid gets mired in corruption and the institutional regime becomes even more autocratic for the masses, as has been the experience of some Afro-Asian countries.

What needs to be answered is why is it that the debate of governance is limited only to state agencies and not extended to other bodies—the international financial institutions, the corporations, the NGOs, and so on? The complex relationship between the state and globalization and questions the popular myth of the "end of the nation state." There are several arguments to explode this myth. First, we need to closely look at the extent of the present phase of globalization; in fact, it is only the latest phase of capitalism, which was always globalised and in some ways the last phase of pre-second world was, if anything, more globalised in a certain manner like the free movement of labour. Second primarily, the present phase is being spearheaded by TNCs which themselves are concentrated in a few industrialized countries and even their transactions are primarily located within the boundaries of a handful of developed nations. Moreover, these corporations need the support of the state to promote their activities at all times. First, they need the prop of the first world states to promote their interests within and then beyond to the third world. They also need state protection in the third world to further their interests. So when we talk about the end of the nation state, we are mostly talking about the "state receding" from certain domains, mostly related to development like infrastructure, education and health. While the state is becoming proactive in protecting property rights and elite privileges through law, policing and controlling labour. Furthermore, TNCs are primarily represented by the host states in the international arena. It is pointless to criticize globalization because there is no alternative to it. Hence, those who are pointing fingers at it are branded "pessimists," "negativeminded," "rabble rousers," and so on. Worldwide, people are not only criticizing globalization but are also seeking alternatives, both in theory and practice.

Globalization Retreats

In the early 1990s, 'globalization' was supposed to create the so-called borderless world. The process by which relatively autonomous national economies become functionally integrated into one global economy was touted as "irreversible."

And the people who opposed globalization were disdainfully dismissed as modern-day incarnations of the Luddites who destroyed machines during the Industrial Revolution.

Fifteen years later, today, despite runaway shops and outsourcing, we have a collection of national economies interdependent, domestic factors still largely determine their dynamics. Globalization, in fact, has reached its high-water mark and is receding (Walden Bello: Frontline: 24, January, 2007).

During globalization's heyday, we were told that state policies no longer mattered and that corporations would soon dwarf states. In fact, states still do matter. The European Union, the United States government, and the Chinese state are stronger economic actors today than they were a decade ago.

Growing Social Divide

Triggered by globalization, the growing social divide would unleash a new ideological counter current while in India cities are booming rural areas are languishing. If we are not convinced of the stresses and strains of globalization, ideological counter currents will emerge. Globalization is not a bed of roses. There is a need to be watchful. Globalization had integrated nation economies into a world economy unheard of in the last century. The last century also characterized by a shifting of manufacturing bases and R & B units of and the west to east south Asia in particular.

Moreover, state policies that interfere with the market in order to build up industrial structures or protect employment still make a difference.

Fifteen years ago, we were told to expect the emergence of a transnational capitalist elite that would manage the world economy. Indeed, globalization become the "grand strategy" of the Clinton administration which envisioned the U. S. elite being the *primus inter pares*—first among equals—of a global coalition leading the way to the new, benign world order. Today, this project lies in shambles (Walden Bello: 24.01.2007).

Propellers of Globalization

A decade ago, the World Trade Organization (WTO) came into being, joining the World Bank and the International Monetary Fund (IMF) as the pillars of the system of international economic governance in the era of globalization. The coordination of the neo-liberal policies of the three institutions in order to ensure the smooth, technocratic integration of the global economy is yet to be completed.

Sebastian Mallaby, pro-globalization commentator of The Washington Post, now complains that "trade liberalization has stalled, aid is less coherent than it should be, and the next financial conflagration will be managed by an injured fireman."

The IMF is practically defunct now; the Fund precipitated and worsened the Asian financial crisis, more and more of the advanced developing countries are refusing to borrow from it or are paying ahead of schedule, with some declaring their intention never to borrow again. These include Thailand, Indonesia, Brazil and Argentina.

Crisis of Legitimacy

The World Bank, having been central to the debacle of structural adjustment policies that left most developing economies in greater poverty, is also suffering a crisis of legitimacy. According to former IMF chief economist Kenneth Rogoff, the Bank has been systematically manipulating its data to advance its proglobalization position and conceal globalization's adverse effects (*Frontline*: 24.01.2007).

But the crisis of multilateralism is perhaps most acute at the WTO Slast, July, 2006 the Doha Round of global negotiations for more trade liberalization. The so-called Group of Six broke down in acrimony over the U.S. refusal to budge on its enormous subsidies for agriculture.

Fred Bergsten, the pro-free trade American economist, once compared trade liberalization and the WTO to a bicycle: "they collapse when they are not moving forward." First of all, the case for globalization was oversold. Second, rather than forge a common, cooperative response to the global crises of overproduction, stagnation, and environmental ruin, national capitalist elites have competed with one another to shift the burden of adjustment. While cooperation may be the rational strategic choice from the point of view of the global capitalist system, national capitalist interests are mainly concerned with not losing out to their rivals in the short term.

A third factor has been the corrosive effect of the double standards brazenly displayed by the hegemonic power, the U.S. Fourth, there has been too much dissonance between the promise of globalization and free trade and the actual results—more poverty, inequality and stagnation—of neoliberal policies.

The globalization of finance proceeded much faster than the globalization of production. But it proved to be the cutting edge not of prosperity but of chaos. The Asian financial crisis and the collapse of the economy of Argentina were the two decisive moments in reality's revolt against theory (Frontline: 24.01.2007).

Unenduring Growth

Another factor unraveling the globalist project derives from its obsession with economic growth. Unending growth is the centrepiece of globalization, the mainspring of its legitimacy. While with rapid growth resulting in the increasing tribe of expanding the global middle class, other environmental events such as global warming and peak oil, are making it clear to people that with globalization there is a surefire prescription for an ecological disaster.

The final factor is popular resistance to globalization. The battles of Seattle in 1999, Prague in 2000 and Genoa in 2001; the massive global anti-war march on February 15, 2003, when the anti-globalization movement morphed into the global anti-war movement; the collapse of the WTO ministerial meeting in Cancun in 2003 and its near collapse in Hong Kong in 2005; the French and Dutch people's rejection of the neoliberal, pro-globalization European Constitution were all critical junctures in a decade-long global struggle that has rolled back the neoliberal project. But these high-profile struggles were merely the tip of the iceberg, the summations of thousands of anti-neoliberal, anti-globalization agitators throughout the world involving millions of peasants, workers, students and indigenous people.

Corporate Driven Globalization

While corporate-driven globalization may be down, it is not out. Many pro-globalization neoliberal policies remain in place in many economics, for lack of credible alternative policies in the big trading powers are emphasizing free trade agreements (FTAs) and economic partnership agreements (EPAs) with developing countries.

When it comes to FTAs, the global south is becoming aware of the dangers and is beginning to resist. Key South American governments under pressure from their citizens derailed the Free Trade of the Americans.

The Retreat

The retreat from neoliberal globalization is most marked in Latin America, long exploited by foreign energy giants, Bolivia under President Evo Morales has nationalized its energy resources. Argentina gave an example of how a developing country faces down finance capital when it forced northern bondholders to accept only 25 cents of every dollar Argentina owed them.

From today's vantage point, globalization appears to have been not a new, higher phase in the development of capitalism but a response to the underlying structural crises of this system of production. Today globalization seems to have less a brave new phase of the capitalist adventure than a desperate effort by the global capital to escape the stagnation and disequilibria overtaking the global economy in the 1970s and 1980s. The collapse of the centralized socialist regime in Central and Eastern Europe deflected people's attention from this reality in the early 1990s.

Many academics still think that the task at hand is to "humanize" globalization. Globalization, however, is a spent force. Today's multiplying economic and political conflicts resemble, following the end of what historians refer to as the first era of globalization, which extended from 1815 to the eruption of the First World War in 1914.

Dynamics of Globalization

Alan Greenspan was, till, mid-2006, the Chairman of the United States Federal Reserve System ("the Fed"), one of the highest official positions in that country which he had occupied for almost two decades. The Fed is a statutory body which enjoys almost complete independence to attend to its mission of "putting in place the monetary conditions needed for maximum sustainable longterm growth and employment."

The manner in which other countries watch movements in the U.S. shows what an impact the Fed can have on the rest of the world as well. One can understand without much difficulty.

Alan Greenspan, as the head of the Fed was, thus, one of the most powerful players in the global economy during the past two decades which he aptly describes as an "age of turbulence." He authored The Age of Turbulence (2007) in which he championed the cause of globalization.

Greenspan describes himself as a "renowned defender of capitalism" and an ardent admirer of Ronald Reagan and Margaret Thatcher, Ayn Rand and her "objectivism" which championed laissez faire capitalism as the ideal form of social organization. Adam Smith's treatment of the invisible hand and the working of the free market, the collapse of the Soviet Union and its communist allies, the spread of property rights and markets in China, the transformation of the Labour party in the U. K. under Tony Blair, India's rejection of bureaucratic planning and its reliance more and more on the market, all these development are indications to Greenspan of the inevitable acceptance of capitalism globally. He concedes, though, that the intellectual battle for free market capitalism and globalization is far from won.

The thrust of the argument is that in the short run there may be uncertainty and some disruptions. But as globalization makes cross-border ownership of property more natural, economic relationships will turn out to be between economic units, basically households and firms everywhere, irrespective of national boundaries. Hence, if markets, competition, and capitalism are good for individual national economies, they have to be good for the global economy too.

But it overlooks the fact that within national economies there are non-market arrangements (such as the U.S. government and the Fed) to supervise and regulate the economic units.

An oft-repeated statement is that markets work best when they are not interfered with. One of the incidents that Greenspan discusses is the manner in which public authorities including the Fed itself, the central bankers of G7 and the government of the U.S. thought it necessary and wise to intervene when one of the economic units they were watching and admiring, a hedge fund named Long Term Capital Management (LTMC), suddenly showed signs of collapse. The details are not important. But the crucial question is, "Why?" This was not the only instance of public intervention in "private" economic affairs in recent U.S. experience either. They take such interventions as very much a part of the system. There are other things that they ask for so that markets can work effectively and, capitalism and globalization can succeed.

Dynamics of Capitalism

Equally significant is the failure to note the problems that the dynamics of capitalism poses to its working. Greenspan affirms frequently that "creative destruction is the underlying principle of capitalism" and "free competition is required for the efficient working of the market." He also admits that creative destruction leads to the emergence of increasing concentration of incomes and wealth. If so, doesn't the normal working of capitalism itself generate conditions that give undue economic advantage to the strong and make it not possible to have fair competition? Does it take much effort to see that in the international arena, economic strength is normally reinforced by political and military clout as well? If there is any doubt on these matters, recall that Thomas Friedman, another ardent supporter of competition, capitalism, globalization and all that announced to the world that "the hidden hand of the market will never work without a hidden first" and that in today's world, that hidden first" is called the US Army-Navy and Marine Corps."

"Rapid rise of India, China and other Asian countries to world prominence has disposed of the idea that globalization benefits the West at the expense of the rest," said the eminent social-theorist Prof. Anthony Giddens. Globalization was not just a synonym for the global dominance of the U.S. or of the West.

"It is obvious that the affluent countries tend to dominate the major world institutions. Virtually all of the technologies of communication that have been so important in creating greater global interdependence emanated from the developed states. These countries have also taken the lead in opening up world markets. Yet globalization is by definition a two-way set of processes not just a system of imbalanced power," said Prof. Giddens, the former Director of the London School of Economics and Politics. (*The Hindu*: 29.10.2007)

Noting that globalization has produced major new tensions and cleavages within many nations, Prof. Giddens said that the rapid pace of change and uncertainties had been ably, handled by most societies, including Western and non-Western. But others saw their ancient traditions as being under threat and they yearned for the certainties of an earlier age.

"India is the most pointed challenge to those who say that authoritarian government is the condition of rapid economic development. India has always had a cosmopolitan elite. In the global arena, peace and security depended upon the cooperation of nations, as well as the recognition that no nation, however powerful, could cope with the problems alone.

"In an age of interdependence we are partners not only in prosperity but also in adversity, in respect of the threats the world faces. The U.S. has explored the limits of unilateralism, with disastrous consequences. Ideals of freedom, democracy, freedom of the press may have originated in the West but they are universal in their implications." (The Hindu: 29.10.2007)

The European Union is the most important attempt in the world today to sustain real sovereignty through the common pooling of resources.

A new stage in the evolution of the global justice movement was reached with the inauguration of the World Social Forum (WSF) in Porto Alegre, Brazil, in January 2001.

The WSF was the brainchild of social movements loosely associated with the Workers' Party (PT) in Brazil. Strong support for the idea was given by the ATTAC (Association for the Taxation of Financial Transactions to Aid Citizens) movement in France. In Asia, the Brazilian proposal, floated in June 2000 received early, enthusiastic endorsement from, among others, the research and advocacy institute focus on the Global South Based in Bangkok (Walden Bello: *Frontline*: September 21, 2006).

Porto Alegre was meant to be a counterpoint to "Davos," a resort town in the Swiss Alps where the world's most powerful business and politicians met to discuss the ways and means to expand corporate activities. The highlight of the first WSF was a televised transcontinental debate between George Soros and others in Davos with representatives of social movements gathered in Porto Alegre.

With the decline the U.S. economy and the widespread slidedown due to recession almost all advanced countries including the USA are resorting to protectionism. They have virtually reduced imports to the minimum and the U.S. president is very much against BPO (outsourcing the business process), against the inflow of immigration slogan like "jobs in Britain are for Britishes only" has cought up with the French citizen also. This is a clear indication of the retreat of globalization. Of all the developing countries this "retreat" hurts India very much as already our real estate, garments and textile exporting sectors facing severe crises; which employ a sizable number of people who have lost their earnings now.

Is an Alternative to Globalization Possible?

The world of Davos was a contrast to the world of Porto Alegre—the world of the global rich with the world of the rest of humanity. It was this contrast that gave rise to the resonant theme "another world is possible." While Seattle was the site of the first major victory of the transnational anti-corporate globalization movement the collapse amidst massive street protests of the Third World Trade Organisation Ministerial Conference—Porto Alegre represented the transfer to the South of the centre of gravity of that movement.

The WSF became a magnet for global networks focused on different issues, from globalization to communalism to racism to gender oppression to alternatives. Regional versions of the WSF, a sun off, the most important being the European Social Forum and the African Social Forum; and in scores of cities throughout the world, local social meetings were held and at that level movements were institutionalized.

World Social Forum

Since its establishment, the WSF has performed three critical functions for global civil society: First, it represents a space—both physical and temporal—for this diverse movement to meet, network and, quite simply, to feel and affirm itself.

Second, it is a retreat during which the movement gathers its energies and charts the directions of its continuing drive to confront and roll back the processes, institutions and structures of global capitalism. Naomi Klein, author of No Logo: Taking aim at the Brand Bullies, underlined this function when she told a Porto Alegre audience in January 2002 that the need of the movement was "less civil society and more civil disobedience." (Walden Bello: Frontline: September 21, 2006).

Third, the WSF provides a site and space for the movement to elaborate, discuss and debate the vision, values and institutions of an alternative world order built on a real community of interests. The WSF and its many offsprings are significant not only as cited of affirmation and debate but also as direct democracy in action. Through a combination of periodic face-to-face meetings and intense e-mail and Internet contact in between, the WSF network was able to pull off events and arrive at consensus decisions. Finally, the central principle of the organizing approach of the new movement is that getting to the desired objective is not worth if the methods violate democratic process, if the goals are reached through authoritarian means. The movement has no future if its future is military.

Is WSF an Annual Festival?

The WSF has, however, not been exempt from criticism, one charge, is the WSF as an institution is unanchored in actual global political struggles and this is turning it into an annual festival with limited social impact. Many of the founders of the WSF have interpreted the "open space" concept in a liberal fashion, that is, for the WSF not to endorse explicitly any political position or particular struggle though its constituent groups are free to do so.

The reason that the WSF was so exciting in its early years was its effective impact: it provided an opportunity to recreate and reaffirm solidarity against injustice, against war, and for a world that was not subjected to the rule of empire and capital. This is why the sixth WSF, held in Caracas in January 2006, reinvigorated some 50, 000 delegates into the storm centre of an ongoing struggle against the empire, where they mingled with militant Venezuelans. Caracas was an exhilarating reality check. This is also the reason why the seventh WSF, held in Nairobi, was so disappointing, since its politics was diluted and the big business interests liked to the Kenyan ruling elite.

The worries on the economic front were not merely focused on the gross domestic product (GDP), but also about real everyday issues such as job, prices (particularly housing and fuel) and wages. The slowdown in the housing sector has been worrisome because it is a major provider of jobs. In 2005, this sector accounted for 15 per cent of the new jobs created by the economy. The job market had been slowing down, the increase was concentrated mainly in temporary and part-time jobs, which are low-paying and offer curtailed access to benefits that normally accompany tenured employment. About 39, 000 jobs in factories were lost in October, 2005 the quality of employment has been deteriorating, which cannot be captured solely by the unemployment rate. More crucially, the average length of unemployment of those seeking employment has reached its highest level in 10 years.

The minimum wage, at $ 5.15 an hour, has been at its lowest level in 50 years. The political elites' refusal to raise the minimum wage was a quiet war against "a poor." The minimum wage rate, which implies an annual wage level of $ 10, 300 for a fulltime worker, is about 20 per cent below the poverty of around 13, 000. About eight million people eke out a living on the minimum wage. More significantly, these workers bring in about two-thirds of their families' income, despite the fact that each household at the very top of the economic structure enjoyed wealth averaging about $ 15 million. The "average" American household's wealth, in sharp contrast was about $ 80, 000. Output per worker has increased by about 80 per cent since then. A growing proportion of women with children have been pushed into the labour force. In 1996, about half of low-income mothers were in the labour force; by 2002 this proportion had increased to two-thirds (V.Sridhar: Frontline: September 1, 2006).

In fact, the gap between productivity gains registered by the U. S. economy and the wage levels is regarded as lying at the root of the widening inequalities in American society. In 1962, the average wealth per household in the richest one per cent of America was 125 times the wealth of a typical household in the middle of the wealth scale. By 2004 the richest 1 per cent had 190 times the wealth of an ordinary household. Tax cuts show that only the crème de la crème of American society—the top 0.01 per cent were benefitted from the tax cuts—the cuts are mainly meant for the wealthy.

Pulitzer Prize-winning journalist David Cay Johnston calculated that between 1990 and 2002, for each additional dollar earned by the bottom 90 per cent of America, the richest one thousand earned an extra $ 18, 000 each (V. Sridhar: Frontline: September, 1, 2006).

In the realm of healthcare and health insurance, too, a growing number of Americans are being excluded from coverage. This is mainly because of the continued erosion of employer – provided health insurance, which is the primary means of health insurance. Almost 50 million Americans were uninsured in 2005.

Neoliberalism by its very nature stricts the range of policy options available to politicians and political parties "the centre of gravity of the system (political, economic and social) has shifted steadily to the right over the past generation."

Gore Vidal's observations, made before the last U. S. Presidential election, captured this problem of choices "We have only one political party in the United States, the Property Party with two right wings, Republican and Democrat.

Confronting Globalization

We are living in the world of the United States military-industrial complex. Whether one likes it or not this is a fact as the U.S. imperialist designs have become more naked with the aggression on Afghanistan and the annexation of Iraq to the interests of the U.S. domestic corporate sector.

David Harvey, the political historian remembers in his recent book on imperialism, the picture of the British monarch on stamps from India. Sarawak, Rhodesia and Jamaica, which was enough to make evident the history of imperialism the idea of the British Empire and Western hegemony. However, we saw the empire fast crumbling with the Indian independence signalling its demise. The Suez Canal crisis of 1956 led to the British and the French entering into a military conflict with Nasser, only to receive, a "rap on the knuckles" by the U.S. which wanted a peaceful containment to the conflict. It is here that we see the fall of one empire and the rise of another. A further blow to Europe came with the rise of American capitalism; international capitalism was no longer controlled from Europe. Now international politics and economic dominance are in the hands of the U.S. than with Europe which previously enjoyed the supremacy in international commerce and poltitics. (Shelly Walia: *The Hindu*: 09.09.2007)

Expansion of American Imperialism

In the words of Michael Ignatieff it is clear from the recent upheavals in West Asia that "America's entire war on terror is an exercise in imperialism."

The forces of globalization have created a novel situation globalization with an American face underpinned by the overwhelming impact of the American brands. In this context, Thomas Friedman's The World is Flat, discusses how globalization has reached a scenario from 2000 onwards when the individual becomes all powerful in contributing to the world. At this stage there are no walls and each individual is powerful in his own right. At least he thinks he is, existing as he does in a world here it is difficult to separate illusion from reality.

Fallout of Neoliberalism

This is the fallout of neoliberalism, the embodiment of free market economy that lays out the rules of the world we live in. We are restricted by transnational corporations, the World Bank, the IMF, symbols of the hegemony of a corporate led global trade. The "third world" becomes an onlooker of the steamrolling effect of the juggernaut of Western capitalism. People of the developing world remain "disconnected from what they produce and what they consume from the earth and from one another living in an "arid homogenized culture." Corporate globalization pushed farmers off their land; crops, water, patents are corporatized with no respect for human rights or ecology or justice.

Using the false message of prosperity and progress from the West is one form of strategic dominance. If this does not work, the alternative of "economic muscle" is ruthlessly employed. It is a known fact that "between 1990 and 1997 developing nations paid out more in servicing their debt than they received in loans a transfer of $ 77 billion from South to North, through the machinery of the IMF and the which ensure the continued dominance of the rich nations (Shelley Walia: *The Hindu*: 09.09.2007).

Latin America Revolts

Opposed to such an overwhelming control of the "third world" economies and life at large, the cries of rebellion by the Zapatista movement have inspired activism manifested in various movements around the world in Scotland where the G8 met to confer on the hunger and poverty in Africa and the rest of the developing world. An estimated 2, 00, 000 people converged on the hotel for a rally organized by Make Poverty History, a coalition of about 450 non-governmental organizations. Protests were intended to draw attention to more than 12, 000 children who die every day from poverty-related diseases: if the millennium targets are not met by 2015, the sub a Saharan Africa will be a burial ground for two in every three child deaths in the world. Such a reaction also highlights that AIDS and other major epidemics like malaria, which kills one child every minute, are all related to the overwhelming shroud of poverty and malnutrition. The lack of clean drinking water and the absence of any national health services or supply of medicines together multiply the burdens of a society that now looks towards the West for some tangible aid programmes to avert one of the biggest tragedies of the human race. Similar demonstrations at Genoa saw 3,00,000 protestors which got the impetus from the Zapatista uprising in Chiapas in Southern Mexico. The agitation gradually spread to many other cities around the world.

To oppose these free market strategies, the protesters in Quebec City tore down the fences surrounding the summit meeting of Free Trade Area of the Americas. The radical guerrillas in South Africa broke the fence of privatization that kept the poor from having electricity by installing illegal connections.

We now witness the encouraging moves by the nations in Latin America putting an end to the interventions of neoliberalism or the eye-catching challenges to the new-liberal agenda as in the Asian uproar to the financial crisis in 1998 and the South's antagonism to the "Singapore conditions."

Time is ripe now to counter the oppression of globalization with a new "language of resistance." In this great globalization debate, we have to ask the pertinent question: "Who rules and in whose interests and to what ends?" We have to snatch ourselves from the stranglehold of the powerful and the rich. Hostility towards the weaker sections, manipulation of the global media led to a deep-seated global antipathy. All discourses on pluralism and multiculturalism stand interrogated and suspect. It is time to counter the blatant support given to the neoconservative agendas of global supremacy and regional control.

All that Matters is Global Finance

Within the realm of the economy, the fastest-growing segment is finance. In a modern economy, finance is the facilitator of all activities. When people buy and sell, they use money and a wide range of money substitutes – cheques, credit cards, IOUs ('I owe you' contract bonds) and so on. When people save, they need instruments to hold their savings—bank deposits, mutual funds and shares for instance. Some of these instruments, typically shares, also represent claims to wealth, and so as wealth increases, more financial activities merge too.

At the 'global' level, finance comes to have a larger and more visible role. National economies have their own currencies and so trade between two countries involves not only a transfer of goods from one country to the other but also a conversion of their currencies for instance, Indian Rupees into U.S. Dollars. Since the exchange values of currencies change, buying and selling of currencies becomes a profitable transaction. As a matter of fact, trade in currencies now exceeds that in any other commodities globally (C.T.Kurien: *Frontline*: July 13, 2007).

The movement of capital from one country to others is a further manifestation of finance. Indeed, free and fast movement from one place to the other, transcending national boundaries, is the natural proclivity of capital. The broad category of "asset management" consists of the way pension funds, insurance assets, mutual funds and the like are administered. In 2004, pension funds globally amounted to $18.8 trillion, insurance assets to $ 14.5 trillion and mutual funds to $ 16.2 trillion, making a total of $ 49.5 trillion. (Mumbai – An International Financial Centre, High Powered Expert Committee, Ministry of Finance, Govt. of India: 2007).

Another source of funds in recent years has been the wealth of those who have a net worth of more than $ 1 million. They handed over their funds to some well-established international bank and the value of such funds in 2004 was over $ 30 trillion. All these funds circle the world in search of high returns at unimaginable speed thanks to modern information and communication technologies.

During the first four decades after Independence, India was a minor player in global finance. With the economy opened up in the early 1990s,. India's global trade increased substantially. Foreign capital has started moving in steadily, multinational corporations have become active in the Indian economy, Indian companies are making their presence felt in other parts of the world; Indian IT services have established contacts all over the world.

Global Financial Centres

But global financial activities do not spread uniformly. Global financial services tend to get located in a few cities in different parts of the world. In fact, there are only three cities world wide that are considered to be truly global financial centres – London, New York and Singapore. They are global in the sense that shares and currencies from all over the world are traded there. Since money is the lubricant of the present "democratic" politics, the person who raises more money with least controversy is declared by the media to be the front runner to higher public office.

Corporate Power

That money corrupts politics is a well known fact. A Washington Post poll found that 66 per cent of the public supports restrictions on the way that political candidates raise money through campaigns and feels that the process has been corrupted by big business. It is a known fact that who shall be the President of America is decided not by the American voters but by the all powerful military industrial corporate combine. They finance the Presidential and the Congress elections.

The money for the US elections comes, largely, from the corporations whose interests are in finance, insurance and real estate (FIRE); pharmaceuticals; media; and retail sales (such as Wal-Mart). These are the beneficiaries of globalization and neoliberal polices, which tend to favour transnational corporations more than the people of nation states. It is virtually impossible for a serious candidate for getting elected to office in the US to be critical of globalization and neoliberalism. At the most they can offer are gentle suggestions about the dangers of inequality. No American politician has shown leadership on the issue of globalization and outsourcing. To do so would mean that they must challenge the power of global financial firms, many of whom are their biggest campaign financiers.

Globalization has a bad image to which every perceived ill in the world attaches: depressed commodity prices, Asian sweet shops, child labour, fast-food imperialism, American cultural hegemony, outsourcing and global warming.

"Globalization is an expression of human desires that date back to the dawn of time, when the first humans left their African homeland and set out in search of a better life. Globalization," as Chanda describes "is not a scheme dreamed up by a few Western finance ministers, corrupt industrialists and the IMF." It is an age-old drive as natural as breathing: "essentially, the basic motivations that propelled humans to connect with others—the urge to profit by trading, the drive to spread religious belief, the desire to exploit new lands and the ambition to dominate others by armed might all had been assembled by 6000 BCE to start the process we now call globalization." Globalization, perceived by its critics as a radical break with the past looks to Chanda like a very familiar phenomenon. The traders, preachers, adventurers and warriors who acted as agents of globalization in ages past now wear different clothes and have access to new technologies. The Spanish missionaries of the 16th century find their modern counterparts in the idealists spreading a secular gospel of social justice (Nayan Chanda: Bound Together: How Traders, Preachers, Adventurers and Warriers Shaped Globalization: 2007).

But the game remains the same, as Chanda points out with telling examples, like the counterfeit Greek wines made by the Italians, thousands of years ago and exported to India in authentic Greek amphorae much as Chinese factories turn out knock-off Rolexes today.

"Globalization may have a positive impact on the market and economy. It may bring the best practices and products to your doorstep, but its contribution to our culture is not a welcome development," India will soon emerge as an Asian leader in networking cultural and literary ethos of countries, but entertainment methods may pose a challenge in doing so. The process of globalization had resulted in the commercialization of almost all aspects of life. "The impact of media, which sets people's entertainment agenda, can never be underrated. It pulls away an individual's attention from what one really needs" (*The Hindu*: 21.08.2007).

Why Harry Potter mania is so arresting about the theme or technique in the series that is so endearing for children? We have the most profound narrative skills in our own literature. *Mahabharata* is just an example. All of us have been brought up on the stories of witches, black magic, witchcraft and dark power. Triumph of good over evil has always been the mainstay of our themes. Yet it is the packaging that has made all the differences in the case of Harry Potter. We have failed in exposing our children to our cultural heritage rooted in our classical literature and its narrative traditions.

In his recent book *Indentity and Violence*, Amartya Sen argues that the anti-globalization movement is one of the most globalised movements today.

The current phase of globalization, beginning after the Second World War and gathering momentum during the 1980s and 1990s is not distinct. The latter half of the 19th century also witnessed an identical process of global integration, but it was followed by "four decades of inward orientation" between 1914 and 1950 (Amartya Sen: *Globalization, Poverty, Inequality*: 2007).

The current phase of globalization is characterized by a rapid expansion of trade followed by a dramatic reduction of barriers of trade decline of absolute level of poverty still leaves at least 12 billion people below the basic poverty line. Furthermore, inequality has risen on a range of dimensions particularly within countries. The geography of production, it argues, is impacted by the combination of effective use of innovation management and concentrated global purchasing in three specific sectors such as clothing and textiles, automobiles and components and furniture. While some Asian countries have benefitted because of globalization, a large part of Latin American and Carribean countries (specially sub-Saharan and African countries) have lost.

Is the current torque of globalization sustainable? The endogenously determined—arising out of us, success would sense setbacks to globalization. This would happen owing to three factors first—global value chains are energy intensive and global—is going to impact the future profitability on this count; second, widespread poverty would cause resentment; and finally, rapid adjustments would induce anxiety and impact distributional patterns triggering further political resistance to globalization.

Globalization—a ubiquitous buzzword "the cliché of our times," the term signifying different things to different people—evokes conflicting connotations and emotions. While Joseph Stiglitz ------- in any instances and episodes of exploitation and expropriation exacerbating inequalities, several others find its unstoppable thrust to a new dimension to human effort and potential. Whereas, Thomas Friedman, argues that globalization was creating a 'flat world,' Jagdish Bhagwati calls it a world of 'kaleidoscopic comparative advantage' rather than 'flat.' Kavaljit Singh, (*Questioning Globalization*: 2007) views globalization essentially as a process of capital transfer;" for some others, the Third World MNCs blur the battle lines in the globalization debate, driven as it is by the dynamic of merit based competition.

Global economic integration has been responsible for adverse living conditions, financial crises, social and political conflicts, as also deterioration in education, health and other social indicators and, above all, income inequalities. Globalization together with liberalization and privatization has led to job losses in the financial sector, fall in social sector spending no less than in employment opportunities. A global investment regime has impaired the regulatory capacity of governments and becomes subservient to the interests of foreign capital.

Is the IMF on the Wane?

The IMF has scarcely any influence left among the big developing countries and is groping for a new role. Ten years after the Asian financial cataclysm of 1997, the economics of the western Pacific Rim are growing, though not at the rates they enjoyed before the crisis. There is no doubt that the region has been scarred indelibly by the crisis, the key indices being poverty, inequality and social destabilization greater than before the crisis. South Koreas' painful labour market reforms, for instance, have produced a quiet desperation that is resulting in one of the highest suicide rates among the developed countries. There is no mechanism to regulate the massive movements of capital shooting through global financial networks at cyber speed.

The markets are getting bigger, information is moving faster, flows are larger and trade and capital markets have continued to integrate. No one can predict in what area – emerging markets, or whatever else – the next crisis will occur.

Flight of Speculative Capital

The amount of speculative capital sloshing around in global financial circuits is truly mindboggling. According to the McKinsey Global Institute (MGI), the global stock of "core financial assets" stood at $ 140 trillion in 2005. Traditional commercial banks held a significant amount of global financial assets, but non-bank financial operators, accounted for $ 46 trillion in 2005, hedge funds for $ 1.6 trillion, and private equity investors about $ 600 billion. These figures and other data on the stupefying rise and scale of global finance capital were presented by economist C.P. Chandrasekhar. (Walden Bello: *Frontline*: 24 August, 2007)

The explosive growth of finance capital is the outcome of the overcapacity which is plaguing the global economy. This has resulted in a market slowdown in investment in major parts of the global economy, with notable exceptions such as China and the United States. With stagnation, capitalists are less motivated to invest in more productive capacity and have more incentive to move their money to speculative activity that is, to try to squeeze more value out of already created value.

Speculative activity as a mode of profit-making has also outrun trade, with the daily volume of foreign exchange transactions in international markets standing at $ 1.9 trillion of trade in goods and services that is speculative activity in a single day amounted to 20 per cent of the annual value of global trade. "The new financial capitalism represents the triumph of the trader in assets over the long-term producer"(Martin Wolf).

Hedge Funds

The movements and mutations of speculative capital have outrun the capacity of national and multilateral regulatory authorities. In addition to traditional credit stocks and bonds, new, esoteric financial instruments such as derivatives have exploded on the financial scene. Derivatives represent the financialisation or the buying or selling of risk of an underlying asset without trading the asset itself. Emergence of hedge funds and private equity funds are the most dynamic players in the global casino. Hedge funds, numbering over 9,500, take short and long positions on a variety of investments, with a view of minimizing overall risk and maximizing profits. Private equity funds target firms with the aim of controlling them, restructuring them and then selling them for a profit.

With the absence of global financial regulation to tame the whirlwind of global finance, Asian countries have taken measures to defend themselves from the volatile global speculators that brought down their economies by pulling $ 100 billion in panic from the region in a few fateful weeks in July and August, 1997. The countries of the Association of Southeast Asian Nations (ASEAN) have banded with China, South Korea and Japan to form the "ASEAN plus will enable the member countries to swap reserves in the event their currencies are targeted by speculators as they were in 1997."

Even more important, they have built up huge financial reserves by running massive trade surpluses, an objective they have achieved by keeping their currencies undervalued.

This has resulted in a highly paradoxical situation. In a global economy marked by strong tendencies towards stagnation, China as producer and the U.S. as consumer are the twin engines that keep the world economy afloat. Yet, keeping the U.S. economy going necessitates a constant flow of credit from China and the other East Asian countries to the U.S. to finance middle-class consumption of goods from China and Asia. In the meantime, countries that really need the capital from East Asia, such as of in Africa, get very little of these reserves since they are not considered creditworthy.

Why has IMF Lost Credibiltiy?

The building up of massive reserves on the part of the Asian countries is directly related to their bitter experience with the IMF. First, the Fund, along with the U.S. Treasury Department, pushed them to liberalize their capital accounts which resulted in the easy exit of foreign capital that brought down their currencies. Then, the IMF provided them with multibillion dollar loans, not to rescue their economies but to rescue foreign creditors. Then, as their economies wobbled the Fund told them to adopt pro-cyclical expenditure-cutting policies that accelerated their plunge into deep recession.

Never Again

"Never again" became the slogan of a number of the affected government. Thailand declared its "financial independence" from the IMF after paying off its debts in 2003, vowing never to return to the Fund. Indonesia has said it will pay off all its debts to the IMF by 2008. The Philippines has refrained from contracting new loans from the fund, while Malaysia defied it by imposing capital controls at the height of the crisis.

Latin America Shows the Way

In 2006, Brazil and Argentina, following Thailand's example, paid off all their debts to the Fund in order to achieve financial independence .Boycott by its biggest borrowers is translating into a budget crisis for the IMF. Over the past two decades, the IMF's operations have been largely funded from the loan repayments of its developing-country clients rather than from the contributions of wealthy Northern governments. But with the biggest borrowers refusing to borrow, debt repayments are being reduced to a trickle. The upshot of these developments is that payments of charges and interest, according to Fund projections, will be cut by more than half, from $ 3.19 billion in 2005 to $ 1.39 billion in 2006 and again by half, to $ 635 million in 2009. These reductions have created what Ngaire Woods, an Oxford University specialist on the Fund, describes as "a huge squeeze on the budget of the organization."

This left the IMF with scarcely any influence among the big developing countries and groping for a new role. But the unravelling of the authority and power of the IMF is due not only to the resistance by the developing countries. The U.S. itself contributed to eroding the Fund's search for a meaningful role in global finance when it vetoed a move by the conservative American deputy director of the Fund, Ann Krueger, to create an IMF-supervised "Sovereign Debt Restructuring Mechanism" (SDRM), which would have allowed the developing countries a standstill in their debt repayments while negotiating new terms with their creditors. Washington's veto showed was that the U.S. was not going to tolerate even the slightest controls on the international operations of the U.S. financial institutions.

Neoliberalism Boomerangs

It is not only the IMF but neoliberalism, the dominant ideology of the 1990s, that came crashing down in the aftermath of the East Asian crisis. Malaysia imposed capital controls and stabilized the economy allowing to it weather the recession in 1998-2000 better than other afflicted countries. It was, however, Thailand that most dramatically broke with neoliberalism, government propelled countercyclical, demand-stimulating neo-Keynesian policies to get the economy back on track. Rural debt was frozen, government-financed universal healthcare was instituted, and each village was given one million baht to spend on a special project. Despite dire predictions from the neoliberal economists, these measures contributed to propelling the economy into a moderate growth path.

The 1997 financial crisis, which saw one million Thais drop below the poverty line in a few weeks, turned the theme against neoliberal globalization. Popular sentiment went against free trade. On January 8, 2006 several thousand Thais tried to storm the building where negotiations for a free trade agreement (FTA) were taking place between the U. S. and Thailand. The negotiations were frozen.

The souring on globalization has been paralleled by the rise in popularity of an economic paradigm promoted by the country's popular monarch, King Bhumibol.Dubbed "sufficiency economy" it is an inward-looking strategy that stresses self-reliance at the grassroots and the creation of stronger ties among domestic economic networks. Whatever the case, globalization is an unpopular word in Thailand today.

While Thailand broke with neoliberalism and the IMF South Korea followed almost to a "T" IMF management, has become a much more liberal economy than Japan. Denationalisation of its financial and industrial firms has taken place with "appalling speed," with foreign ownership now accounting for over 40 per cent of the shares of South Koreas to financial and industrial conglomerates or Chaebol Samsung now has 47 per cent foreign ownership; Posco, the steel company, over 50 per cent; Hyundai Motors 42 per cent; and LG Electronics 35 per cent.

Increasing Social Costs

The IMF has touted South Korea as a "success story." However, Koreans hate the Fund and point to the high social costs of the so-called success. Poverty has increased sharply with people living under the "minimum livelihood income," a measure of poverty rising from three per cent of the population in 1996 to 11.6 per cent in 2006 with emigration, family desertion and divorce rising alarmingly, along with the skyrocketing suicide rate (Walden Bello: Frontline: August 24, 2007).

In retrospect, the Asian financial crisis of 1997 may have brought about the downfall of the IMF, it also marked the demise of the East Asian developmental state that had aggressively and carefully managed the integration of the national economy into the world economy so that the domestic economy would be strengthened, not marginalized by global economic forces. The crisis marked the end of their being at the forefront of the development, as models to be emulated. The 21st century, which was supposed to be their century, slipped away the cataclysm market, the passing of the torch to China, while the smaller East and Southeast Asian economies have now become increasingly dependent on the dynamism imparted by their giant neighbour.

17

Neo-Imperialism's Hegemonism

Yet another attempt to formulate America's post-Cold War role comes from Zbigniew Brzezinski Second Chance: Three Presidents and the Crisis of American Superpower and the Crisis of American Superpower (Basic Books, New York, 2007). Although expressing confidence in a "Second chance" for America, he is more aware of "Something rotten in the state of Denmark" and the worldwide hostility the United States currently attracts to itself. Barack Obama expresses a similar discomfort: "There is a running thread in the American history of idealism that can express itself powerfully and appropriately, as it did after World War II with the creation of United Nations and the Marshall plan, when we recognized that our security and prosperity depend on the others. But the same idealism can express itself in a sense that we can remake the world any way we want because we are technologically superior or we're wealthier or we're morally superior (through a) kind of naivete and unwillingness to acknowledge history and the weight of other cultures, we get ourselves into trouble (M.S. Sondhi: *Deccan Chronicle*: 07.08.07).

Reviewing the personalities, policies and advisers of the three self-crowned post-1989 "global leader," Brzezinski traces a route to the present crisis and suggests lessons for the future. The first leader, George H.W. Bush, is a "policeman," a traditional, experienced pragmatist who rode out the break-up of the USSR but committed the "original sin" of failing to bring the Gulf war to a successful conclusion or settling the Israel-Palestine imbroglio. This triggered a series of malign effects in West Asia culminating in the disastrous Iraq and Lebanon Wars.

Soft-Welfare Advocates

The second, Bill Clinton, the "soft-welfare advocate," subscribed to a rosy belief in a benign globalizing determinism (almost a "force of nature") radiating from America, which would usher in universal democracy. Despite initiating Nato expansion, transatlanticism, and the WTO (soon followed by the Asian financial crisis), Clinton, with his preference for domestic affairs, stands accused of "strategic timidity."

Reacting to him, the third global leader, George W. Bush, the "vigilante," abetted by neocon advisers, provided "catastrophic" leadership post 9/11, through according to Nicolas Krist, Bush actually scored some major humanitarian accomplishments on the world stage.

Neo-conservatism is more belief than theory, asserts Brzezinski, belief that West Asian rage towards the United States is sheer nihilism, unprovoked and unrelated to history (although Bernard Lewis' thesis regarding Arab frustration over lost supremacy received much popular acceptance) that Arabs respect only force, without specifying how much force is needed to elicit Arab "respect;" and that electoral democracy can be forcibly injected into any kind of socio-political corpus with benign results. These beliefs when acted upon led to disaster, especially in West Asia. Altogether he suggests America has not come to grips with the new universal responsibilities that attend sole superpowership which are qualitatively different from the focused antagonism of the Cold War.

Brzezinski assumes that a Hobbesiam world of "global systemic instability" needs hegemonic leadership, and for the immediate future, only the US, in terms of military, economic and technological power, fits the bill. Other would-be competitors like Russian and China are currently disadvantaged. Though experiencing some economic recovery and stability, the former is still torn by the conflict between its residual authoritarian, imperialist proclivities and its humanism which failed to morph into democracy at first attempt. China is fast growing economically and militarily, and though this is not emphasized, suffers from a huge democratic deficit.

So what advice can he give to the next President of America? The bedrock for global action is consolidation of the transatlantic partnership (for despite the advantages mentioned, America cannot manage the world on her own), which can then tackle West Asian peace (by withdrawing from Iraq and settling the Israel-Palestinian imbroglio), and nuclear non-proliferation, with special concern for Iran and North Korea. He emphasizes the key role played by values and quotes Raymond Aron: "In the twentieth century the strength of a great power is diminished if it ceases to serve an idea." "The relativist hedonism" of self-indulgence and social shortcomings in American society adds to her already tarnished image, and Brzezinski, would that the embattled hegemon learn to exhibit a universal concern for human dignity, implement an agenda for remedying human injustices worldwide, all within a frame inherently respectful of cultural diversity. Forcing elections onto hitherto authoritarian societies is more likely to result in electocracy than democracy, self-defeating if a successfully elected party votes out or cripples the democratic system. Brzezinski, therefore, advocates, as did Natan Sharansky, a phased cultivation of human rights, till the populace at large is familiar and comfortable with the rights and duties of modern citizenship. Both presume that freedom and democracy are the natural if obscured goals of the human race. Few would argue with such impeccable sentiments, but exactly how they translate into policy prescriptions is not clarified.

Moreover, understanding cultural and civilisational diversity is a wide open field. The start of the last century heralded the writings of civilisationists in historical and sociological disciplines (such as Toynbee and Sorokin) or philosophy (Basanta Kumar Mallik), but the misuse of eugenic theories by the Nazis brought this field of study, post Second World War, into disrepute until Samuel Huntington's Clash of Civilizations caught the public imagination. Brzezinski conforms to Huntington's civilisational prescription by insisting on the transatlantic (Western Christian humanist) partnership.

From within this comfort region of compatibility, believing that freedom and democracy are the common goals of humankind even when large portions of humanity are either ignorant of or deny them, he would encourage adoption of this social and political organization for the rest of humankind, with some allowances for local colour. It is not clear how much he is aware of the cultural conditioning of non-Christian, non-individualistic cultures whose sociological and psychic impulses continue under the more superficial globalization or westernization of their international elites.

In the face of worldwide hostility stemming from American brashness and insensitivity to local sensitivities, be it in South America, Eurasia or anywhere else, and apart form the inevitable antagonism the mere fact of being a sole superpower would invite, Brzezinski offers three guiding principles: first that America, apart from safeguarding its own interests, promote global well-being and security; second that American society develop some self-restraint, and third, the US understand that its own future is linked with the "pulsating aspirations of the newly politically awakened masses all over the globe," George Bush could hardly disagree, the question remains, how?

House in Disorder

As manufacturing jobs disappear in the U.S. and as retraining remains more a *mantra* than a reality, the disposable population drifts towards service jobs, often poorly paid ones.

In 2006, the U.S. economy created 200,000 fewer jobs than it did in 2005. Since the 1980s, there has been a steady decline in manufacturing jobs. The new jobs being created are largely in the service sector. An estimated 30 million U.S. workers have lost their full-time jobs over the past two decades. Three quarters of them either never worked again or else found jobs with limited recompense.

Rise of New Technologies

The rise of new technologies, new competition and new markets abroad is bringing changes. There was a time when most people expected they'd keep a job for life. Now the average American has 10 jobs before the age of 40." For many Americans, change means having to find a new job or to deal with a new boss after a merger or to go back to school to learn new skills for a new career" (Vijay Prashad: *Front line*: April 4, 2007).

The promise of job retaining has been around for more than a decade. The former President Bill Clinton's "lifetime learning" as a way for laid-of workers to conceptualise their need for new skills. In a startling new book (The Dispsable American: Layoffs and their Consequences), The New York Times' economic reporter, Louis Uchitelle, recounts a visit to re-employment centre for aircraft mechanics dried up funds for social programmes and threw billions of dollars at the military. The "War on Terror" has allowed Bush to continue Reagan's polices, with the federal deficit reaching such alarming levels that even the generally loyal International Monetary Fund cautioned the U.S. government to change course with the point being that the current course is economically unsustainable and politically dangerous. Excess capital did not go into the creation of new industries but towards Wall Street, whose bubble burst towards the end of the Clinton presidency. The current U.S. debt is $9 trillion. When Bush took office, the debt was $5.6 trillion. The Iraq war is estimated to have cost $2 trillion so far

Wither the American Dream?

"We're in a class war, and our middle class is losing and losing badly. But I do blame and have blamed the rich corporate America and our political elites in both parties who have permitted the unabated assault on middle-class working men and women and their families. The titles of Dobbs' two recent books express his anger and his ideology: "Exporting America: Why Corporate Greed is Shipping American Jobs Overseas" (2004) and "War on the Middle Class: How the Government, Big Business and Special Interest Groups are Waging War on the American, Dream and how to Fight Back" (2006). Senator Jim Webb of Virginia wrote an opinion piece in The Wall Street Journal (November 15, 2006) entitled "Class War," in which he argued that the government had "no greater duty than to confront the growing unfairness of globalization."

Dobbs and Webb inflame the resentment of the section of America abandoned by both its political elite and its corporate parts. But rather than offer a platform to "reclaim America," they recycle xenophobia. Dobbs correctly identifies corporate power for its callous indifference to the U.S. workers, but he also points the finger at the "illegal alien invasion" as well as at India and China. On the U.S. Mexico border, Dobbs is virulent with his accusations that the Mexican government is "exporting poverty. They are overcrowding the major schools in Los Angeles. They are creating a crime wave in point of fact in certain parts of the country."

Dobbs is blind to the power differential between corporate America and the migrants, with the former playing a causative role in joblessness and the latter simply responding to the destruction of their economy by free trade agreements and to the need for cheap labour within the U.S. "Two Americas" theme the growth of poverty (roughly 37 million people), the lack of health insurance (roughly 47 million people), and the remarkable rise of hunger (9.6 million people, including three million children).

Since 2006 the housing market, which gave a lift to a sagging stock market has begun to leak. This month the sub-prime housing market bubble burst and sent a tremor through the world of finance. Uchitelle's emphasis on lay-offs reveals both the economic and cultural shifts in the U.S. Bush was statistically correct when he said that the average American would have 10 jobs before turning 40. Uchitelle cites a government study of 10,000 people, conducted from 1979, when "most were teenagers and the permanent lay-off was just becoming a national phenomenon.

As manufacturing jobs disappear in the U.S. and as retraining remains more a *mantra* than a reality, the disposable population drifts towards service jobs. When Wal-Mart announced interviews for a new retail outlet it was opening in Chicago, 25,000 people applied for 325 poorly paid jobs. This is the underlying reality of the job market for the bulk of the U.S. Population.

"The United States is the first country in history destroy the prospects and living standards of its labour force. It is amazing to watch freedom-loving libertarians and free-market economists serve as apologists for the dismantling of the ladders of upward mobility that made the America of an old opportunity society. America is seeing a widening polarization into rich and poor. The resulting political instability and social strife will be terrible."

The binary opposition between that is called 'globalization' and protectionism defines the mainstream discussion of the economy in the U.S. Both the Democratic party and Republican party are fundamentally committed to 'globalization,' which to them means to defer to corporate power over economic activity and to ask their domestic workforce to be essentially experts in their careers. Corporate interests are preponderant and criticism is deemed irrational.

18

New Resistances to Globalization

The internationalization of capital is making this an epoch of extraordinary conflict, upheaval and uncertainty. Michel Chossudovsky in the globalization of poverty contends that the new international regime of capital has had disastrous consequences for the poor.

The globalization of poverty in the late 20th century is unprecedented in world history. This poverty is not, however, the consequence of a "scarcity" of human and material resources. Rather it is the result of a system of global oversupply predicator on unemployment and the worldwide minimization of labour costs . Capital on a global scale is appropriating more and more of the planet's income and wealth while driving down living standards for large swaths of the world's population. The old breakdown of the world into North-South, core-periphery, or first and third worlds, is diminishing in importance. Hans-peter Martin and Harald Schumann in their book, *The Global Trap*, portray this as the creation of a "20:80 society" in which the top 20 per cent of the globe's population takes more and more of the world's income while the other 80 per cent suffers economic decline or stagnation as they argue.

The concepts of core and periphery, or North and South, are increasingly not geographic per se as much as they are social class in character. The global economy is incessantly churning out new variations, specializations, and asymmetries that cut across nations and regions. The end of socialism has brought dramatic increases in poverty along with the creation of a new rich and ostentatious upper class. As of 1998, the world's 225 richest individuals with total assets of $311 billion, had a combined wealth of over $1 trillion equal to the annual income of the poorest 47 per cent of the entire world's population. The two richest countries, the United States and Canada have experienced a growing polarization and decline of the influence of the working classes and trade unions that event adversely affects sectors of their societies referred to as "middle class." Even the so-called advanced economies too third world "zed" to some extent because of increasing marginalization, expanding third through a cheapening and casualization of the work force, all of which are related to the process of globalization. (Michel Chossudovsky: The Globalisation of Poverty, Impacts of IMF and World Bank Reforms, 1997, P.26)

The United States, with the highest per capita income in the world also has the greatest percentage of its population living in poverty among the industrialized countries. Between the late 1970s and the end of the 1990s the average real income of the richest fifth of the U.S. population increased by 30 per cent, while that of the lowest fifth dropped by 6 per cent. Even the U.S. economic expansion in the 1990s, with its declining unemployment and right labour markets, did little to alter this picture as the upper fifth saw its income rise by 15 per cent between 1988 and 1998 while the income of the lowest fifth increased by mere 1 per cent. Interestingly, New York, the leading financial centre of the new global economy, experienced the greatest increase in income inequality of any state between the late 1970s and the late 1990s, while California, the technological heart of the so-called "new economy," numbered among the top five states with the greatest growth in economic disparity.

Edward Wolff, author of *Top Heavy*: A Study of the Increasing Inequality of Wealth in America commented that:

Capital Capitalises Capital

"Generally what's happening in the U.S. economy is that capital is what's being rewarded, and not labour. Average wages have been stagnant now for almost 25 years, and the share of income going to the owners of capital has been rising dramatically in the last 10 years particularly."

This ever-liberal policies pursued by many of the world's states are central to explaining the growing polarization of wealth and poverty. Neo-liberalism, meaning economic deregulation, reduced taxes and laissez faire markets, was the economic philosophy of a new bloc of social forces that began to take control of national states in the 1980s, as epitomized by the Reagan and Thatcher regimes. However, the dictatorship of Augusto Pinochet in Chile actually served as the first laboratory for an experiment in neo-liberal economics in the mid-and late 1970s with its bloody repression of the working class, privatization of state companies, and dismantling of the public health system.

Neo-liberalism was consolidated as an integral part of the globalization process in the 1990s by democratic and social democratic governments around the world.

To the extent that local productive apparatuses are integrated into the transnationalization process, the logic of local and global accumulation tends to converge and the earlier rivalries between capitalists no longer take the form of national rivalries. Competition between capitalists and corporations continues, of course, to be as intense as ever. But given the separation of accumulation from determined territories and the transnational integration of capitalists, competition is now between oligopolistic clusters in a transnational environment. The rapid growth of transnational investments, particularly in the telecommunications and the high-tech sectors, illustrate this new pattern of competition.

Transnationalised Bourgeoisie

The transnationalised bourgeoisie in the globalization epoch, and it has now become the hegemonic class faction globally. This denationalised bourgeoisie is class conscious, and conscious of its transnationality. At its apex is a managerial elite that controls the levels of global policymaking, and which responds to transnational finance capital as the hegemonic faction of capital on a world scale.

As Manuel Castells notes in his three volume study, *The Information Age*: "The instrumental capacity of the nation-state is decisively undermined by the globalization of core economic activities, by the globalization of media and electronic communication and by the globalization of crime. The determinant feature of the current epoch is the supersession of the nation state as the organizing principle of capitalism, and with it, of the inter-state system as the framework of capitalist development.

There is no longer anything external to the system of global capitalism. As the organic and internal linkage between people become truly global, the whole set of nation-state institutions is becoming superseded by transnational institutions.

In order to understand the position of the nation state in the age of a location we should analyze in a dialectical manner the nature of states and the social forces that congeal in state structures and practices in particular historic periods. "Markets" are the site of material life while states spring from economic relations and represent the institutionalization of social relations of domination. State practices and the very structure of states are negotiated and renegotiated in specific historic periods through changes in the balance of social forces as capitalism develops and classes struggle. Newly strengthened ruling classes can quickly constrict state autonomy as they make more intensive use of the state in times of major capitalist restructuring. In the late twentieth century, capital abandoned earlier reciprocities with labour precisely because the process of globalization has allowed it to break free of nation-state constraints.

State Serves the Captalists

Governments are undertaking restructuring and serve the needs of transnational capital not simply because they are "powerless" in the face of globalization. A particular historical constellation of social forces now exists that presents an organic social base for neo-liberal restructuring. Here the case of Mexico is once again illuminating as to how this process occurs even in third world countries. When the transnational faction of the Mexican bourgeoisie undertakes neo-liberal restructuring and integration into the global economy, it is not doing so merely because the Mexican government became "powerless" in the face of globalization, but because the interests of this class faction lies in integration into global capitalism.

And the peso crisis might have thrown millions of poor Mexicans into dire straits, but it saved the necks of the Mexican bourgeoisie just as surely as it saved those of its counterparts in the U.S. and elsewhere.

The "dinosaurs" in the power struggle represent the old bourgeoisie and state bureaucrats whose interests lay in Mexico's corporatist-import substitution model of national capitalism. The new "technocrats" are the transnational faction of the Mexican bourgeoisie that captured the party, and the state, with the election in 1988 of Carlos Salinas de Gortari. Since then, this transnationlized faction has implemented neo-liberal structural adjustment, including the accelerated privatization of public spheres and commodification of non-market spheres.

Transnational capital and the transnational bourgeoisie utilize national state apparatuses to create the conditions for global capital accumulation. Moreover, "strong" states will impose adjustment on "weak" states. The transnational bourgeoisie exercises its class power through two channels. One is a dense network of supranational institutions and relationships that increasingly bypass formal states. The other is the utilization of national governments as territorially bound juridical units, which are transformed into transmission belts and filtering devices, but also into proactive instruments for advancing the agenda of global capitalism.

National states continue to exist and many will be powerful entities, but, instead of serving the "nation" they now increasingly respond to transnational economic interests, particularly those of footloose deterritorialized finance capitalists and transnational corporations.

Among the key global financial institutions imposing order for the capitalist world are the IMF, the World Bank, and the World Trade Organization. The annual meetings of the G-8 also play an important role in coordinating the policies of the key capitalist countries, along with the Organization for Economic Cooperation in Europe (OSCE). The United Nations also is a factor in the efforts to create a "new world order," as exemplified by the UN-backed war against Iraq and the interventions in Somalia, Bosnia and the Congo.

Global Capitalism

Hence, global capitalism is organized in a set of institutions. These institutions include: the transnational corporations that own and manage the world's resources and appropriate its wealth; the international financial agencies that impose the conditions necessary for global capital accumulation to take place; the states of the North, and their junior counterparts of the South that create the global and the local political, administrative, and legal environment that allow the system to function; and the formal and informal transnational elite forums, such as the G-8, the Trilateral Commission, and the World Economic Forum, which develop strategies for the maintenance and reproduction of the system and supervise its overall operation.

Transnational Capitalism

Transnational capital currently enjoys an unprecedented structural power over popular classes worldwide, but this is a historic conjuncture and not a fixed feature of the system. Capitalism has always been a violent and unstable system wracked by contradictions. The confidence exuded by the transnational bourgeoisie with its "end of history" thesis and so on conceals a fragility in the foundations of the system.

Therefore, the most critical question is what will be the role of the popular classes around the world in this process? Globalization has also led to an increasing popular awareness that transnational, rather than merely national, perspectives are necessary to deal with many issues of popular grassroots concern. The Battle of Seattle in the late 1999 revealed that all these different social forces are beginning to coalesce and work together in opposition to a corporate agency. In the long term the question is whether these movements can build a transnational platform to challenge capital and to make the new global economy serve the needs of the many rather than the interests of the rich and powerful as it currently does.

High-Tech Robber Barons

With globalization the "information age," has become an age in which technology and the manipulation of knowledge are at the cutting edge of the new global economy. During the twentieth century, industries like steel, automobiles, chemicals and petroleum were the most dynamic centres of economic activity. Today they are surpassed by information age enterprises such as software suppliers, telecommunications companies, computer manufacturers and online commercial firms. Globalization and information age are completely intertwined. One could not exist without the other. But these two concepts need to be distinguished: globalization by and large refers to the expansion of capital, production and markets on while the informational age denotes the technologies that facilitate the globalization process. The spread of computers, digital technologies and new communication networks provide the basic infrastructure for globalization to occur. At the same time continued advance of globalization generates an ever-increasing demand for these new technologies.

Fortune Magazine, in its commentary on the top 500 corporations in 1998, took note of the rise to the prominence of companies linked to the Information Age, or what it call the "New Economy." "The Year "1998," proclaimed Fortune, "when the New Economy fundamentally parted ways with the old and high-tech consolidated its role as the driving force behind the growth of big business" in order of revenues. The Fortune 500 is still dominated by the likes of General Motors, Mobile and Coca Cola, but these companies are "battling their shrinking top and bottom lines," while challengers "like Microsoft, Dell Computer, Cisco Systems and Sum Micro systems, with their high rates of revenue growth and their stock option-rich employees" make it clear "that one day the Fortune 500 will be theirs."

Information Highway

While today's business magnates have built immense fortunes via the "information highway" and the technological infrastructure related to it, the robber barons of the nineteenth century accumulated their wealth by building a new transportation system, the railroads and seizing control of many of the emergent industries that were linked up by the rails. The major difference between the two is their economic "playing field;" while the robber barons dominated the U.S. national economy, the new corporate, or "cyber," barons of the information age have their sights set on controlling the markets, resources and assets of the planet.

The dynamic and emergent enterprises of our aggressive economic age are: computer, communications and Internet firms; media conglomerates; bio-technology corporations and finance and banking companies. While the rise of the corporations of the information age appeared first in the United States and are more readily discernible here.

The information age has thrown up a number of U.S. corporate magnates whose economic appetites are every bit as voracious as those of the earlier robber barons: Bill Gates of Microsoft has control of most of the global market for software operating system; John Malone, the cable mogul of TCI, has gouged the public, exercising local monopolies and charging exorbitant cable rates to build his business fiefdom; Rubert Murdoch of the Fox Media conglomerate has brought out of destroyed local competitors and smashed newspaper unions around the globe; Michael Eisner of Disney World stands over and enormous entertainment empire that inflicts its cultural preferences of the world's populace; and Craig Barrett of the Intel Corporation is the tycoon of the computer processing chips, controlling over 80 per cent of the global market.

The greed, perniciousness, and fortunes of the original robber barons are rivaled and in some cases surpassed, by the owners and executives of the corporations of the information age. (According to Fortune Magazine, Bill Gates, the richest outclass the wealthiest robber baron of the late nineteenth century, John D. Rockefeller, by a factor of 311 to 1. The top five are all key players in corporations involved in globalization and the information age: Michael Eisner of Walt Disney, Mel Karmazin of CBS, Sanford Weill of Citigroup, Stephen Case of AOL, and Craig Barrett of Intel.

In Silicon Valley, the birthplace of the personal computer and the microchip, antiunion policies have characterized most of its leading businesses for years. High-tech companies in the valley during the past half century have operated in a largely paternalistic fashion, paying relatively low wages while striving to keep the trade union at bay by providing some benefits.

Business Process Outsourcing

Business process outsourcing has become the order of the day. Several U.S. firms have engaged the services of call centres in having developing countries including India to reduce the work done at home. Thirty-one per cent of the valley workforce had annual incomes under $15,000, hardly a living wage in a country that has one of the highest costs of living in the world.

A study released in early 1998, declared that "Silicon Valley is experiencing a dramatic growth in income inequality and economic insecurity," the report found that as of 1996, while wages for the bottom quarter had declined by 13 per cent about 19 per cent of all jobs in the area paid less than the living wage for a single adult, while almost 40 per cent earned too little to keep a single parent and a child out of poverty, and 55 per cent did not earn enough to support a family of four.

In the age of "flexible employment" companies throughout the valley have abolished many permanent jobs and contracted work out to agencies for temporary staff, where they have few or no benefits. Regular employment in major computer companies, like Sun, Hewlett-Packard, and Apple is stagant or declining while these same companies subcontract for many of their components with manufactures who pay 30 per cent less to their employees.

On the national level, high-tech companies have set the pace in mergers and acquisitions, which inevitably leads to downsizing or in simple words, the elimination of jobs. Characteristic of this trend is the buyout by AOL in 1999 of Netscape, an Internet browser company based on the Silicon Valley. Immediately after the buyout, AOL, based on Texas, announced that 700 to 1, 000 employees would be eliminated, about one-tenth of the labour force of the combined companies.

Another is the tendency of many Internet businesses that force free labour to promote and expand their companies in exchange for free monthly accounts.

Mergers and Downsizing

Mergers and the use of volunteers aside, downsizing of the labour force is a salient characteristic of corporations related to the information highway and high-tech activities. Cutting benefit packages is also commonplace among these giants. In May, 1999, with its earnings at record highs, IBM announced that it was phasing out traditional pensions for over 1,40, 000 employees, replacing the pensions with "flexible retirement benefits" that cost the workers $200 million in payments per year.

The elimination of jobs due to new technologies and the slashing benefits explains in part why the U.S. economy in the late 1990s had high growth rates while incomes were almost stagnant. Monopolistic tendencies are prevalent among today's high-tech barons. Many of the days cyber barons, such as Bill Gates of Microsoft, have carved out monopolies based more on patent claims and the control of knowledge than on the manufacture of specific products. The manipulation of knowledge assets by imformation age corporations "makes the monopolies of the nineteenth century robber barons look like penny pinchers."

In the nineteenth century, patents were usually granted for specific products rather than for particular ideas. Thomas Edison, for example, the greatest inventor of the late nineteenth and early twentieth century, saw most of his patented inventions through the production, be it the light bulb, the phonograph, or the mimeograph. Today, however, patents on ideas and specific areas of knowledge are of particular importance and can have more market value than a final manufactured product.

Privatization of Knowledge

The most momentous consequence of the "privatization of knowledge" by corporate interests is in bio-technology and the life sciences. Currently, the big rush is on top map out of the complete genetic structure of the human genome. Once it is done, this knowledge will give us the power to alter our gene structure, control diseases, and even to prolong life itself. While some researchers of the genome have openly published their results on the Internet, it is estimated that access to at least 15 per cent of the research completed thus for is restricted by private firms seeking to use their knowledge for private gain.

In the agricultural sciences, a handful of corporations are intent on dominating the market for bio-engineered crops. By splicing new DNA strands into selected plants, new seeds can be grown that are resistant to insects and fungus, or new plants can be developed that contain added nutritional is a leader in bio-engineering, particularly with its production of genetically altered soybeans that are resistant to the company's Roundup weed killer, which kills all unaltered vegetation. Not to be outdone, Dupont spent $7.7 billion to take controls of Pioneer Hi-Bred the world's largest corn seed company.

Critics argue that the creation of uniform seeds threatens crop diversity around the world. Further more, the spread of bio-engineered crops resistant to certain insects or weeds could lead to the development of "super" weeds or insects that would have devastating consequences for traditional crops grown in the same region, the most controversial area of bio-engineering is the development of what are called "terminator seeds." To protect their patents and prevent farmers from replanting the bio-engineered seeds, genetic material is spliced into the new plants so that their seeds are rendered sterile. According to Pat Mooney "these technologies are extremely dangerous because over 1.4 billion farmers, primarily poor farmers in Africa, Asia and Latin America depend on far-saved seed as their primary seed source. If they can't save seed, they can't continue to adapt crops to their unique farming environments, and that spells disaster for global food security.

The media corporations are unceasingly involved in shaping and intruding into our daily lives. The sway of these corporations has expanded enormously with the technologies of the information age.

In the early twentieth century, the media came to include the radio and the cinema, and then in the 1950s, television and the TV Networks. In the last 15 to 20 years, the size and scope of the major media corporate holdings have exploded to include Internet, satellite and cable TV as well as newspapers, book and magazine publishing Hollywood studios, and TV and radio networks.

The media conglomerates serve as the primary boosters of globalization in the information age, shaping cultures and societies in the name of market capitalism. As Edward Herman and Robert McChesney write: "The global media are the missionaries of our age, promoting the virtues of commercialism and the market loudly and incessantly through their profit-driven and advertising-supported enterprises and programming. As the media monopolies spread their tentacle virtually into every facet of our existence never have so, few had so much power to shape the lives of so many.

19

Globalization and Micro Movements

In the process of opposition to globalization, micro-movements have begun to raise a new discourse on democracy and invent political practices, expanding the arena of politics beyond the representational institutions of elections and political parties. They see globalization as undermining and de-legitimizing the institutions of democratic governance and as a force which seeks to undo Indias democratic revolution. This paper analyses the discourse and politics of micro-movements and their role in reinventing participatory democracy as the form of social action and political practice, creating new spaces and infusing deeper meaning to democracy in the globalizing world (D.L.Seth: *EPW*, January 3, 2004)

When the Indian state has lined itself to the vertical hierarchy of global economic and political power, significant countervailing processes have emerged in the form of political and social movements at the grass roots making new provincial and national-level alliances aimed at countering the state's policies of globalization. These movements led by small groups of social activists have been active in different parts of India working on disparate issues, albeit all concerning struggles of the economically marginalized and socially excluded poorer populations. In the decade of the 1990s, many of them have come together and have joined larger, worldwide alliances and forums protesting against hegemonic policies of the institutions and organizations representing global economic and political power. Though the micro-movements have been fighting politically on several issues concerning the poor much before they joined the debate on globalization, it is the challenge of globalization that has brought many of them together on common political platforms at provincial and national levels, making issues of participatory democracy a part of their ongoing struggle.

Movements and Globalization

The micro-movements in india represent a varied and complex phenomenon. They are variously referred to as grass roots movements, social movements, non-party political formation, social-action groups and movement-groups. Although there is no systematic survey, compilations made from different sources by researchers and guesstimates provided by observers in the field suggest a figure in the range of 20-30,000 such movement groups in the country (Kapoor, 2000). A large number of them existed as fragments of the earlier political and social movements, which had their origins in the freedom movement but were subdued and dispersed soon after independence when the liberal, modernist English-educated ruling elite begun to nominate public discourse in India. These were the groups which had their lineage in the Gandhian, socialist, communist and social reform movements but, by and large, had stuck out as groups of party independent social and political activists (Sheth and Sethi, 1991). But within three decades of independence, with the decline of institutional politics, which began in the late 1960s, giving rise to several mass-based movements of protests. The organizational or a pressure group, it was that of a civil-associational group, leading political struggles on issues articulated by the people themselves.

Discourse of Globalization

In the early 1990s, the grass roots movements confronted an entirely new set of terms justifying the hegemony of the newly established post cold war global order. Earlier, till the end of the cold war, a significant section of grass root movements in India were active in protesting against the exclusionary elite-oriented development model that was conceived and sought to be made uniformly and universally applicable the world over, by the Bretton Woods institutions and their sponsor countries. The campaign for 'alternative development' propagated and practised in India for long by Gandhian activists, after independence was marginalized within the development discourse dominated by India's modernist ruling elite.

Some concepts developed by the proponents of alternative development became buzzwords for activists of new social movements: appropriate technology, small is beautiful (a la Schumacher), pedagogy of the oppressed eco-friendly life-styles, limits to growth were only a few among them. This discourse of the new social movements in the West found a great deal of resonance among the social activists in India, particularly for the apolitical, westernized ones, for whom it had almost an emancipator effect. It gave cultural meaning to their activism and even helped them to re-discover their own alternatives. M.K. Gandhi's deep anxieties were felt and expressed about the growing consumption habits of the idle classes. For, it was feared that may lead to state policies resulting in rapid depletion of the world's natural resources.

The discourse of globalization was conceived and led by the victors of the cold war, it claimed to establish a new global order which would put an end to the old one that had kept the world divided-economically, culturally and politically. In its place it not just promised, but communicated a virtual experience of the world becoming one culture and one polity such a world could do, globally, without the messy institutions of representational democracy, even as such institutions were to be made mandatory internally for every individual country. It assured that this new global order would be managed by a set of global institutions (served by experts and freed from the cumbersome procedures of representational accountability), which, being set up and controlled by the world's few 'self-responsible' and 'advanced' democracies, would guarantee peace and order to the whole world. Moreover, since the monopoly of violence (including its technology) will be withdrawn from a large number of individual and often 'irresponsible' nation sates (whose natural location is in the south) and be placed collectively in the hands of a few nation states, which also are 'responsible' and civilised' it not only will eliminate international wars, but alleviate poverty wherever it exits. These outlandish ideological claims of globalization made and propagated globally by the world's most powerful (G-8) countries have been lapped up by large sections of the Indian middle class and the media, as if they represented a policy package offered by some really existing and democratically legitimate World Government.

Counter Discourse of Movements

By the end of the cold war and two decades after the movement-groups were by and large fragmented into an almost isomorphic existence of each group fighting its own little battle independently. Much larger quantities of funds were now made available to them by the international donor agencies which had their own agenda for influenzing the politics of discourse in peripheral countries. Most movement-groups had thus become reutilized in their activities and functioned as NGO bureaucracies. In short, in the early 1990s, the mood among grass roots movements in India was marked by widespread pessimism among the observers and participants of the movements in the mid-1990s, protests against globalization led by the few movement-groups kept the tradition of struggles alive as different sections of the poor in India began to acutely feel globalization's adverse impact. It revitalized the entire spectrum of grass roots movements in the country, giving rise to a new discourse and politics aimed at countering the forces of hegemonic globalization. First, globalization has intensified and expanded the destructive forces of development-forces which disrupt communities, cultures and livelihoods of the poor without offering any viable and dignified alternative. Similarly, words for the constituent elements of its power structure—the techno-scientific, bureaucratic, military, managerial and business elites and a small consumerist class.

Second, a section of social activists, have become acutely aware of the role that politics of discourse plays globally and nationally, in influencing policy choices of governments and international organizations. Consequently, some of them now are participating actively in shaping the terms of discourse, globally on issues such as biodiversity, global warming, construction of big dams, regulations concerning international trade and intellectual property rights and so on. Their aim is to create global politics of popular movements with a view to building an alternative institutional structure of global governance, based on democratic principles of political equality, social justice, cultural diversity and non-violence, and ecological principles of sustainability and maintain biodiversity (Sheth, et al. 2002).

Third, another type of movement, representing largely the Left and social democratic strands referred to earlier, see globalization as intensifying further the already existing economic and social inequalities in the country (Sainath, 2000). While the votaries of globalization celebrate the growth of the middle class, the social activists see this phenomenon quite differently. In their view the programmes of economic reforms being implemented as a part of globalization package, have consolidated and enriched the old middle class. The growth of this class in their view, largely represents the rise in the purchasing power of the small idle class that emerged during the colonial rule and expanded during the initial four decades after independence, covering largely the upper and middle strata of the traditional social mented in the name of economic reforms improving living standards of the poor, have pushed them further down the social and economic ladder, and below the poverty line some fragments of the traditional lower social strata have entered the middle class but this has been due to the long existing social policies of the state—like affirmative action. In fact, with the state shrinking in the process of globalization, there has been a reversal of this process.

The few avenues of upward mobility that the policies of the Indian state had opened up for the disadvantageously located populations in the traditional social structure are now narrowing. The market is increasingly becoming the only avenue for upward mobility, and that too is monopolized by the upper strata of the society. Thus economic globalization offers ever rising standards of living to those who entering the market with some entitlements usually available to the members of upper castes, given their resources: land, wealth, social privilege and education. For large segments of the population outside the charmed circle of the market, and disadvantageously located in the traditional structure, it means malnutrition, starvation, disease and destitution. This relationship of the traditional social structure and globalization is emphasized by strangely, ignored in the academic debates on globalization. Colonial type exploitation of primary producers (the vast populations of tribals, artisans, small and marginal farmers and landless labourers) by a small urban-industrial elite, and their cognate groups of upper caste rural elite persists, even thrives, in the so called open economy of the market. In brief, in India the market-economy instead of making a dent on the iniquitous social structure is being absorbed by it.

Fourth, the movements reject the claim of the Indian state that in the process of globalization, it has been playing a positive role for the poor, giving a 'human face' to economic reforms. For enabling the poor to enter and find places in the market the state undermines their rights to sold on to whatever sources of livelihood that are still available to them. The Indian state in fact, systematically and blatantly discriminates between the rich and the poor in the implementation of economic reforms [Kishwar 2001a]. The result is, a vast population affected adversely by the market-led model of economic globalization is today unable to make a forceful entry in mainstream politics for their survival, let alone 'development.'

Fifth, the combined impact of the retreat of the state and the globalizing economy, is that the poorest among the poor are neither able to become full wage-earners in the economy nor even full-fledged citizens in the polity. For them there is no transitional pathway in sight that can lead them to the market. They have even lost the claims on the state which the bureaucratic-systemic nature of their exclusion continues under globalization as it did underdevelopment. State policies which, until recently, aimed at removing the structural barriers facing the poor and bringing into the mainstream of political economy are now being discarded as 'market-unfriendly.'

Finally, the new ideology of globalization has made issues of poverty and social deprivation in the peripheral countries of the world ever more unintelligible in the global discourse. In effect, the agencies of hegemonic globalization have been able to produce new terms of justification for the old development project i.e., of retaining the political and economic hegemony of the few rich and militarily powerful countries globally and of a small metropolitan elite within the country. The result is, development is seen and measured in terms of the extent to which a country can 'integrate' (read subjugates its economy to the world economic system).

Global Protests

This has resulted in the agencies of hegemonic globalization seeking, to depoliticize development and undermine democratic movements by co-opting, financially and politically, some protest movements in the developing countries and in the global arena. In the process issues such as environment, gender, human rights and even democracy are being redefined in terms radically different from those that were developed by the grass roots movements in the earlier paradigm of alternative development. For example, the issue of environment is no longer seen as one involving a political process for re-organising the economy and social, cultural life locally and globally on the basis of primary ecological principles. Instead ecological issues are being recast in constantly shifting terms of 'tolerable limits' and 'admissible costs' of environmental damage that is expected in higher proportions with escalation rates of economic growth.

These considerations pertains not only in establishing their oligopolistic rule over the world, but also in guaranteeing 'smooth' functioning of the multinational corporations in the peripheral countries. This is sought to be achieved by compelling governments of the peripheral countries to yield to conditions and terms the MNCs dictate and think are necessary for such functioning. In the process the multinationals have emerged as powerful global actors, often more powerful global actors, often more powerful and wealthy than many nation states, which often undermine fundamental human rights—rights to livelihood, habitat and culture of the poor in peripheral countries, but remain unaccountable to any agency of global governance or a nation-state.

In the new hegemonic discourse the thinking on human rights has been dissociated from concerns like removing poverty, fulfilling basic human needs and social justice. Poverty is increasingly seen as the poor people's own failure in creating wealth. It is no longer seen as an oral issue. In other words, the global discourse on human rights has ceased to be a discourse regarding social and political transformation; it is easy for the global hegemonic powers to target some poor peripheral countries 'not playing ball' with them for human rights violations, even as they ignore similar violations by governments of the countries pliable to their hegemonic designs. It is a measure of their dominance over the global culture of protests that despite practising such double standards, the global hegemonic powers are able to the claim 'commitment' to the universalisation of human rights.

Hence, it is not difficult for an organization like the WTO to function without reference to any principle of transparency or representational accountability, and also autonomously of the United Nations institutions, even when it sits in judgement on issues that fall in the purview of international law and representative bodies such as the ILO. The institutions of global governance are thus supposed to be self-responsible, not accountable outside their own ambit. They are 'accountable' only to their sponsors who are often the few militarily and economically powerful nation states.

In the global feminist discourse, sensitivity about the social structural, economic and cultural complexities faced by women in poor countries in securing their rights has vastly receded; in its place the legalist and metropolitan concerns about women's rights in a consumerist society have acquired prominence. Hegemonic globalization is bent upon monopolizing the global discourse of protests, with a view to legitimizing the hegemonic global order and undermining the processes of social and political transformations.

In this globally homogenized culture of protests some movement-groups in India show insensitivity to the historical and cultural contexts on which the issues are embedded. As a result, these groups often even refrain for articulating their opposition to the Indian state in terms and forms which, in their view may delegitimise the role of the state in a society. Globalization is a new, post-cold war ideology justifying the rule of a hegemonic structure of global power seeking to establish monopoly of a few powerful countries over resources of the whole world. As such, globalization to be inimical to the basic democratic and ecological values: liberty, equality, diversity and sustainability. To them, its impact on poorer countries has been to produce new and more dehumanized forms of exclusion and inequality—worser than those created by the cold war development model, or even by the colonial rule. We are particularly concerned about its adverse impact on democracy in India. For, when the poorer classes have found long-term stake in democracy and have begun to acquire their due share in governance, the power of the state (elected governments) itself is being denuded and undermined by the global power structure in collaboration with the country's metropolitan elites. In other words, globalization is undermining and delegitimizing the institutions of democratic governance.

Grass roots Movements

They are formulating old issues of development in new political terms, although their objective remains the same as before, namely, those at the bottom of the pile find their rightful place as producers in the economy and citizens in the polity. Accordingly, they don't view development as a political struggle for people's participation in defining development goals and devising means to achieve them. Rather than altogether 'opting out' of development they now seek to change the power relations on which the conventional model of development is premised. In the process some new elements have entered in the grass roots movements' thinking and practice of development.

First, the old post-colonial critique of development which invoked pre-modern nostalgia has ceased to appeal to a large section of these movements. Thus, at one level movement groups see the power elements of the old development model being encoded in the hegemonic structure of globalization which they oppose. But at the level of national politics they see the idea of development as representing political and economic rights of the people who have been denied access to it because of their disadvantageous locations in the power structure. This change in perspective was effectively articulated by a well known social activist Aruna Roy when she left a development NGO in mid-1980s to found a movement-group. According to her the need of the time was to "redefine the paradigm of development – to see the whole process of development for a different perspective." In her words: "Development is political and there can be no development without political will. In fact, all acts of social and economic living are determined by the nature of politics" [Roy, Aruna, 1996]. Second, with the global development promise of universalizing development for all, they are now able to see the real face of global hegemonic power. The cold war structures of aid and assistance were and in their place a new global economic regime of trade and fiscal control has been set up. This change representing a new political agenda on the part of the global power structure which aims at the dispersal of state control over the economics of the peripheral countries on the one hand, and centralization of global political and military power in the hands of the world's already rich and powerful countries on the other.

Third, all types of grass roots groups today, including even some conventional development NGOs, articulate basic issues of development in the framework of right. For example, they no longer view poverty purely as an economic problem. They see it as a function of social-structural locations of the poor, because of which they are excluded from development and imprisoned in poverty. They do not perceive the classical division between the two worlds in unidimensional terms of polarization between two economic classes. Their mobilisational strategies, therefore, focus on the new social-political formations which combine the categories of class, caste, ethnicity and gender.

Need for New Political and Civic Space

But in creating and expanding new political and civic spaces for them by converting the survival and developmental needs of the poor and the deprived into struggles for their economic, political and cultural rights and these not only of individual groups and communities surviving on the margins of the civil society. In the process, these movement activists link rights of access to and benefits from the development process with the issues of ethnic identity and human dignity, and view the satisfaction of material needs as a pursuit not detached from the spiritual and cultural aspects of human existence.

Similarly, the ecology movements at the grass roots do not view ecology as merely a cost factor in development, as some development specialists do. Instead, they view ecology as a basic principle of human existence, which if reactivated, can yield higher level for reorganizing the economy in a humane way and refocus development in terms of well being, in which, to use Gandhiji's well known phrase, "everyone shall have enough to satisfy one's need, but not greed."

The activists of the women's movements fusion of the ecological and gender principles, the argue, is conducive for a more humane economic and political organization of the society than that of development which, in their view, is founded on the principle of male domination over all aspects of human life and nature [Shiva, 1988]. Guided by this broad perspective, movements are often able to forge links with each other in fighting for issues at the grass roots. Women are in the forefront of the movements fighting for the rights of the population displaced by development projects, especially in Madhya Pradesh and Maharashtra, Anti-arrack movement in

Andhra Pradesh. Similarly, human rights organizations often team up with women's organizations on the issues of dowry, sati, rape, and equal wages that the roots of rural poverty lie in the pattern of urban growth in India. This has led to greater interaction and building of new organizational linkages between the city-based and village-based social action groups, different groups and movements, which began to converge in mid-1990s, have acquired a common direction and a fairly durable organizational base. The convergence has been attained on the point of resisting the ongoing efforts of the bureaucratic, technocratic and the metropolitan elites to support the policies of globalization and depoliticize development. It is only through politicization of the poor that they can counter the negative impact of globalization and make development a just and equitable process.

Participatory Democracy and Political Theory

In the course of implementing the structural adjustment programmes and other globalization-related policies, the state has been actively assisting the Indian and multinational corporations to acquire land and other resources of the villages at a nominal cost. This involves withdrawing constitutional guarantees given to the tribal regarding alienation of their land and in effect, extending such guarantees to MNCs as making land, water and forest-resources available to them cheaply, but at a great cost to the livelihood of the people and ecology of the area. The proceedings of public interest litigations which earlier had remained by and large confined to the courtrooms as contentions between the state and the social-legal activist, have now become matters of direct concern and involvement for the people themselves, constituting everyday politics of the movement groups. The most effective and innovative mode of consciousness raising and of political mobilization developed in this process, which has now become a common practice for movement groups all over the country, is organizing big walkathons (*padyatras*). The *padyatras* are usually organized by the activists representing the organizations for different parts of the country but sharing a common perspective on and concern for a particular issue they together wish to highlight for mobilizing public opinion. They walk long distances along with the people drawn from different locals but facing a similar problem, for eg; a threat posed to their livelihood by the project of the government or MNC—in a specific area. In the course of the walk, they take halts in villages—interact with people, show films, stage plays—highlighting the issues.

One among any such cases is the movement against bauxite mining in tribal areas of Vishakapatanam in Andhra Pradesh. In 1991 a walkathon, known as the *manya prante chaitanya vatra*, a consciousness raising walk of the area facing ecological destruction was organized by a couple of movement groups, SAMTA and SAKTI, active in the area. Over 50 other social action groups joined the march and prepared a report on ecological destruction they saw and experienced during the march. The report described how the region had come under severe threat to its ecology and to the livelihood of people inhabiting it and how if the damage was not controlled could cause ecological disaster for the entire peninsula of south India. The report also spoke of the displacement of 50,000 tribals, the massive deforestation and the problem of flash floods and silting that resulted.(Report by P. Sivaram Krishna of SAKTI, (Mimeo): also report in Newstime, March, 13, 1991). Largely accepting the SAMTA plea, the Supreme Court of India gave a 400 page judgement in 1997, outlining the steps which needed to be taken to make the tribal partners in the development of scheduled areas (i.e, constitutionally protected areas populated by tribals). The court ruled that all private and public sector organizations functioning in these areas should give not less than 20 per cent of jobs to local people and an equal amount of seats to their children in educational institutions. The court also stipulated that each industrial unit in the area part with

20 per cent of its profit and make it available for the kind of development that would be in the interest of the local people.

Although the movements usually work in local areas they invariably define local issues in trans-local terms. Theirs is thus a new kind of local politics which unlike the conventional politics of local governments is not linked vertically to the macro structures of power and ideology, either of a nation state or of the global order; nor is this politics parochially local. It expands horizontally through several micro-movements of people living in different geographical areas and socio-cultural milieus but experiencing the coon situation disempowerment caused by mal-development and contemporary forms of governance which are imperiously distant yet close enough to feel their coercive edge.

In a nutshell, the movements conceive participatory democracy as a parallel politics of social action, creating and maintaining new spaces for decision-making (i.e., for self-governance) by people on matters affecting their lives directly.

All Said and done, it is for the people to resist the adverse fallout of globalization, which in the course of line like any other bubble is bound to buss. Meanwhile, the developing countries such as India with a strong population of 1.10 billion should promote labour intensive industries to provide gainful employment to its marginalised section of America, the citadel of capitalism and no holds bar individualism is investing large sums to arrest meltdown and revive closed banks, is it not high time for India to guard herself against worldwide recessions through state intervention?

Bibliography

Agarwal, M. (2007). *Globalization and the millennium development goals : negotiating the challenge.* New Delhi: Social Science Press.

albrow, M. (2006). *Global Civil Society.*

Bardhan, P. K., & Bowles, S. (2006). *Globalization and egalitarian redistribution.* New Delhi: Oxford University Press.

Bartholomew, A. (2008). *Empire's law : the American imperial project and the 'war to remake the world'.* New Delhi: Sage Publications.

Basu, R. (2008). *Globalisation & the changing role of the state : issues & impacts.* New Delhi: New Dawn Press Inc.

Behera, M. C. (2006). *Globalising rural development : competing paradigms and emerging realities.* New Delhi: Sage Publication.

Bhagwati, J. N. (2007). *In defense of globalization.* New York: Oxford University Press.

Black, J. N. (2006). *Inequality in the global vilage.*

Bohramita, R. (2008). *Liberalisation from liberalization-gender and globalization in South East Asia.* Bangaluru.

Brar, B., Kumar, A., & Ram, R. (2007). *Globalization and the politics of identity in India.* New Delhi: Sage Publications.

Choudhary, K. (2007). *Globalisation, governance reforms, and development in India.* New Delhi: Sage Publications.

Custers, P. (2007). *Questioning globalized militarism : nuclear and military production and critical economic theory.* New Delhi: Tulika Books.

Damodaran, H. (2008). *India's new capitalists : caste, business, and industry in a modern nation.* Ranikhet.

Dasgupta, B. (2005). *Globalisation : India's adjustment experience.* New Delhi: Sage Publications.

Dasgupta, S. (2006). *Globalization and after.* New Delhi: Sage Publications.

Dasgupta, S. (2004). *The changing face of globalization.* New Delhi: Sage Publications.

Desai, M. (2005). *Development and nationhood : essays in the political economy of South Asia.* New Delhi: Oxford University Press.

Deshpande, A. (2008). *Globalization and development : a handbook of new perspectives.* New Delhi: Oxford University Press.

Friedman, T. L. (2005). *The world is flat : a brief history of the twenty-first century globalization.* New Delhi: Penguin Books.

Gandhi, P. J. (2008). *Inclusive growth in globalised India : challenges and options.* New Delhi: Deep & Deep Publication.

Goldman, M. (2007). *Imperial nature : the world bank and struggles for social justice in the age of globalization.* orient longman.

Greenspan, A. (2007). *The age of turbulence : adventures in a new world.* New York: Penguin Press.

Huchel, J. F. (2007). *Globalization in China, India and Russia.* New Delhi: Academic Foundation.

Jhunjhunwala, B. (2007). *Globalisation and Indian economy.* Delhi: Kalpaz Publications.

Joseph, Y. (2005). *Globalization and challenges for education.* New Dehi: Shipra Publications.

Kaplinsky, R. (2007). *Globalization, poverty and inequality : between a rock and a hard place.* Jaipur: Rawat Publictions.

Kraidy, M. M. (2007). *Hybridity, or the cultural logic of globalization.* New Delhi: Dorling Kindersly (India) P. Ltd.

Krishna Rao, V. (2008). *Battle for Seattle.* New Delhi: Academic excellence.

Krishna Rao, V. (12-18 February, 2007). Indian currents, 11 June, 2006 the road to Americanization Indian currents. *Why reservations in the age of globalization?*

Lal, D. (2004). *In praise of empires : globalization and order.* New York: Palgrave Macmillan.

Maira, A. (2008). *Transforming capitalism : business leadership to improve the world for everyone.* Gurgaon: Nimby Books.

Maitra, P. (2007). *Higher education and global challenges.* New Delhi: Saurabh Pub. House.

Nayar, B. R. (2007). *Globalization and politics in India.* New Delhi: Oxford University Press.

Nissanke, M., & Thorbecke, E. (2008). *Globalization and the poor in Asia : can shared growth be sustained?* New York: Macmillan.

O'Connor, D. E. (2006). *Encyclopedia of the global economy : a guide for students and researchers.* New Delhi: Academic Foundation.

Pathak, A. (2005). *Modernity, globalisation and identity towards a relative quest.* New Delhi: Aakar Books.

Patnaik, B. N., & Hasnain, S. I. (2006). *Globalization, language, culture, and media.* Shimla: Indian Institute of Advanced Study.

Radhakrishna, R. R. *India in a globalization world.* New Delhi: Academic Foundation.

Rai, R. (2006). *Globalisation of human rights.* Delhi: Authorspress.

Rao, C. H., & Bhattacharya, B. B. (2005). *Indian economy and society in the era of globalisation and liberalisation : essays in honour of prof. A.M. Khusro.* New Delhi: Academic Foundation.

Rao, C. N. (2007). *Globalisation, justice, and development.* New Delhi: Serials Publications.

Rao, V. Krishna. (2008). *Expansion of cultural imperalism through globalisation.* New Delhi: Manak Publications.

Ravindra Sastry, V. Krishna Rao. (Jan-March 2006). *The rise of the imperialist information economy and its impact on India, Third World Impact.*

Rudolph, L. I., & Jacobsen, J. K. (2006). *Experiencing the state.* New Delhi: Oxford University Press.

S., J. K. (2006). *Globalization under hegemony : the changing world economy.* New Delhi: Oxford University Press.

Saul, J. R. (2005). *The collapse of globalism : and the reinvention of the world.* New Delhi: Penguin Books.

Saul, J. S. (2007). *Decolonization and empire : contesting the rhetoric and practice of resubordination in Southern Africa and beyond.* Gurgaon: Three Essays Collective.

Sebastian, T. (2006). *Globalization and uneven economic development.*

Seernau, S. R. (2008). *Contempory readings in globalization.* New Delhi: Sage Publication.

Sennett, R. (2007). *The culture of the new capitalism.* Orient Longman.

Sharma, S. (2007). *New mantras in corporate corridors : from ancient roots to global routes.* New Delhi: New Age International.

Singh, C. P. (2007). *Indian education in emerging society.* New Delhi: Lotus Press.

Singh, K. (2005). *Questioning globalization.* Delhi.

Sudan, F. K. (2005). *Globalization and liberalization : nature and consequences.* New Delhi: Serials Pub.

(June, 2007, Vol. iv). *The wonder that is India: her unparalled march from Harappan valley to I.T.Industry Pol-sym.*

Thomas, A. O. (2006). *Transnational media and contoured markets : redefining Asian television and advertising.* New Delhi: Sage Publication.

Vanita-Koti-Khandekar. (2006). *The Indian media business.* New Delhi: Sage Publications.

Index

Abdali, Ahmed Shah, 80
Adverse Environmental Impact, 180
advertising, 138
AES Corp, 73
African Social Forum, 203
Agarwal, Aarti, 151
Agarwal, K.C., 33, 73
Age of Turbulence, 199
Agnew, John, 23
agricultural sciences, 242
All India Management Association, 57
Alternative Technology, 178
Amar Singh, 157
Americanization, 8, 172
Amin, Ash, 23
Amnesty International, 49
Anti-Americanism, 92
Anti-arrack movement, 255
Anti-Globalism, 90
Anusha, 59
AOL, 239, 240
Aron, Raymond, 224
Asian financial crisis, 98, 195, 196, 221, 223
Azadi Bachao Andolan, 178
Babar, 80
backward castes, 56
Balakrishna, 151
Bangaru Laxman, 156
Barrett Craig, 238, 239
Basic Amenities, 64
Baudrillard, 172
bauxite mining, 257
Bell, Daniel, 117
Bello Walden, 98, 99, 102, 194, 195, 202, 203, 216, 221
Bergsten, Fred, 196
Bhagwati, Jagdish, 215
bilateral agreements, 190
Bill Gates, 40, 238, 239, 241
bio-tech manufacturing jobs, 13
Blair, Tony, 199
Bondurant, Joan, 170
Boomerang, 219
Brand Bullies, 203
Bretton Woods, 179, 246
Briberisation, 184, 186
Brown, Mulloch, 12
Brzezinski, 222, 223, 224, 225
Bush, George H.W., 223
Byers, Stephen, 13
Cable News Network of Atlanta, 143
capitalism, 207
Capitalism Retreating
  CRAS Consumerism, 96
  Global Social Democracy, 101
  Mafia Capitalism, 98
  Marginalised Masses, 97
  Neo-Liberalism, 99
  New-Structuralism, 99
  Primitive Capitalism, 96
Capitalist Concept, 108
capitation fee, 64
Careerists, 50
Case, Stephen, 239
Castells, Manuel, 233
Chaebol, Samsung, 220

Chakrabarti, Amitabh, 156
Chakravarthy, Ranajit, 137, 139, 143
Chanda, Nayan, 89, 213
Chatterjee, Basu, 141
Chavez, Hugo, 100
Chipko Andolan, 178
Chomsky, Noam, 17, 105
Chopra's, B.R., 143
Chossudovsky, Michel, 230, 231
Cisco Systems, 237
Clinton administration, 194
Cococolanisation, 172
Commodification, 43, 125
Computer software, 118
Confronting Globalization, 206
Corporate Chaos, 46
Corporate Power, 211
corporation, 17
corporatist-import, 234
Counter-narratives, 26
CRAS Consumerism, 96
Crass, 51
Credibiltiy, 218
Cultural Homogenisation, 8, 172
Cultural Hybridisation, 51
Cultural Imperialism, 8
Dalit-Minority International Conference, 161
de Gortari Carlos Salinas, 234
deindustrialisation, 42
Dell Computer, 237
Denationalisation, 220
dependency theorists, 169, 170
Desai, Santosh, 155
deterritorialisation, 22
development, 66
Development Communication, 136, 138
Die Zeit, 158
Dobbs, 227, 228
Doctor Sobha, 139
Drug Administration, 61
ecology movements, 255
Economic Commission, 100
Economic Cooperation, 235
economic globalization, 7, 22, 27, 107, 115, 249, 250
economic liberalisation imports, 70
Economic Oppression, 16
economic reforms, 191, 192, 248, 249, 250
Editorial Priorities, 150
Education
  Global Impact, 49
  Quality Education, 56
Eisner, Michael, 238, 239
Electronic capitalism, 117
  Civil Participation, 132
  Commodification, 125
  Hypersaturation, 121
  Ideological Determinants, 120
  Media Dominance, 119
  Revenue, 129
  Serious Questions, 129
electronic media, 119, 120, 129, 131, 132, 134, 135, 136, 146, 150, 152, 155, 158, 163, 165
electronic transactions, 28
employment, 4, 5, 9, 17, 18, 19, 61, 62, 240
environmental destruction, 40, 45
environmental organisations, 49
Ezrahi, Yaron, 92
Fed, 198
Film Based Programmes, 144
financial crisis, 209, 220

financial liberalization, 188, 189
first generation reforms, 191
Fiscal austerity, 8, 9
Forays, 100
Foreign Direct Investment, 72, 175, 189
Foreign Participation, 73, 75
Fortune Magazine, 237, 239
Fox Media, 238
Frank, Robert, 95
Free Trade Agreements, 190
Free Trade Area, 209
Gandhi, Mahatma, 7
Genealogy, 25
General Motors, 61, 237
geographical territory, 22
Ghos, Jayati, 66
Ghraib, Abu, 106
Giddens, Anthony, 201
Gill, Barry, 31
Girijan Cooperative Corporation, 84
Global Economy, 59
global negotiations, 196
Global Social Democracy, 101
global systemic instability, 224
Globalization, 1
- Business Process Outsourcing, 13
- Cultural Globalization, 7
- Economic Activity, 3
- Economic Oppression, 16
- Liberalisation, 11
- Military Pressure, 16
- Privatisation, no, 9
- Rich Countries, 12

Godzilla, 53
Golden Arches, 50
good governance, 98, 191, 192
Green Peace Movements, 178
Greenspan, Alan, 198, 199
growth-modernisation model, 177
Harry Potter mania, 213
health insurance, 206
health sector, 58, 61, 81
Hedge Funds, 216, 217
Hegelian, 114
Held, David, 171
Herman, Edward, 243
High Quantity, 60
high-tech economy, 44
High-Tech Robber Barons, 236
Hirst, Paul, 39
Hobbesiam, 224
housing market, 228
human capital, 98, 100
human rights, 49, 102, 106, 182, 208, 225, 251, 252, 255
Human Rights, 182
Huntington, Samuel, 225
hypercommodification, 172
Hypersaturation, 121
idealism, 50, 55, 222
Ignatieff, Michael, 207
IMF on the Wane, 215
imperialism, 27, 40, 207
- Adverse Environmental Impact, 180
- Bretton Wood, 180
- Briberisation, 184
- Kickbacks, 185
- Privatisation, 184, 185
- Reduced Services, 183
- Small Farmers Plight, 181
- Violation, 182

Incompatible, 59
Industrial Revolution, 193

Inegalitarian Global Order, 175
Inequality, 232
Information Age, 236, 237, 243
Information Highway, 238, 240
Information Technology, 2, 50, 68
international division, 2
International Financial Centre, 211
International Forum, 7
Internet, 43, 47, 93, 118, 119, 127, 132, 133, 134, 147, 149, 150, 158, 159, 161, 162, 203, 238, 240, 242, 243
IT-enabled services, 59
Jain, Girilal, 151
Janasakthi, 160
Jasti, Venkat, 57
Jha, Avinash, 83, 86
Jobs Plenty - Hands Few, 58
Joshi Committee, 141, 144
Justification, 109
Karmazin, Mel, 239
Kaushik, Asha, 169, 174, 176
Kellner, Douglas, 38
KFC, 76
Kick-Backs, 11
Klein, Naomi, 203
Knowledge Capital, 65
Kothari, Rajani, 169
Krishna Murthy, T., 3, 8, 16
Krishna Rao, V., 58, 65
Krishnan, G. Anantha, 146
Krist, Nicolas, 223
Krueger Ann, 219
Kyoto Protocol, 6
Larner, Wendy, 21, 31, 32
lay-offs, 228
Legitimacy
  Victors Gobble, 195
Leisure Class, 96
Lenin, 169
Lewis, Bernard, 223
Liberal Democracy Sans Liberalism, 114
Liberalisation, 11, 33, 34
Libertarian liberals, 111
local production, 86
Locke, John, 108
Lopsided development, 4
Louis, Uchitelle, 228
Luddites, 193
Macdonaldization, 8
mafia capitalism, 98
Mallaby, Sebastian, 195
Mallik, Basanta Kumar, 225
Malls, 55
Malone, John, 238
manufacturing, 105, 228
manufacturing sector, 107
Marcuse, 177
Marginalised Masses, 97
Marine Corps, 200
Market economy survive
  anti-globalism
  Anti-Globalism, 90
  Momentum, 92
  Protest, 92
  State Failure, 93
Market fundamentalism, 9
Marshall plan, 222
Martin, Hans-peter, 230
Maruti Udyog, 61
Marxist, 22, 40
Mass Media
  Commercial Values, 148
  Development
    Communication, 138
  Editorial Priorities, 150

  Electronic Media, 136
  Evolution, 136
  Giant Channel, 143
  Ignores Masses, 145
  Joshi Committee, 141
  Mega Serials Era, 142
  Original Agenda, 137
  Regional Media, 151
  Sensational, 151
  Serials Selling Brands, 140
  Soap Operas, 138
  Soft Porn, 149
  Stench Afar, 153
  Tele Revenue, 139
  Top Priority, 148
Mass, Mathias, 158
Materialism, 50
McChesney, Robert, 243
McDonaldisation, 46
McKibben, 130
McKinsey Global Institute, 216
Media Dominance, 119
Media Mania, 165
Mega Serials Era, 142
Metro Channel, 141
Micro Movement
  Counter Discourse, 247
  Discourse, 245
  Global Discourse, 251
  Participatory Democracy, 256
  Political Theory, 256
Microsoft, 67, 237, 238
Military Pressure, 16
minimum wage, 205
Mitra, Ananda, 143
Mittelman, 31
Modernisation, 83
Monopolisation
  Capitalism, 109
  Capitalist Concept, 108
  Justification, 109
  Market Economy, 112
  Neo-Liberalism, 112
  Oil Crisis, 111
  Sans Liberalism, 114
Mooney, Pat, 242
Moraes, Frank, 151, 166
More, Thomas, 112
Motion pictures, 121
Multi-cultural Traffic, 52
Multi-Dimentional Concept, 39
multilateral institutions, 99
multinational capitalism, 171
Murdoch, Rubert, 238
NAFTA, 177
Naidu, Chandrababu, 165
Nass, 158
Nasser, 207
National Association, 59
national capitalism, 234
National Economy, 82, 83
National Science, 65
nation-states, 30, 175, 176
Neo-conservatism, 223
Neo-Imperialism, 41
  Culmination, 171
  Cultural Homogenisation, 172
  Inegalitarian, 175
  Multinational Capitalism, 171
Neo-Imperialism Hegemonism
  Soft-Welfare Advocates, 223
Neo-Liberal State, 45
Neo-Liberalism, 6, 8, 99, 112, 113, 219, 232
  Neo-Liberalism, 208
neostructuralism, 99
Neostructuralist, 100
New Resistance

Bourgeoisie, 233
Downsizing, 240
High-Tech Robber Barons, 236
Information Highway, 238
outsourcing, 239
Privatization, 241
news media, 146
newspaper circulation, 127
Newspapers, 127
non-proliferation, 224
Northernisation, 27
Nozick, Robert, 112
Obama, Barack, 222
Oil Crisis, 111
Opportunities Abroad, 35
Oracle, 60
padyatras, 257
Paehlke, Robert C., 117, 128
Parasitic Culture, 74
Participatory Democracy, 256
Paul, Vivek, 90
peso crisis, 234
pharma sector, 61
Pinochet, Augusto, 232
Pliant Journalism
Anti-Rural Bias, 161
Biased Programmes, 160
Cultural Policy, 160
Declining Credibility, 162
Ethical Restraint, 157
Mass Media Sans Mass Interests, 164
Media Mania, 165
Migration, 162
Powerful Role, 157
Print Media, 158
Plural cultural identities, 172
plutonomy, 95
Polanyi, Karl, 104
Police State, 113
Poor Work Culture, 77
population, 231
Population mobility, 51
Porto Alegre, 202
Posco, 220
post-Cold War, 222
post-war consensus, 113
poverty alleviation, 94
poverty-related diseases, 209
Prashad, Vijay, 226
primary education, 175
Primary Sector, 76
Primitive Capitalism, 96
print industry, 149
print media, 127
Private industries, 75
privatisation, 8, 9, 10, 183, 184, 185, 186, 187, 241
productivity gains, 205
Propellers, 195
public school system, 64
public sector reforms, 191
quota system, 55
Quota-vs-No-Quota, 56
Ram, J., 162
Ram, N., 162
Rama, Rao N.T., 164
Rand, Ayn, 199
Rao, Rammohan, 57
Reagan, Ronald, 179, 199
Reaganomics, 112
Reduced Services, 183
regional media, 150, 152
Re-Politicising, 253
reservations, 61
Resistance, 104
Retreat, 193
Robertson, 53

Rockefeller, John D., 239
Rodrik, Dani, 1, 18
Rogoff, Kenneth, 195
Ruggiera, Renato, 19
Runyan, 22
Sagar, Ramanand, 142
Said, Edward, 106
Sainath, P., 152, 248
Samaritans, 110
Sarawak, 206
Sardesai, Rajdeep, 155
Sassen, 28
sati, 256
Scholte, Jan A, 25
Schumann, Harald, 230
semi-knocked down, 76
Sen, Amartya, 214
Sen, Sukomal, 182
Sengupta, Mugdha, 137, 139, 143
service sector, 35, 36, 79
Seth, D.L., 244
Sharansky, Natan, 225
Silicon Valley, 239
Singh Patwant, 97
Singh, Manmohan, 90
situatedness, 28
Sivaram Krishna, P., 257
Small Farmers Plight, 181
small scale industries, 4
Smith, Adam, 110, 199
Social Costs, 183, 221
Social Divide, 194
socialism, 231
Sondhi, Madhuri S., 96, 97, 222
Soros, George, 202
Special Economic Zones, 10, 96
speculative capital, 216
Sridhar, V., 205, 206
Star News, 153, 156, 157
Stiglitz, Joseph E., 11, 16, 179, 184
stone, Feather, 172
structural adjustment, 98, 183
subaltern, 53
Subba Rao, Kasa, 151
Subba Rao, Kasa, 166
Suez Canal crisis of 1956, 207
Sum Micro systems, 237
Superpower, 222
supranational government
institutions, 42
Supreme Court, 55, 56
Swadeshi, 168
Swaraj, 169
system theorists, 38
Tabassum, 138
TATA, 5
TCI, 238
technical manpower, 68
technology, 22, 33, 41, 61, 181, 190,
236
Tele Revenue, 139
telecommunication, 54, 67
television game, 138
Television Rating Point, 142
Tendulkar, Priya, 141
Thatcher, Margaret, 179, 199, 232
Thatcherism, 112
Third World MNCs, 215
Thomson, Grahame, 17, 27, 39
time-space compression, 21
tolerance' philosophy, 33
Tormey, Simon, 114, 115
trade deficit, 18
trade liberalisation, 12, 101
Trade-Related Aspect, 101
training centres, 65
Transformation, 85

Transformation of Tribal Life and Economy, 85
transnational capital, 234, 235, 236
transnational corporation, 190
transnational media, 42
Transnationalised Bourgeoisie, 233
transnationalism, 42
Trappings, 84
tribal economy, 83, 85, 87
Tribal Economy
 local markets, 86
 local production, 86
 National Economy, 82
 Transformation, 85
 Trapping, 84
 Tribal Life, 85
U.S. economy, 226
Uchitelle, Louis, 226
underdevelopment, 100
Unemployable Professionals, 57
unemployment, 9, 113, 231
Varman, Rahul, 189
Venkateswar Rao, Narla, 166
Victors Gobble
 Alternative, 202
 Boomerangs, 219
 Confronting Globalization, 206
 Corporate Driven Globalization, 197
 Corporate Power, 211
 Credibiltiy, 218
 Dynamics, 198
 Fallout, 208
 Global Finance, 210
 Hedge Funds, 217
 Neoliberalism, 208, 219
 Retreat, 193, 197
 Social Costs, 221
 Social Divide, 194
 Speculative Capital, 216
 Unenduring Growth, 196
 World Social Forum, 203
Vidal, Gore2, 206
video games, 118
Violation, 182
Virtual senate, 17
Walia, Shelly, 207
Wall Street Crash, 111
Wallerstein, 170
Wal-Mart, 9, 10, 212, 228
Walters, William, 21, 31, 32
Washington Consensus, 6, 8, 97, 99, 184
weaker sections, 61
Webb, Jim, 227
Weill, Sanford, 239
Wendt, 180
Western capitalism, 208
Western cultural imperialism, 172
Westernization, 8
Who benefits from globalization
 Liberalisation, 34
 Service Sector, 36
Why is globalization
 Counter-narratives, 26
 Genealogy, 25
Williamson, John, 6
WIPROS, 75, 79
Wolf, Martin, 217
Wolff, Edward, 232
women's movements, 255
Women's Woes, 182
Woods, Ngaire, 219
Workers' Party, 202

World Bank study, 68
World Economic Forum, 236
world richest individuals, 231
World Slunk Miuly, 68
World Social Forum, 202, 204
World Trade Organization, 6, 12, 34, 101, 103, 179, 195, 197, 202, 223, 235, 252
World War I, 198
World War II, 179, 222
Young, 60
Zapatista movement, 208, 209
Zbigniew Brzezinski, 222